# OXFORD

## TEACHING GUIDES

### HOW TO

# Teach Mathematics For Mastery

## SECONDARY SCHOOL EDITION

# DR HELEN DRURY

## OXFORD

# OXFORD
## UNIVERSITY PRESS

Great Clarendon Street, Oxford, OX2 6DP, United Kingdom

Oxford University Press is a department of the University of Oxford.
It furthers the University's objective of excellence in research, scholarship, and
education by publishing worldwide. Oxford is a registered trade mark of Oxford
University Press in the UK and in certain other countries

British Library Cataloguing in Publication Data
Data available

978-0-19-841409-4

Kindle edition

978-0-19-841701-9

10 9 8 7 6 5 4 3 2 1

Paper used in the production of this book is a natural, recyclable product made
from wood grown in sustainable forests. The manufacturing process conforms to
the environmental regulations of the country of origin.

Printed in Great Britain by Clays Ltd., Bungay

The publisher would like to thank the following people for offering their
contribution in the development of this book: Anne Watson, Steve Lomax, Jo
Walker, Robert Wilne and Anthony Haynes.

For Robin Rogers

# About the author

Dr Helen Drury has taught mathematics for over a decade, including as a head of mathematics and senior leader, in Oxfordshire and London (UK). She is passionate about bringing research and best practice into the classroom to close the attainment gap and raise achievement for all. As Director of Mathematics for Ark, Helen founded the charitable, not-for-profit *Mathematics Mastery* programme to build up an evidence base to demonstrate that every  student in mainstream education can succeed with mathematics, and that the high achievement of UK students can rival that of students anywhere in the world. In 2015, Helen published *Mastering Mathematics: Teaching to transform achievement.*

# Contents

# Acknowledgements

I would like to thank the many colleagues I have worked with over the years for all they have done. Whether in practice, academic or policy roles, your insight, creativity and commitment are what have led to this book and I am enormously grateful for that. To pick out two individuals: Anne Watson and John Mason are responsible for igniting my passion for looking at mathematics education in the broader view – bringing together classroom experience and the research world – and have persistently fanned that flame over many years. This book wouldn't have happened without them.

With thanks to all my incredible colleagues at *Mathematics Mastery* and Ark for your expertise and dedication. It's a real pleasure working with and learning from you all. A special thanks to Alexi Makris and Laura Shenker for leading the secondary programme with such aplomb and keeping me sane as the book finally approached completion.

I am very grateful to everyone who read some or all of this book during the writing process. Your feedback was immensely helpful. In particular, the comments of Steve Lomax, Zoe Noonan, Jo Walker, Anne Watson and Rob Wilne on early (and late!) drafts significantly shaped the book. Of course, any errors or failings are my responsibility entirely.

Most of all, I thank my husband Robin and our children Oliver and Peter for their unfailing love and support and for making time spent *not* writing such a joy.

# Origins

This book is grounded in two things: a belief that every child can enjoy and succeed in mathematics – regardless of background – and a dedication to transform mathematics education.

I began teaching secondary mathematics in 2002. I taught in comprehensive schools in England – in rural Oxfordshire and inner-city London. After several years, I found myself becoming frustrated at the many barriers standing in the way of student achievement.

Teachers, myself included, were increasingly overwhelmed by the daily challenges of bureaucracy, lack of staff and an unmanageable workload. Professional development, when time was allowed for it, was generic and patchy.

In short, teachers were unable to thrive. It didn't matter how talented, dedicated or hard-working we were. The essence of great mathematics teaching was getting lost. Why? Because mathematics teaching was playing second fiddle to a multitude of other demands.

Unsurprisingly, these challenges were reflected in classroom attitudes and attainment. Students were often disengaged. They struggled to push beyond a surface-level understanding of mathematical ideas. Mathematics was seen as too hard, too boring or irrelevant to everyday life.

International league tables such as the Programme for International Student Assessment (PISA) told the same story. The United Kingdom was trailing behind a whole host of countries in mathematics. What on earth had gone wrong in such a well-resourced nation, full of well-intentioned people working in education?

Teachers in the UK work in a high-stakes environment where exam results are paramount. But the pressure to ensure students perform well on paper – alongside all the other challenges – comes at a price. Time and resources are invested in playing catch-up instead of planning for the long term. The 'system' has trapped schools in a false economy.

As my years in the classroom progressed, I realised I had a deep motivation to change things. Not just for one class, one year group, or even one school. I wanted to help bring about change on a national scale.

Teachers wanted to do the best job they possibly could. Students were capable of achieving significantly more. But a step change was needed.

In my role as Director of Mathematics at the education charity, Ark, I began to research how to best support teachers in mathematics. How could we improve mathematics teaching across a range of different school contexts and enable more students to achieve their goal?

Specifically, I was interested in what could be done here and now to provide support and raise standards. While the growing issues of workload, school funding and policy changes were beyond my reach, I was convinced that positive change was still possible.

I was struck by the level of success seen in high-performing jurisdictions such as Shanghai and Singapore. What did they do differently that enabled their students to achieve their goal in such great numbers?

I was faced with questions: are the teachers in Shanghai and Singapore simply better? Are the children simply more 'able'? The answer to both questions is a resounding no.

It can't be denied that certain cultural differences support the high levels of achievement in these nations. Parental engagement and the societal value placed on education – and specifically mathematics education – do go a long way.

But that's certainly not all there is to it – and to claim otherwise is nothing but a convenient excuse to maintain the status quo.

What I discovered in my research wasn't dramatic or revolutionary. These countries weren't hiding a mysterious 'silver bullet' that could magically fix a broken education system. They weren't doing anything that couldn't be done – at least in part – in countries across the world.

So what were these countries doing differently that led to their sustained success in mathematics? Now, answering this could take up an entire book in itself, but there were three core elements that excited me most:

- Teachers have ongoing access to high-quality professional development throughout their career, with an emphasis on mathematics-specific pedagogy. Time is carefully allocated for training, engaging in research, collaborative planning and knowledge sharing – and the value of this activity is widely understood.

- Teachers have high expectations for every single learner, rooted in a belief that anyone can become an excellent mathematician. Teachers reinforce this attitude to build confidence and resilience.

- The curriculum is designed to promote mathematical thinking and time is given to ensure every learner truly understands the mathematical concepts taught. Mathematical discussion, multiple representations and problem solving play a central role in lessons that have been carefully crafted. Misconceptions are rapidly addressed to ensure all learners progress at the same pace.

As part of my research, I also began considering the purpose of mathematics education. The vast majority of people – teachers, parents, politicians, and yes, even students – agree it's important. But it's not always clear *why* it's important.

Do we want learners to be able to reproduce standard techniques, such as solving simultaneous equations? Do we want learners to know when it is appropriate to use one technique rather than another? Do we want learners to appreciate how ideas and techniques are connected? Do we want learners to be able to solve unfamiliar problems?

Without clarity concerning the underlying purpose of mathematics education, how can we agree on which classroom practices best enable us to achieve our goal?

In high-performing jurisdictions, the purpose of mathematics education is clear and centrally communicated. This lends structure and continuity to how it's taught across the country.

My research has led me to argue that the ultimate aim of mathematics education is to enable learners to solve new problems in unfamiliar contexts. This belief underpins the arguments and recommendations I make throughout this book.

To achieve this aim, everything we do in mathematics education should support students in developing a deep structural understanding of mathematical ideas and how they fit together. Students need to build fluency in applying mathematical techniques and develop skills to communicate mathematical ideas.

It should also go without saying that students must be exposed to rich mathematical content that enables them to problem-solve on a regular basis. Crucially, this rich content should be accessible to all students – not just the students who have been labelled as 'gifted' or 'more able'.

Eventually, my research evolved into the development of an approach to the teaching and learning of mathematics: *Mathematics Mastery*. This is a structured, whole-school programme of mathematics-specific professional development, integrated with a complete curriculum framework and classroom resources. The programme was launched in schools in England

and Northern Ireland in 2012. Five years in, the programme runs in around 500 primary and secondary schools around the country.

In launching this programme, I set out to bring together schools that share my ethos concerning how and why mathematics should be taught. I wanted to find teachers who believed that mathematics was for everyone. Teachers who believed that deepening understanding was a better use of time than accelerating through the curriculum. Teachers who believed that the ultimate aim of mathematics education was to be able to solve new problems in unfamiliar contexts.

'Mastery' was coined as an umbrella name for the set of principles and effective classroom practice underpinning our approach. While an hour's lesson might be sufficient for someone to say that they have *learned* something, *mastery* is a much longer-term investment. Mastery, at its heart, is about the entire journey of learning a discipline – in this case, the discipline of mathematics.

In the last few years, the term 'mastery' has taken hold across the country as a standard of mathematics education to aspire to.

It remains to be seen whether giving this approach a name – 'mastery' – is of benefit or not. Perhaps it doesn't matter. In this book, I have sought to look beyond the name and simply focus on what it means to put the underlying principles into practice. I set out to transform mathematics education in the UK and this remains my aim. I am humbled, excited and highly motivated by the number of teachers, school leaders and educationalists across the country who share this goal and are making a positive difference to the lives of young people.

As mentioned already, the journey to mastery is a long one. We are still refining and evolving our approach every day. But the importance of recognising incremental shifts in attitude and standards cannot be underestimated. Over time, these gradual changes morph into something much more significant.

Gradually, classroom by classroom, a transformation in mathematics education is taking place. Thousands of students are benefiting from increased understanding, enjoyment, resilience and achievement in mathematics.

No teacher has ever said this was easy. It took investment, dedication and perseverance to make this transformation happen, often in the face of huge pressure and resistance.

If a national transformation in mathematics education is going to take hold, we must aim for more students to reach – and exceed – our national standards. However, this is only viable if we invest in developing our teachers over the long term, and if we refocus our efforts on building a deep foundation of mathematical understanding among learners.

The evidence is clear. The leading countries in mathematics education have shown what is possible. The single most powerful thing we can now do is aim high.

# Using this book

This 'How to' book has been written for teachers and school leaders who share a commitment to transforming mathematics education.

This book introduces the principles, frameworks and classroom approaches teachers are using to ensure every learner gains a deep understanding of mathematics that equips them to solve unfamiliar problems.

It draws on the key principles of the mastery approach and the range of research that underpins it. Though international successes have provided much of the inspiration, the mastery approach we explore here is grounded in UK classrooms. Throughout this book, examples of classroom practice are given to illustrate why or how to apply key principles of the approach. The vast majority of these examples are from the inspirational practice of schools adopting the *Mathematics Mastery* programme.

 **Discuss**

To support this book's use as a professional development resource, discussion points are included at relevant points. These could be used to initiate discussion in staff training.

 **Consider**

These may provide a prompt for individual reflection. They are intended to give you the opportunity to ponder what you think about a particular issue.

 **Try this in the classroom**

These sections, usually centred on a mathematical task, give ideas as to how you might try out an idea in your own classroom.

 **Preparing to teach – do the mathematics!**

One of the best ways to prepare to use a task with students is to tackle the task yourself. These prompt you to complete a mathematical task and reflect on the strategy, language and resources you used.

Initially inspired by the high performance of countries such as Singapore, the underpinnings of the mastery approach provided in this book are both theoretical and practical, and also local and international. It draws on national and international evidence and research findings, and has been further developed through ongoing action research in schools in the UK.

As we consider the evidence from higher-attaining countries, it is important to remember that this is not a one-way process. Just as the UK looks to gain insights from high-performing jurisdictions, these nations have also looked to and learned from the UK over time.

The book begins with an overview of the ideas behind teaching mathematics for mastery, and an introduction to the dimensions of depth that underpin it.

In Chapter 2, we look at the importance of high expectations for every learner. This is followed by a chapter exploring the purpose of teaching and learning mathematics. The curriculum structure required for students to meet these expectations is explored next, followed by the role of assessment.

From Chapter 6 onwards, our focus is firmly on the classroom. These chapters will explore what is meant by deep understanding, and how teachers might best support students to achieve it. Chapter 6 discusses the important role of practice. Chapters 7 to 9 focus on the three dimensions of depth: conceptual understanding, mathematical thinking and language and communication.

While an individual teacher can adopt a mastery approach, it is a challenge much better tackled together, across a school's mathematics department. This not only makes it easier for teachers to transform their practice, it also ensures that students benefit from a consistent approach to mathematics teaching. Departmental leadership and whole-school change is the focus of Chapter 10.

# Chapter 1

## What is Mastery?

To teach for mastery is to teach with the highest expectations for every learner, so that their understanding is deepened, with the aim that they will be able to solve non-standard problems in unfamiliar contexts.

*A mathematical concept or skill has been mastered when, through exploration, clarification, practice and application over time, a person can represent it in multiple ways, has the mathematical language to be able to communicate related ideas, and can think mathematically with the concept so that they can independently apply it to a totally new problem in an unfamiliar situation.*

This is how I described mastery – the ultimate aim of teaching and learning mathematics – in my first (primary-focused) book,[1] and it is as true for secondary mathematics as it is for primary.

As the phrase at the end makes clear, problem solving is at the heart of mastering mathematics. Teaching for mastery involves holding problem solving as the ultimate aim of learning mathematics for every student, whatever their home background or prior attainment. Every student can learn to solve complex problems in unfamiliar contexts.

In addition to ensuring that students become fluent in the fundamentals of mathematics and can reason mathematically, the National Curriculum for mathematics in England aims to ensure that all students: 'can *solve problems* by applying their mathematics to a variety of routine and non-routine problems with increasing sophistication, including breaking down problems into a series of simpler steps and persevering in seeking solutions'.[2]

According to these aims, problem solving means *all* students should be able to:

- apply the concepts and skills they have learned to problems

- learn to tackle both routine and non-routine problems

---

[1] **H. Drury**, *Mastering Mathematics: Teaching to Transform Achievement* (Oxford: Oxford University Press, 2014) p. 9.

[2] **Department for Education**, *Mathematics Programme of Study* (London: Department for Education, 2013), p. 2.

- independently break down problems into a series of simpler steps

- persevere in seeking solutions.

Setting aside the strong case to be made that once a problem becomes 'routine' it ceases to be a problem at all, this is a list that many could agree with.

---

**Problem solving in Singapore**

In Singapore, problem solving is the focus of the mathematics curriculum.

Their national curriculum documents state that problem solving is the focus of the mathematics curriculum. They emphasise that learning should avoid an over-emphasis on recalling facts or reproducing procedures, and instead must focus on understanding and reasoning.

---

Holding problem solving up so absolutely as the ultimate aim of mathematics education does *not* inevitably equate to teaching by discovery, or enquiry-based learning. Naturally, experience of solving problems is vital for success in problem solving, but Singapore's commitment to problem solving does not result in problem solving taking centre stage every moment of every lesson. We can distinguish, then, between the ultimate goal – problem solving – and the classroom pedagogy that will best achieve that goal.

# Mastery takes time

Some teachers get frustrated that a student who, having 'learned' to add fractions, say, in one lesson, appears to have entirely 'unlearned' this skill by the end-of-term test, or in class the following week or even day.

This can happen when the focus of lessons is on 'learning' mathematics in unconnected chunks, rather than on 'mastering' the subject over time.

As Daisy Christodoulou describes, the widespread use of descriptor-based assessment in England has led teachers and students to over-value short-term performance across the curriculum.[3] There can be a tendency to assess students' understanding of a topic at the start of a lesson, and expect to have significantly moved that understanding on by the end of the lesson.

As it is about the full journey of learning, teaching for mastery is about progress along a continuum. Mastery is a goal for a lifetime of learning,

---

[3] **D. Christodoulou**, *Making Good Progress? The Future of Assessment for Learning* (Buckingham: Oxford University Press, 2016).

rather than for a single lesson or even series of lessons. In adopting teaching for mastery, teachers commit to working hard to enable every student to increase their level of mastery.

Let's take the example of mastering ratio. The National Curriculum in England specifies that Key Stage 3 students should be taught to divide a given quantity into two parts in a given part:part or part:whole ratio.[4] What would it mean to master this?

A student might *explore* the concept of ratio by experiencing it in a wide variety of contexts. They have the skill *clarified* when they are reminded, or realise given a context, that ratio is multiplicative rather than additive, and connect ratio to fractional parts. They *practise* dividing in a given ratio when sharing, cooking and tackling problems involving this skill. Subsequent lessons will offer further opportunities to *explore* the idea, moments of *clarification* and plenty of *practice*. As the student moves towards mastery of dividing a quantity in a given ratio, there will be many chances to *apply* this skill. It is through this *application* – once sufficient *exploration* and *practice* have taken place and there is no longer any need for *clarification* (as errors are so rarely made) – that the student comes to *master* the skill.

Setting out with the intention that your class will ultimately *master* dividing a given quantity into two parts in a given part:part ratio, the first thing that is clear is that this is not going to happen in 60 minutes. There may well be a lesson which begins with many students flummoxed by the question 'divide £60 in the ratio 2:3' and ends with them all confidently and correctly answering it – but this in itself is not necessarily a sign of successful mathematics teaching.

Rather, the curriculum throughout the year (in fact across several school years) must be planned so that the necessary concepts and skills have already been explored, clarified and practised (the skill of adding and multiplying positive integers, for example, and the concepts of equivalence and fractions). Furthermore, appropriate relevant opportunities to apply the skill of dividing a quantity with a ratio should be built in to the subsequent months. This includes recognising the presence of ratios in situations where the words and symbols are not used.

---

[4] **Department for Education**, *Mathematics Programmes of Study: Key Stage 3 National Curriculum in England* (London: Department for Education, 2013).

# Mastery is about deep understanding

The term 'mastery' tells us nothing about the level of challenge of the thing being mastered. I might say that I have *mastered* differential calculus. I might claim to have *mastered* the use of Pythagoras' theorem to find the length of an unknown side in a right-angled triangle, when the other two lengths are given. Equally, I might state that I had *mastered* counting from one to ten. It is not the difficulty of the thing being learned that merits the term mastery, but rather the deep understanding that it implies.

With the example of Pythagoras' theorem, a learner who has *mastered* this might be expected to be able to:

- find the length of the hypotenuse given the lengths of the other two sides

- find the length of one of the two shorter sides

- apply the theorem to find missing lengths in three-dimensional situations

- apply the theorem in area and volume problems

- recognise when the theorem might usefully be applied, even when it is not named

- prove the theorem.

---

### Students who are enabled to gain a deep understanding have increased motivational effort

**Kyriacou, C. and Goulding, M.** (2005).[5]

**The study:** A review of the literature investigated how to increase the motivational effort of Key Stage 4 students.

**What it tells us:** The extent to which students saw themselves as mathematicians was the most important area to emerge from the studies in the review. Not seeing themselves as mathematicians tended to create barriers to putting effort into mathematics. For example, some students viewed mathematics as a subject that only clever people did well in and believed that any effort they put in to learning mathematics would make little difference.

---

[5] **C. Kyriacou and M. Goulding**, 'A Systematic Review of Strategies to Raise Pupils' Motivational Effort in Key Stage 4 Mathematics,' in *Proceedings of the British Society for Research into Learning Mathematics* 25(3), edited by D. Hewitt (November 2005).

By 'seeing themselves as mathematicians', the reviewers meant students who, regardless of their level of ability and set placement, enjoyed mathematics, were interested in the subject, and could do the mathematics they were set.

Students work harder when they develop a more positive identity of themselves. To achieve this, teachers need to:

- provide a caring and supportive classroom climate
- provide activities that students find challenging and enjoyable
- enable students to gain a deeper understanding of the mathematics
- provide opportunities for students to collaborate
- enable students to feel equally valued.

Of these, they found that the most important was helping students to gain a deeper understanding of the mathematics they were doing.

So, valuing students equally and providing a caring and supportive classroom climate – as we will discuss in Chapter 2 – are important factors in raising achievement for all, but they are insufficient in isolation. Students must find learning mathematics challenging and enjoyable, have opportunities for collaborative learning, develop the will and drive to persevere and, *most important of all*, gain a deep understanding of the mathematics.

## Dimensions of depth

A major motivation for developing the approach described in this book was that I found, in working with passionate, committed and skilled teachers in excellent schools, that something more was required to truly transform achievement.

Time and again I found myself in classrooms – my own included – where teachers had high expectations of all their students and were spending longer on each topic when it was first taught, but were disappointed by the lack of progress made by some lower-attaining students, or by the superficial nature of the understanding of even their highest-attaining students.

In founding the *Mathematics Mastery* programme, I was looking to answer the question 'How can teachers ensure that every student gains the required depth of understanding to apply mathematics successfully to unfamiliar problems?'

I considered this as two sub-questions:

- What is standing in the way of previously lower-attaining students succeeding with mathematical problem solving?

- What are the mathematical working practices that high-achieving mathematicians need to strengthen further?

These two questions were my motivation for developing the 'dimensions of depth' framework. Interestingly, the answers to these two questions result in the same three dimensions of depth.

Whether struggling or excelling, all learners benefit from deepening their conceptual understanding, improving their mathematical communication and developing their mathematical thinking.

There are a number of potential barriers to success in mathematics. Students can find it difficult to make sense of mathematical concepts in a meaningful way. They can struggle to verbalise their mathematical thinking. They can be challenged by such thinking itself.

To overcome these barriers, I argue that there are three key dimensions to deepening students' understanding:

- Deepening *conceptual understanding* through using and making connections between concepts, and between physical, diagrammatic and symbolic representations (including those that are computer supported), as demonstrated so effectively in places such as Singapore, Shanghai and the Netherlands.

- Encouraging students to *think like mathematicians*, through giving them opportunities to seek patterns and rules, and to ask and answer open questions.

- Developing students' *communication*, through explicitly teaching them to discuss mathematics in grammatically correct full sentences with accurate terminology – a key priority in Asian economies such as Shanghai, where exposure to a more 'formal' treatment of mathematics has been credited with their success in PISA.

I have given these the name 'dimensions of depth' because they are activities that all learners do to a greater or lesser extent, and because students can work on deepening each of them while focusing on the same content area. They are three dimensions in which learners can deepen their understanding, as an alternative to racing on to cover a new topic.

Since I introduced the three dimensions of depth as part of a model for transforming achievement they have proven to be a useful framework for curriculum and lesson design, as well as for lesson observation and feedback.[6]

The three dimensions of depth resonate with the findings of a review of how students learn mathematics. The team, from the University of Oxford, drew the following conclusions:

*To solve problems posed for pedagogic purposes, secondary mathematics learners have to:*

- *be able to read and understand the problem*

- *know when they are expected to use formal methods*

- *know which methods to apply and in what order and how to carry them out*

- *identify variables and relationships, choosing which variable to treat as independent*

- *apply appropriate knowledge of situations and operations*

- *use mental, graphical and diagrammatic imagery*

- *choose representations and techniques and know how to operate with them*

- *know a range of useful facts, operations and functions*

- *decide whether to use statistical, algebraic, logical or ad hoc methods.*[7]

---

**◯ Discuss**

How do each of the items on the above list connect with the dimensions of depth? Which relate to language and communication? Which concern conceptual understanding? Which are about mathematical thinking? Are there any items the researchers included that surprise you? Or are there any that are missing?

---

When teaching for mastery, carefully crafted lesson design provides a *conceptual journey* through the mathematics, engaging students in *thinking mathematically* and developing their *mathematical communication*.

---

[6] **H. Drury**, 'Joining the dots: transforming mathematics education with a coherent whole school approach', *Mathematics Teaching* (Association of Teachers of Mathematics, 2014).

[7] **A. Watson**, 'Paper 7: Modelling, Problem-Solving and Integrating Concepts' in *Key Understandings in Mathematics Learning* (London: Nuffield Foundation, 2009).

There are three dimensions to the mathematics that students require in order to become proficient and persistent problem solvers. Everyone needs to develop their understanding of key mathematical concepts, to seek and use patterns and rules, and to explain and reason.

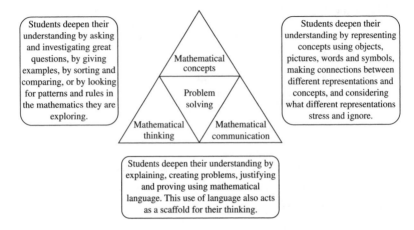

**Figure 1.1:** A framework for understanding the three dimensions of depth

Although this framework is theoretical, there is substantial evidence that each of these three dimensions is systematically developed in higher-performing countries, particularly in East Asia. For example, towards the end of the twentieth century, Shin-Ying Lee set out to account for the differences in academic achievement between students in China, Japan and the United States.

Lee reported detailed observational and qualitative analyses of classroom interactions. She compared cultural expectations about teaching and learning and instructional practices of teachers.

## Dimensions of depth in East Asia and America

**Lee, S.Y.** (1998)[8]

**The study:** The researchers noted the frequency of four different kinds of instruction in each country: using different examples of a problem; extending students' answers; relating answers to abstract concepts; and facilitating deeper understanding.

---

[8] **S.Y. Lee**, 'Mathematics Learning and Teaching in the School Context: Reflections from Cross-Cultural Comparisons,' in *Global Prospects for Education: Development, Culture, and Schooling*, edited by S.G. Garis and H.M. Wellman (Washington, DC: American Psychological Association, 1998), pp. 45–77.

**What it tells us:** Although the stereotypical Asian education system places a strong emphasis on drilling procedural skills, this study's data illustrated that East Asian students also have frequent classroom experience that facilitates their conceptual understanding of mathematics. Japanese and Chinese teachers were found to be more likely than American teachers to provide learning experiences with concrete operations first, followed by abstract concepts. The practice of presenting one mathematical concept in a number of different ways was more common in East Asian classrooms than in American classrooms. Lee argued that students in American classes had fewer opportunities to construct meaning and to understand the mathematical concepts presented in the curriculum.

It was found that American teachers were less likely to use techniques that facilitate students' mathematical thinking than teachers in the East Asian countries. Teachers were also applying their own teaching strategies to lead students to construct mathematical concepts.

East Asian students were found to have more opportunities to produce, explain and evaluate their solutions when solving mathematical problems. The frequency of East Asian students offering their ideas was significantly higher than for American students.

Lee's study offers some support to the idea that East Asian students' success may be due to differences in pedagogic approach. It indicates that teachers in East Asian economies may do more than their Western counterparts to deepen students' conceptual understanding, advance their mathematical thinking, and develop their language and communication.

The theoretical and evidence-based foundations behind each of the three dimensions of depth are introduced in Chapters 7, 8 and 9. In those chapters, we also look in further detail at what we can do as teachers to support students in developing these three facets of the successful mathematician:

**1** Conceptual understanding

**2** Mathematical thinking

**3** Language and communication.

Before considering the dimensions of depth in greater detail, we give due consideration to the mindset behind teaching for mastery, as well as the principles behind curriculum and assessment for mastery.

## Developing problem solving through the dimensions of depth

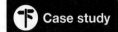 Case study

**The school context:** The mathematics team at Skinners' Academy, London, are aware that high expectations and taking their time are essential starting points in transforming their students' achievement.

Alongside the introduction of a curriculum for mastery, the team meet weekly to work on the mathematical tasks they will be setting students the following week. In discussing each task, they consider the three dimensions of depth: conceptual understanding, mathematical thinking, and language and communication.

*Mathematical concepts:* The teacher leading on the mastery approach across the department reports greater use of multiple representations to build understanding. For example, pictorial representations are used to support students' understanding in lessons on sequences, area, multiplying decimals and forming equations. When teaching students about multiplying decimals, pictorial representations are used alongside the abstract representations and several different abstract representations are used to deepen understanding.

*Mathematical thinking:* On a learning walk, almost all lessons observed included the teacher asking 'why?' Students were keen to understand 'why' as well as 'how'.

*Mathematical communication:* The school has increased teacher and student discussion of mathematics. Walking through Year 7 lessons you might hear students explaining that 1.5 is '10 times smaller' than 15 and also equal to '15 ÷ 10', or discussing the difference between the identity and equals symbols when forming equations.

**Their impact:** Through explicitly supporting students with each of the three dimensions of depth, the team at Skinners' Academy has developed students' abilities and confidence in solving problems. Teachers find that Year 7 and Year 8 students are more willing to attempt challenging problems than older students. Students are now keen to question why things work, rather than just following procedures. In their first year of focusing on the three dimensions of depth in this way, the Year 7 students outperformed their Year 8 peers in the United Kingdom Mathematics Trust (UKMT) Challenge.

# Summary

Two ambitions form the aim of success for all – every student succeeding and many more excelling. These ambitions give rise to two important questions:

- What is standing in the way of some students succeeding in mathematics?

- What are the mathematical working practices that high-achieving mathematicians could do with strengthening further?

There are three main barriers to success with mathematics: lack of *conceptual understanding*, underdeveloped *mathematical thinking* and poor mathematical *communication skills*. These three dimensions are also necessary for mathematics at higher levels.

There are therefore three dimensions of depth:

**1** Deepening *conceptual understanding*, through making connections between representations.

**2** Encouraging students to *think like mathematicians*, through giving them opportunities to seek patterns and rules, and to ask and answer open questions.

**3** Developing students' *communication skills,* through explicitly teaching them to discuss mathematics in grammatically correct full sentences with accurate terminology.

When teaching for mastery, carefully crafted lesson design provides a *conceptual journey* through the mathematics, developing students' *mathematical thinking* and engaging them in *communicating mathematically*.

Teaching for mastery, as advocated in this book, is grounded in the idea that all three of these dimensions of mathematics education are vital and should be pursued for *every* student.

# Chapter 2

## What are students really capable of?

Success in mathematics is often used as an indicator of 'innate' intelligence, rather than something that everyone can achieve with effort. This attitude is more prevalent in some countries than others, seeming to be particularly common in the United States and the United Kingdom. Many people believe that mathematical ability is a 'gift' that some people have and others don't. The assumption is often made that students' capacity to learn is determined by an innate endowment of fixed intelligence.[1]

In the UK, for example, the current system of teaching and assessment seems to develop a 'fixed' theory of ability[2] that results in teachers and students believing that they are either good at mathematics or they are not. This belief has informed the way learning and assessment are organised. It has had a negative influence on expectations of achievement. High-performing systems take a radically different approach from this to student progression, and to differentiation.[3]

Students can achieve in, and enjoy, mathematics, whatever their socio-economic background or prior attainment, as long as they are given the appropriate learning experiences. Thinking that some students are 'naturally good at mathematics', and that others are not, fast becomes a self-fulfilling prophecy.

Underlying a mastery approach is a belief that all students are capable of understanding and doing mathematics, given sufficient time. In this chapter, we consider the importance of high expectations.

In practice, a focus on success for all can be separated into two ambitions: success for all (no learner left behind), and a higher proportion of students excelling (higher achievement for all).

---

[1] **R.J. Herrnstein and C. Murray**, *The Bell Curve: Intelligence and Class Structure in American Life* (Free Press, 1994).

[2] **C.S. Dweck**, *Self-Theories: Their Role in Motivation, Personality and Development* (Philadelphia, VA: Psychology Press, 1999).

[3] **D. Reynolds and S. Farrell**, *Worlds Apart? A Review of International Surveys of Educational Achievement Involving England* (London: HMSO, 1996).

**Consider**

- What do these two ambitions mean for you and the students you teach?

- Can 'every student' mean just that, or are there any students with specific learning needs for whom success will have to be defined differently?

- What proportion of students will have such a deep understanding and enjoyment of mathematics that they will wish to continue with the subject once it is no longer compulsory?

# Success for all

Countries with higher achievement tend also to have less variation in student achievement than others.[4] Increased variation in student achievement is associated with lower overall student achievement.[5]

Whereas, notably, the UK seems to have become used to a 'tail' of underachievement, other countries demonstrate that this is far from inevitable. Many more children can succeed with mathematics than are doing so in the UK at the moment.

**In East and South-east Asian countries more students are mathematically prepared to participate in modern society**

 **Evidence**

**OECD** 2016.[6]

**The study:** The Organisation for Economic Co-operation and Development (OECD)'s 2016 report, *PISA 2015* considered students from East and South-east Asian countries, such as Singapore, Japan, South Korea and China.

---

[4] **R. Wilkinson and K. Pickett**, *The Spirit Level: Why More Equal Societies Almost Always Do Better* (London: Allen Lane, The Penguin Press, 2009).

[5] **E.A. Hanushek and L. Woessman**, *The Economics of International Differences in Educational Achievement* (Vol. 4925). (Bonn: Forschungsinstitut zur Zukunft der Arbeit, 2010).

[6] **OECD**, *PISA 2015 Results (Volume I): Excellence and Equity in Education* (Paris: OECD Publishing, 2016). DOI: http://dx.doi.org/10.1787/9789264266490-en accessed on 11 August 2017.

At PISA level 2, students can use basic algorithms, formulae, procedures or conventions to solve problems involving whole numbers. For example, they can:

- convert an approximate price to a different currency

- compare the total distance across two alternative routes.

The report describes PISA level 2 as 'a baseline level of proficiency that is required to participate fully in modern society'.

*These low-achievers can solve problems involving clear directions and requiring a single source of information, but cannot engage in more complex reasoning to solve the kinds of problems that are routinely faced by adults in their daily lives.*

**What it tells us:** So how many 15-year-olds don't even make it to this level?

- 23 per cent across the OECD

- 22 per cent in the UK

- 10 per cent in Singapore and China.

These jurisdictions demonstrate that it is possible to have half as many students struggling as the UK currently does.

In 2013 professor Zhu Xiaohu of the Shanghai PISA Centre observed that Shanghai:

> rank[s] world best in Maths and Science, not because of the performance of our top students, but because of the small gap between high and low performers. High quality is matched by high equality.[7]

Results from the Trends in International Mathematics and Science Study (TIMSS) report in 2016 showed that in England, in contrast, the gap between the lowest-performing and the highest-performing children remains unacceptably wide, even though England has risen to its highest point in these rankings for 20 years.[8]

---

[7] **National College for School Leadership**, *Report on Research into Maths and Science Teaching in the Shanghai Region* (Research by National Leaders of Education and Subject Specialists in Shanghai and Ningbo, China, 11–18 January 2013), p. 7.

[8] **I.V.S. Mullis et al.**, *TIMSS 2015 International Results in Mathematics* (2016). Retrieved from Boston College, TIMSS and PIRLS International Study Center website: http://timssandpirls.bc.edu/timss2015/international-results accessed 11 August 2017.

The difference in mathematics performances *within* OECD countries is even greater than the difference *between* the countries, with over 300 points – the equivalent of more than seven years of schooling – often separating the highest- and the lowest-achieving students in a country.[9]

Expecting that some children will struggle with mathematics quickly becomes a self-fulfilling prophecy.

A headteacher once took me to a Reception class and pointed out a little boy who was chatting with the teacher. She proudly told me how good he was at mathematics, and confidently predicted that, in the formal assessments that would be conducted in seven years' time (when the boy would be 11), he would be exceeding national expectations in mathematics. Later in the same lesson, she drew my attention to another little boy, who she said was already struggling. 'We'll do what we can,' she explained, 'but I can tell you right now that he's going to need booster classes in Year 6. It's very unlikely he'll meet national expectations.'

When I recount this story to secondary practitioners, there can be a tendency to fall into passing the buck – no wonder so many students are underachieving at the start of secondary school: their primary teachers had such low expectations for them. But before putting the blame on the shoulders of primary colleagues, it's worth just reflecting on the experience of that same little boy at secondary. Let's say his headteacher's prophecy comes true (and, of course, her thinking this makes it so very much more likely) and, despite 'booster classes', he arrives at secondary school below national expectations in mathematics.

Do his secondary teachers wonder:

- how many positive mathematics experiences he enjoyed in the early years?

- how equipped and empowered his primary school teachers were to provide him with the learning experiences he needed?

Or is the assumption made that he's just one of those people who, for whatever reason, simply 'isn't good at mathematics'?

In fact, in a study of students who had been identified as 'having a learning problem in mathematics', roughly *half* 'did not show any form of cognitive deficit'.[10] It is very likely that this boy was born with just as much potential to learn mathematics as his higher-attaining peers. His under-attainment is very likely no reflection on his natural ability, but rather is the consequence of the limited quality of the opportunities he has been given to learn.

---

[9] www.oecd.org/pisa/keyfindings/pisa-2012-results-volume-I.pdf accessed 11 August 2017.

[10] **D.C. Geary**, *Children's Mathematical Development: Research and Practical Applications* (Washington, DC: American Psychological Association, 1994), p. 157.

Even given a fairly standard offer of three hours of mathematics per week (and many schools dedicate more time to mathematics than this, plus intervention time on top) this boy will receive almost 600 hours of secondary mathematics education. Given 600 hours, surely his mathematics teachers can influence his learning outcomes? In a sense, that time is wasted if it is decided right from the start that he does not have the potential to succeed in mathematics.

Nearly all school learners are able to learn significant mathematics given appropriate teaching.

 **Consider**

- 'Nearly all school learners' – who does this include? Who might this exclude?

- 'Significant mathematics' – what mathematics is this?

- 'Appropriate teaching' – what is this?

## 'Success for all' – who does this include?

We have focused so far in this chapter on the importance of having high expectations for every student. In this section, we'll consider what is meant by 'every' student. In particular, to what extent might teachers have high expectations of students with low prior attainment? What about students with special educational needs or disabilities?

All students have the right to access a broad and balanced curriculum. There is no need for teachers to assume that students with special educational needs or disabilities will be unable to study the full national curriculum. Throughout this book, the expression 'every student' is used to refer to all students in mainstream education.

Some students may have particular medical conditions that prevent them from reaching national expectations for their age. There will be many aspects of the curriculum where these students can work on the same curriculum content as their peers. A few students may need to work on earlier curriculum content than that intended for their age. However, these students can still benefit from a focus on deep understanding and problem solving.

Teachers can set high expectations for every student, whatever their prior attainment. By planning and teaching to remove barriers to student achievement, it is often the case that students with special educational needs and disabilities will be able to study the full national curriculum.

Teaching for mastery should mean that students who, under other teaching approaches, risk falling a long way behind, are better able to keep up with their peers. Gaps in attainment are narrowed while the attainment of all is raised. As primary schools increasingly adopt teaching for mastery, the need for separate catch-up programmes at secondary school, due to some students having fallen behind, should decrease.

# More students excelling

PISA 2012 results show wide differences in mathematics performance between countries. The difference between the *average* mathematics performances of the countries that took part (245 score points) is the equivalent of almost six years of schooling.

Performance in the PISA tests for 15-year-olds show that – across the OECD countries – around one in ten students is a top performer in mathematics. In Singapore, more than one in three students are high achievers in the subject.

While students in the UK achieve above the OECD average for science and reading, performance in mathematics is around average and has remained stable since 2006.

Teaching for mastery is not just about closing the gap between the highest and lowest achievers. It's about raising achievement for everyone. This not only means more students achieving the highest grades, but more students loving mathematics, more students deeply understanding mathematical concepts, and more students choosing to continue studying mathematics and mathematics-related subjects once it is not compulsory.

This means teaching every concept or skill in a way that promotes understanding and problem solving, so that mathematics is not just a collection of memorised techniques, but rather a coherent body of interconnected knowledge that can be flexibly applied to solve problems in unfamiliar contexts.

## More students excel in East and South-east Asian countries

**OECD** 2016, *op. cit.*

**The study:** According to the OECD's Programme for International Student Assessment (PISA) study, students from East and South-east Asian countries, such as Singapore, Japan, South Korea and China, perform relatively strongly. Their results are, on average, up to three years ahead in mathematics compared with 15-year-olds in, for example, England, France, Italy, Sweden, Australia and New Zealand.[11]

**What it tells us:** The 2015 study found that more than one in four students in Beijing, Shanghai, Jiangsu and Guangdong (China), Hong Kong (China), Singapore and Chinese Taipei are top-performing students in mathematics, meaning that they can handle tasks that require the ability to formulate complex situations mathematically, using symbolic representations.

At PISA level 5, students can:

- develop and work with models for complex situations

- select, compare and evaluate appropriate problem-solving strategies for dealing with complex problems related to these models

- work strategically using broad, well-developed thinking and reasoning skills, appropriate linked representations, and symbolic and formal characterisations.

In the UK, 11 per cent of students achieve level 5. In the four jurisdictions of China that participated in the study (one of which was Shanghai), 26 per cent of students achieved it. This figure was 27 per cent and 28 per cent in Hong Kong and Chinese Taipei respectively, and an impressive 35 per cent in Singapore.

The PISA study gives some indication of what can be achieved through high expectations, with a focus on depth and problem solving. Secondary education is, for many students, a last chance to learn the mathematics that will prepare them for everyday adult life, to gain the foundations for success in the workplace and to grasp the opportunities to discover the creative and intriguing nature of mathematics.

There is a real danger that, even within a predominantly comprehensive system, teachers find themselves mentally 'streaming' students at the beginning of their secondary school careers, deciding at this young age that some students need only the basics of everyday numeracy, that others require preparation for the workplace, and that only an elite minority will develop a real interest in the subject and might pursue mathematics-related disciplines to degree level and beyond.

---

[11] Also Austria, Vietnam, Russia, Czech Republic, Portugal and Iceland.

Such decision making, whether conscious and explicit or not, fast becomes a self-fulfilling prophecy. What if, instead, teachers worked together and held each other to account in the belief that every student might come to discover the power and beauty of mathematics?

## Choosing to continue studying mathematics

**M. Brown, P. Brown and T. Bibby** 2008.[12]

**The study:** Margaret Brown and her colleagues studied the reasons why students choose not to continue studying mathematics after the age of 16. Their study included free response and closed items in a questionnaire with a sample of over 1500 students in 17 schools in London, close to the moment of choice.

**What it tells us:** The analysis supports findings that perceived difficulty and lack of confidence are important reasons for students not continuing with mathematics, and that perceived dislike and boredom, as well as lack of relevance, are also factors. There is a close relationship between reasons for non-participation and predicted grade. Students who perceive mathematics as difficult, and do not see themselves as good at it, are less likely to choose to continue studying the subject.

# Why are high expectations important?

There is some evidence to suggest that any brain differences children are born with are less important than the different experiences they have from birth. Studies are emerging that suggest that brain differences present at birth can be eclipsed by the learning experiences we have from birth onwards.[13]

[12] **M. Brown, P. Brown and T. Bibby**, '"I would rather die": Reasons Given by 16-year-olds for Not Continuing Their Study of Mathematics', *Research in Mathematics Education* 10(1) (2008): pp. 3–18. www.tandfonline.com/doi/full/10.1080/14794800801915814 accessed 11 August 2017.

[13] **B. Wexler**, *Brain and Culture: Neurobiology, Ideology, and Social Change* (Cambridge, MA: MIT Press, 2006).

**Discuss**

Identify a 12- or 13-year-old student who started secondary school working below national expectations. What do you believe is possible for that student?

- What messages might that student have received about what they are capable of? Consider decisions made about grouping or setting, marks and feedback on tests, classwork and homework.

- What expectations might this student perceive that others have of them?

- What expectations might this student have of their own potential to succeed in learning significant mathematics? How might these be informed by the expectations of others? What might be the impact of this self-perception?

## Teaching makes a difference

Low attainment in mathematics has been found to be a result of not a single factor but the interplay of mathematical difficulties, students' intellectual and behavioural characteristics and shortcomings in the quality of teaching.[14] But of these three challenges, which has the most impact?

Most student underachievement, according to evidence collected by Kurt Reusser, is due to deficiencies in teaching and learning environments rather than to the students' genetic make-up.[15] He makes the case that effective teaching positively impacts students' mathematics attainment levels regardless of grade levels or mathematical 'ability'.

Differences in teaching can significantly raise achievement, with the most significant impact for students at risk of underachieving.[16]

High-quality teachers, according to a study by Helen Slater, Neil Davies and Simon Burgess, benefited low-achieving students most, and thus narrowed the range of achievement.[17] The impact of particular teaching strategies on student achievement has been synthesised by John Hattie.[18]

---

[14] **D. Haylock**, *Teaching Mathematics to Low Attainers, 8–12* (London: Paul Chapman Publishing Ltd, 1991).

[15] **K. Reusser**, 'Success and Failure in School Mathematics: Effects of Instruction and School Environment', *European Child & Adolescent Psychiatry* 9(11) (2000): pp. 17–26.

[16] **P. Black and D. Wiliam**, 'Assessment and Classroom Learning', *Assessment in Education: Principles, Policy and Practice* 5(1) (1998), pp. 7–75.

[17] **H. Slater, N. Davies and S. Burgess**, *Do Teachers Matter? Measuring the Variation in Teacher Effectiveness in England* (Bristol: University of Bristol Institute of Public Affairs, 2008).

[18] **J. Hattie**, *Visible Learning: A Synthesis of over 800 Meta-Analyses Relating to Achievement* (London: Routledge, 2008).

## The importance of good teaching

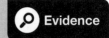

**W. van de Grift** 2007.[19]

**The study:** In a large-scale study, Wim van de Grift provided evidence for the difference that good teaching can make. Mathematics lessons in England, Flanders (Belgium), Lower Saxony (Germany) and the Netherlands were observed in 854 classrooms, with children who were about nine years old when they started the school year. The education inspectorates in these European countries reviewed the results of research on the basic characteristics of effective teaching. The inspectorates from these countries jointly developed an instrument to observe and analyse the quality of learning and teaching.

They agreed five research-informed scales:

- Safe and stimulating learning climate

- Clear instruction

- Adaptation of teaching

- Teaching–learning strategies

- Efficient classroom management.

For the 87 lessons in England, the researchers calculated the correlations between the scales of the observation instrument and student attainment.

**What it tells us:** Higher-quality mathematics teaching resulted in improved student outcomes. The correlations between the five scales and student attainment varied between 0.32 and 0.68. The researchers concluded that all five of the scales on their observation instrument were positively and significantly related with student attainment.

## Teachers' beliefs transform student achievement

Teacher reassurance for students finding mathematics more difficult can focus on how committed the teacher is to supporting the student to deepen their understanding. Such reassurance can focus on how, if they persist and take their time, the teacher will do all they can to ensure it all starts to make

---

[19] **W. van de Grift**, 'Quality of Teaching in Four European Countries: A Review of the Literature and Application of an Assessment Instrument', *Education Research* 49/2 (2007): pp. 127–152.

more sense. This will be of more benefit to them than attempts to reassure them by claiming that it 'doesn't matter'.[20]

## Comforting feedback demotivates

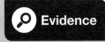

**A. Rattan, C. Good and C.S. Dweck** 2012.[21]

**The study:** Aneeta Rattan, Catherine Good and Carol Dweck investigated the connection between teachers' mindset and the nature of their feedback to students. They explored what this comfort-oriented feedback communicated to students, compared with strategy-oriented and control feedback.

**What it tells us:** They found that teachers holding an entity (fixed) theory of mathematics intelligence were quicker to judge students as having low ability than teachers holding an incremental (malleable) theory. These teachers were also more likely to both comfort students for being 'less able' at mathematics and use 'kind' strategies likely to reduce engagement with mathematics, such as setting less homework.

Students responding to comfort-oriented feedback not only perceived the instructor's entity theory and low expectations, but also reported lowered motivation and lower expectations for their own performance. This research has implications for understanding how teacher mindset can reduce student achievement.

## Students with a growth mindset achieve more

Carol Dweck's research has demonstrated that students and teachers who believe that intelligence is flexible, and that their goal is to learn as much as they can, are more successful than those who focus on passing exams and completing tasks.[22]

*Fixed Mindset: Intelligence is a fixed trait*

*Growth Mindset: Intelligence is a quality that can be changed and developed.*[23]

---

[20] **A. Rattan, C. Good and C.S. Dweck**, '"It's ok, not everyone can be good at math": Instructors with an Entity Theory Comfort (and Demotivate) Students', *Journal of Experimental Social Psychology* 48 (2012): pp. 731–737.

[21] *Ibid.*

[22] **C.S. Dweck**, *Self-Theories: Their Role in Motivation, Personality and Development* (Philadelphia, VA: Psychology Press, 1999).

[23] **C.S. Dweck**, 'Can Personality be Changed? The Role of Beliefs in Personality and Change', *Current Directions in Psychological Science* 17 (2008): pp. 391–394.

Learners with a fixed mindset:

- believe that you either have ability or you don't
- are reluctant to take on challenges
- are worried about making mistakes
- prefer to stay in their comfort zone
- think it is important to seem intelligent in front of others.

Learners with a growth mindset:

- believe that effort creates success
- believe that ability can be increased over time
- view mistakes as an opportunity to develop
- are resilient
- think about how they learn.

Carol Dweck[33] argues that as teachers aiming for success for all, supporting students with their 'orientation to learning' is as important as the design of the curriculum, scheme of work or task. She categorises students' orientation to learning in terms of whether they hold either *performance* goals or *mastery* goals.

Students with performance goals seek to get the correct answers. They evaluate their success based on feedback from a teacher. They give up quickly when challenged. They want to learn but are more comfortable on tasks with which they are familiar.

Students with mastery goals seek to master the content. They evaluate their own success based on whether they feel they can transfer their knowledge to other situations. They remain focused on mastery, especially when challenged. Students with a mastery-goal orientation don't see failure as a negative reflection on themselves. They connect effort with success.

It is clear that students' self-concept – how they feel about themselves as mathematics learners – impacts on their achievement in the subject. As John Hattie emphasises:

> *Achievement is more likely to be increased when students invoke learning rather than performance strategies, accept rather than discount feedback, benchmark to difficult rather than easy goals, compare themselves to*

*subject criteria rather than to other students, possess high rather than low efficacy to learning, and affect self-regulation and personal control rather than learned helplessness in the academic situation.*[24]

Confucian-heritage territories such as China, Singapore, South Korea, Taiwan and Hong Kong Special Administrative Region (SAR) seem to place a greater emphasis on effort than on innate ability. In these high-performing systems, deeper understanding is typically assumed to result from deep engagement with subject matter, including using memorisation where appropriate.[25]

In a study focused on using growth mindset interventions with children at risk of dropping out of school,[26] David Paunesku and colleagues (including Dweck) observed an increase in student attainment.

Teachers adopting teaching for mastery believe that a student's mindset is more important than their prior attainment in determining the progress they will make. Students with a growth mindset will make better progress than students with a fixed mindset.[27]

We have a responsibility to provide the learning experiences that do just that and give every student the opportunity to succeed.

## High expectations for all

 **Case study**

**The school context:** Dunraven school, London, is putting high expectations into practice. Although the school sets students by prior attainment, the mathematics team challenge each other not to lower their expectations when working with students in lower sets. This manifests in a problem-solving approach in every lesson, regardless of students' prior attainment.

The school inspectorate in England, Ofsted, found that 'Teachers and supporting adults unanimously encourage, support and express their very high expectations for every pupil, and the pupils equally expect the very best of themselves.'

Teachers have found that students are getting excited about the mathematics and that they enjoy discussing problems in lessons.

---

[24] **J. Hattie,** *op. cit.*

[25] **J. Cogan, P. Morris and M. Print,** *Civic Education in the Asian-Pacific Region* (London: Routledge Falmer, 2002).

[26] **D. Paunesku** et al., 'Mind-set Interventions are a Scalable Treatment for Academic Underachievement', *Psychological Science* 26(6) (2015): pp. 784–793.

[27] **C.S. Dweck** 1999, *op. cit.*

**Their impact:** The school is seeing students achieve high standards – significantly above average, despite starting Year 7 with mathematics skills broadly in line with their peers nationally.[28] Ofsted found that students 'make fast progress and reach standards which are significantly above average by the time they leave'.

# High expectations in practice

We began this chapter by challenging our preconceptions as to what might be possible for every student, and reconsidering the proportion of students who might have the potential to be high performers in mathematics. We then considered the real impact that teacher beliefs and preconceptions about students can have, establishing the importance of high expectations. In this section, we look at two ways of putting high expectations into practice – removing student labelling and the power of 'not yet'.

## No labels

A crucial aspect of adopting a growth mindset is removing any preconceived ideas about which students have more or less potential. No student is pre-judged due to their prior attainment. It is important that teachers think carefully about how to support students who find a concept difficult, and how to challenge students who find it more accessible. But there is no need to decide in advance which students will require the support and which students will thrive on the challenge.

In education systems with high-stakes national testing, schools' decisions can be based almost entirely on their drive to achieve as many 'good' passes as possible in national tests. This can encourage teachers to adopt a notion of 'fixed ability', grouping students into those guaranteed to achieve 'good' grades, those who might succeed with significant input, and those who are effectively written off.[29]

Teaching for mastery means embracing the challenge of finding and adopting classroom practices that are beneficial for all students. Students with lower prior attainment do not need different teaching. Students with high potential do not need to learn different mathematics. And we must continue to remind

---

[28] **Dunraven Ofsted Report**, https://reports.ofsted.gov.uk/inspection-eports/findinspection-report/provider/ELS/137093 accessed 11 August 2017.

[29] **D. Gillborn and D. Youdell**, *Rationing Education: Policy, Practice, Reform, and Equity* (Buckingham: Open University Press, 2000).

ourselves that there may be many students who fall into both of these groups. A student with low prior attainment may well have the potential to excel in mathematics, if only they are well taught.

If we fool ourselves into thinking that different students have different potential, and that this potential is fixed on entry to secondary school, we deny students the opportunity to progress and excel.

Each new lesson or lesson series is a new start. Teachers can decide which students will work on which task based on observations and questioning during the lesson or series of lessons, rather than on generalised assumptions about overall ability. Better still, teachers can offer the same opportunity to learn to all students, and have all students tackling the same tasks.

David Hargreaves argues that ability labelling leads to 'destruction of dignity so massive and pervasive that few subsequently recover from it'.[30] Rather than creating 'low ability' or 'high ability' sets, we can create flexible in-class groupings as and when necessary, based on students' current depth of understanding of the relevant concept or skill.

 **Discuss**

Does the language that teachers in our school use about mathematics attainment risk giving some students the impression that it's not worth trying, as they'll never be much good?

Teachers in high-performing systems are much less focused on the labelling of differential attainment. Instead, they prioritise ensuring that all students have developed sufficient understanding of the key concepts and content in a block of learning before moving on to the next block of content.[31]

## High expectations in Singapore

Step into a Singaporean classroom and it is extremely difficult to work out which set you are observing. Teachers in every classroom act as if they expect all students to succeed.

This commitment to opportunity for all continues into secondary education. Although students are set, movement between sets is frequent. Perhaps more

[30] **D. Hargreaves**, *The Challenge for the Comprehensive School* (London: Routledge and Kegan Paul, 1982), p. 66.

[31] **Department for Education**, *The Framework for the National Curriculum. A report by the Expert Panel for the National Curriculum Review* (London: Department for Education, 2011), p. 45.

significantly, placement in lower sets does not limit opportunities to learn, as all secondary students are taught the same curriculum for the first three years.

Several schools who have joined the *Mathematics Mastery* partnership in England have taken the opportunity to reduce their use of setting. They group students with mixed prior attainment in Year 7, and in some cases across Key Stage 3. As more primary schools in England teach mathematics for mastery, we can expect to see the spread in students' attainment at the start of secondary school reduce, as attainment for all increases, particularly those previously falling far behind. This will make a shift away from setting by prior attainment increasingly feasible.

The school's own assessment and tracking processes can unintentionally result in many children being labelled as struggling with mathematics – as if there was simply nothing that could be done about it. As we will explore in Chapter 5, the more frequently schools summatively assess students – comparing them with others and labelling their performance with grades – the greater the negative consequences.

Rather than grouping and labelling some students as 'less able', or even 'previously lower attaining', and assuming they must always be treated differently and are destined to achieve less well, why not focus on what can be done to maximise every student's learning?

Yes, some students will find mathematical concepts challenging at times. Yes, some students will seem to find concepts intuitive and grasp them almost instantly. But these might not always be two different groups of people! As part of learning mathematics, everyone experiences challenges and confusion at points, and everyone experiences moments of clarity and insight. These moments are steps on a varied, complex and fascinating journey. Noticing such struggles and insights is important to us as teachers as it helps to inform the decisions we make about the appropriate scaffolding or challenge to provide for particular children at particular times. However, these observations are not useful in making predictions about students' longer-term success or failure with the subject.

This is, of course, much more challenging for teachers of secondary mathematics than for those teaching in the primary phase. By the time they begin secondary school, many students have already reached the conclusion that they 'can't do' mathematics. But the enormity of this challenge does not make it any less worthwhile. It is vital that we do all we can to ensure that the five years of mathematics education that all students receive from age 11 is a valuable and positive one, that deepens their understanding and increases their propensity to continue learning mathematics beyond 16.

What can we do to help all students realise their potential and take a positive view of learning mathematics? Researchers from the University of York carried out a systematic review of the literature. They asked what strategies can raise motivational effort in Key Stage 4 mathematics among students whose attainment ranges between the twentieth and fiftieth percentile in England.

## Grouping and pupil identity

**C. Kyriacou and M. Goulding** 2005.[32]

**The study:** The authors systematically reviewed the literature relating to student motivation in learning mathematics.

**What it tells us:** In their analysis of 25 studies, four key themes emerged. Alongside teaching for engagement and use of innovative methods, grouping and pupil identity were found to be key areas that influence student motivation.

The studies identified a particular issue concerning the impact on motivational effort of how pupils are grouped to form classes. The studies in the review emphasised that if the whole class knew that being in a lower set would deny them access to higher GCSE grades, this could make it very difficult for them to sustain their motivational effort.

Studies focusing on how student identity influences student motivation looked at the extent to which students have a positive pupil identity of themselves as people who can understand and do mathematics. The authors state:

*Developing a more positive pupil identity involves the use of strategies characterised by:*

*(i) providing a caring and supportive classroom climate;*

*(ii) providing activities which pupils find challenging and enjoyable;*

*(iii) enabling pupils to gain a deeper understanding of the mathematics;*

*(iv) providing opportunities for pupils to collaborate; and*

*(v) enabling the pupils to feel equally valued.*

---

[32] **C. Kyriacou and M. Goulding**, 'A Systematic Review of Strategies to Raise Pupils' Motivational Effort in Key Stage 4 Mathematics', in *Proceedings of the British Society for Research into Learning Mathematics* 25(3), edited by D. Hewitt (November 2005), pp. 82–83.

# Change your language – the power of 'not yet'

Students whose parents have high expectations of them perform better: they tend to try harder, have more confidence in their own ability and are more motivated to learn.[33] While we're working on changing students' mindsets, we need to make sure that all adults working with students have the very highest expectations for them.

At its simplest level, this means that where a student doesn't fully grasp a new concept or idea the first time it is taught, instead of using this as evidence to label them as a mathematical 'low achiever', the teacher tries alternative explanations and approaches. In my experience, persistent dedication to every child's success in this way can have an impressive impact.

Carol Dweck describes the power of moving away from using expressions like 'failure' and 'I can't', instead saying 'not yet'.[34]

 **Try this in the classroom**

If a student says 'I can't do it', finish the sentence for them with 'yet'. Work on your students' language – not the way they talk about mathematics but the way they talk about *learning* mathematics. Ban phrases such as 'I can't add fractions', insisting on the addition of the word 'yet' – 'I can't add fractions…yet. I need more practice.' The effect of these 'high expectation behaviours' can be very powerful.

There is a big difference between consistently being offered the 'easy task' and sometimes being offered something different that leads to you making greater progress.

 **Consider**

Think about your own classroom. Do you promote the idea that every student can succeed, or do you reinforce the idea that some students are destined to excel while others will inevitably struggle?

---

[33] **K. Marjoribanks**, 'Family Background, Individual and Environmental Influences on Adolescents' Aspirations', *Educational Studies* 28 (2002): pp. 33–46.

[34] **C.S. Dweck**, Mindset: *The New Psychology of Success*. (New York: Ballantine Books, 2006).

In particular, consider:

- how students are grouped for mathematics
- how mathematics tasks are assigned to students
- how extension groups are formed
- how intervention is given, and who gives it.

# The role of society

Anyone involved in secondary mathematics education – teachers, teaching assistants, school leaders, family members and members of wider society – has a responsibility to aim high for every student.

When Shanghai or Singapore are held up as examples of what might be possible elsewhere, people point to the high levels of parental involvement and investment in private tutoring there. As individual classroom teachers or school leaders, it can be tempting to question whether there is anything teachers can do.

### Tutoring in high-performing countries

An OECD study[35] found that 71 per cent of students in Shanghai use after-school mathematics tutoring. In Singapore, the top-ranked system in PISA 2015, 68 per cent attended such tutoring. However, perhaps it is worth looking first at the quality of teaching and school leadership in successful countries, and only then considering other factors. Parental support, and learning outside school, may well contribute to student success, and efforts to involve parents can only be a good thing. However, we should not despair if such support seems impossible to achieve in a given context.

In schools where a number of students are tutored, they report that this has limited effect on their overall outcomes. In fact, sometimes the effect can be detrimental as students take less responsibility for their own learning in lessons, assuming their tutor will sort out any confusion. If tutors focus on method over understanding, this can reduce rather than increase students' ability to make connections between mathematical concepts and procedures.

---

[35] **OECD**, *PISA 2012 Results: What Students Know and Can Do: Student Performance in Mathematics, Reading and Science (Volume 1)* (Paris: OECD Publishing, 2012).

In my experience, schools in England in the most challenging of circumstances are able to increase achievement through transformational classroom teaching, even in the absence of tutoring, and where parental involvement continues to be work in progress.

In higher-performing jurisdictions, teachers, students and parents believe mathematical success is possible for all. No one assumes that some children will inevitably struggle and fail. The Chinese conception of ability and effort is quite different from the West's. For example, in China, there is a generally held belief that ability is not 'internal and uncontrollable', but something that one can 'develop'.[36]

Of course, some students find mathematics easier than their peers. But we must not underestimate the impact of the teacher.

It is often observed that East Asian societies tend to attribute success to effort, and that they place a high social value on achievement. They are understood to have a strong belief in the maxim 'practice makes perfect'.[37] Teachers in the West often feel envious of the apparent diligence and competitive spirit of East Asian students. However, Ngai-Ying Wong warns that 'over-simplification and generalisation of the characteristics' of learners in East Asia could result in underestimating the importance of curriculum and pedagogy.[38]

There's clearly a societal, cultural advantage in some higher-performing countries – they have a head start. But is it inevitable that societies' expectations and values will determine students' success?

Where individual learners have a fixed mindset, societies' expectations and values can negatively impact on their achievement.

However, the evidence is emerging to show that, even where learners report that negative stereotypes are widespread in their environment, those who hold a growth mindset continue to feel that, with effort,

[36] **T. Good and R. Weinstein**, 'Teacher Expectations', in *Improving Teaching: 1986 ASCD Yearbook,* edited by K. Zumwalt (Alexandria, VA: Association for Supervision and Curriculum Development, 1986).

[37] **D.A. Watkins and J.B. Biggs, J.B.**, eds, *The Chinese Learner: Cultural, Psychological and Contextual Influences* (Hong Kong: Comparative Education Research Centre and Victoria, Australia: The Australian Council for the Educational Research, 1996).

[38] **N.Y. Wong**, Mathematics education and culture: the 'CHC' learner phenomenon (2000). http://ibrarian.net/navon/paper/Mathematics_Education_and_Culture__the__CHC__Lear.pdf?paperid=3897969 accessed 11 August 2017.

they could be successful with mathematics.[39] In other words, even if expectations in wider society are low, students can develop and maintain a growth mindset. This is exciting, as it suggests that changing the culture in the classroom may help to transform achievement even while society catches up.

To see real transformation, a nation must unite behind an effort to ensure that every student succeeds and a high proportion of them excel. Teaching for mastery requires much more than implementing a new programme of study or using specific practices – it involves taking a stand for what is right.

---

### Aiming high for every student

 **Case study**

**The school context:** Oasis Academy South Bank, London, opened as a new school in 2013 with a determination to achieve success for every student. Having set out an aspirational mathematics curriculum for all students, the school invests in extensive planning to ensure that all students can understand the concepts taught.[40] For example, of the five classes preparing for GCSE (i.e., 16+ examinations), four are learning all 'higher tier' content, and the fifth class is learning enough to enable students to access this tier – in no class are students restricted to the foundation tier.

The mathematics team craft success criteria carefully, so that every student has access to the same curriculum. They help each other to aim high even when teaching students who have low prior attainment. This is standardised through the department's 'Mastery Matrix', which tracks each student's understanding of each skill through an exit ticket, homework and a stretch task. Through weekly co-planning sessions, they work together to consistently support and challenge all students to master every skill. Most lessons include visual or concrete representations to aid conceptual understanding. Every lesson includes problem solving.

**Their impact:** The school has taught mathematics for mastery since opening. By the end of their third year, the head of mathematics reported that 95 per cent of students were on track to achieve a 'good' grade at GCSE (with 71 of the

---

[39] See, for example, **C. Good, A. Rattan and C.S. Dweck**, 'Development of the sense of belonging to math survey for adults: A longitudinal study of women in calculus', unpublished manuscript (2007).

[40] Ofsted Report for Oasis Academy South Bank. https://reports.ofsted.gov.uk/inspectionreports/find-inspection-report/provider/ELS/139659 accessed 11 August 2017.

120 Year 9 students already attaining a grade C on past exam papers). Nearly a third of students are expected to achieve one of the two highest grades: in the specific terms of the English assessment system, the school expects 31 per cent of this cohort to achieve the equivalent of A or A* grades. Half the students are entered for the problem-solving intensive UKMT Challenge, with over 30 receiving certificates and at least one student qualifying for the next round.

Teaching for mastery is motivated by a commitment to transforming achievement for all. The argument of this book is that, for mathematics education to result in success for every student – and a significant proportion excelling – teachers need to keep year groups working together, spend more time on teaching topics, and provide opportunities for all students to develop deep understanding. We will consider the curricular aspects of this – one curriculum for all and taking your time – in Chapter 4. The question of how teachers can offer learning experiences so that students develop deep and rigorous understanding will be our focus in Chapters 6 to 9.

# Summary

The starting point for teaching for mastery is the ambition that every student will succeed in mathematics and a significant proportion will excel.

International comparisons strongly suggest that the tail of underachievement seen in many countries is far from inevitable. More students can succeed in mathematics.

The proportion of students excelling in mathematics – and the depth of understanding these high-attaining students achieve – also varies considerably between countries.

Why are high expectations important?

- Teaching makes a difference – students may be capable of more than we realise.

- Teachers' beliefs affect student achievement.

- Students with a growth mindset achieve more.

What do high expectations mean in practice?

- No labels: avoid labelling students as 'more able' or 'less able'.

- The power of 'not yet': if a student says 'I can't do it', finish the sentence for them with 'yet'.

Although some countries have a societal, cultural advantage, teaching with high expectations can make a real difference to student achievement.

# Chapter 3

## Why do students learn mathematics?

**T**eaching for mastery begins with the belief that everyone can succeed in mathematics and a significant proportion can excel. This achievement goes beyond success in national exams. Mathematics is vital both for individual well-being and for the prosperity of societies – in this chapter we'll take a look at why.

Secondary mathematics is transformative. Learners who succeed with mathematics at secondary school are significantly more likely to continue their education beyond 16, to be in employment as adults,[1] and to likely earn more.[2]

---

 **Consider**

Why is learning mathematics important?

- Take some time to think, talk and write about why you believe mathematics education is important.

- Write your own statement that explains your feelings about the significance of mathematics education.

- If a colleague spent some time in your classroom, would your beliefs about the value of mathematics education become apparent?

If, for example, you are passionate about preparing a generation to become a numerate workforce, you might incorporate realistic work-based problems into your lessons. If you believe an important purpose for mathematics education is developing a sense of logic and reasoning, you might ask students questions such as, 'Does it always work?', 'What about for negative numbers?', 'Can I generalise and find a rule?', 'Can I disprove my rule?'

---

[1] **Department for Education and Skills**, *A fresh start: improving literacy and numeracy. The report of the working group on post-school basic skills chaired by Sir Claus Moser* (Nottingham: Department for Education and Skills, 1999).

[2] **C. Crawford and J. Cribb**, *Reading and maths skills at age 10 and earnings in later life: A brief analysis using the British cohort study* (Report No. 3) (UK: Centre for Analysis of Youth Transitions, 2013).

The development of students' ability to think logically and solve mathematical problems is both enjoyable in its own right and vital for success in a wide variety of fields. Inequity in the teaching of mathematics is consequently a serious social issue – every student is entitled to a high-quality mathematics education.

To be in a position to agree on the principles that underpin effective mathematics teaching, we must first agree on what success looks like. Why is mathematics education important? What are mathematics teachers trying to achieve?

Those informing and shaping policy and practice in mathematics education hold a range of views of mathematics, as Paul Ernest has described.[3] This diversity can lead to policy and recommendations that pull in different directions, resulting in confusing or even conflicting advice for mathematics teachers.

High-performing jurisdictions make the purpose of education explicit. In developing the framework for the National Curriculum in England, Tim Oates and colleagues found that:

> High-performing jurisdictions are explicit about the practical and functional contributions that education makes to national development … In almost all cases, schools are expected to contribute, in a balanced way, to development in all of the following domains:
>
> - Economic – the education of pupils is expected to contribute to their own future economic wellbeing and that of the nation or region;
>
> - Cultural – the education of pupils is expected to introduce them to the best of their cultural heritage(s), so that they can contribute to its further development;
>
> - Social – the education of pupils is expected to enable them to participate in families, communities and the life of the nation; and
>
> - Personal – the education of pupils is expected to promote the intellectual, spiritual, moral and physical development of individuals.[4]

Before we can begin to consider recommendations for effective curriculum, assessment and classroom practice, it is vital that we are clear on the purpose of mathematics education. In this section, we address the importance of learning mathematics from three perspectives: mathematics for day-to-day life, mathematics for the workplace, and mathematics for its own sake.

---

[3] **P. Ernest**, *The Philosophy of Mathematics Education* (London: Falmer, 1991).

[4] **Department for Education**, *The Framework for the National Curriculum. A report by the Expert Panel for the National Curriculum review* (London: Department for Education, 2011), p. 15.

# Mathematics is important for everyone

When distinguishing the purposes of studying secondary mathematics, it is vital that we do not separate the students we teach in the same way. It is not the case that one group of students needs school mathematics for academia and further study, another for the workplace, and a third for everyday life.

The reality is quite the opposite, in fact. The reason it is valuable to separate out these three distinct purposes of studying mathematics is *to ensure that all students see the benefits of all three purposes.* As emphasised throughout Chapter 2, mathematical success is not an attribute that an individual has or does not have. These mathematical skills can be acquired and used, to a greater or lesser extent, throughout a lifetime. All school learners have a right to learn key mathematical ideas.

Teaching for mastery means teaching every student to reason mathematically, to use mathematical concepts and techniques to describe, explain and predict phenomena, and to make well-founded judgements and decisions.

An individual learner may end up primarily using the mathematics they've learned in school for academic study, in the workplace, or in their everyday life. But it is not the role of secondary mathematics teachers to make decisions about which 11- and 12-year-olds will need which mathematics for what. In fact, there is evidence to suggest that teachers' ability to assess students' potential, to make judgements about students' understanding, may not be as strong as is sometimes suggested.[5]

# We learn mathematics for our day-to-day life

An important aim in teaching and learning mathematics is as preparation for adult life and as a foundation for understanding the world. People must be equipped to think for themselves and to make judgements on all issues affecting them. A good foundation in mathematics is a key component of this.

---

[5] **A. Watson**, 'Mathematics Teachers Acting as Informal Assessors: Practices, Problems and Recommendations', *Educational Studies in Mathematics* 41 (2000): p. 69.

In daily life, we need to be able to make reasoned and appropriate estimates, and to be able to check the plausibility of mathematical outcomes applied to the real world. We need to be able to understand and interpret risk and data. Everybody needs to be confident in the management of their own money and to appreciate the financial implications of decisions. Students should be numerically competent, and be confident in the use of percentages, fractions, ratios and proportion. We also want students' mathematics education to equip them with well-developed spatial, number and probability awareness, and for them to be able to solve problems relating to real-life situations.

Through learning mathematics, students develop their logical thinking skills and their ability to reason. As Sir Michael Wilshaw, Chief Inspector for England's school inspectorate, Ofsted, from 2012 to 2016, emphasised in the introduction to its *Mathematics: Made to Measure* report, 'Mathematics is essential for everyday life and understanding our world.'[6]

Learning mathematics prepares students for citizenship. Through learning to understand statistics, compare choices and understand large numbers, they are prepared to play an active role as informed citizens.

# We learn mathematics for the workplace

Mathematics education should provide students with the knowledge and skills that they need in the world of work. By teaching mathematics, we enable people to contribute to the development of a productive economy. We need a suitably equipped workforce ready to adapt to the needs of a growing economy, ready and willing to devote themselves to scientific and industrial research and development, and to the finance and IT industries.

Recent reports have stressed the serious shortage in the UK economy of people qualified in science, technology, engineering and mathematics (STEM), with rising demand outstripping a declining supply. The Smith report[7] in particular, stressed the national need for more young people to study mathematics for longer. The report emphasised that:

*Mathematical concepts, models and techniques are also key to many vital areas of the knowledge economy, including the finance and ICT*

---

[6] **Ofsted**, *Mathematics: Made to Measure* (London: Office for Standards in Education, 2012), p. 4.

[7] **A. Smith**, *Making Mathematics Count: The Report of Professor Adrian Smith's Inquiry into Post-14 Mathematics Education* (London: The Stationery Office, 2004).

*industries. Mathematics is crucially important, too, for the employment opportunities and achievements of individual citizens.*

Not only can the techniques and skills learned in mathematics be usefully applied to a large range of technical and scientific contexts; the need for such skills extends far beyond the 'STEM' industries. As the Advisory Committee on Mathematics Education (ACME) in England noted in its 2011 *Mathematical Needs* report:

> *In the workforce there is a steady shift away from manual and low-skill jobs towards those requiring higher levels of management expertise and problem-solving skills, many of which are mathematical in nature.*[8]

A mathematics education must prepare students to understand, interpret and use mathematical models. We need students to be confident in the management of budgets and appreciate the financial implications of decisions made in relation to those budgets. Students need to be able to manipulate and interpret data sets, and to be able to identify trends and spot anomalies.

To prepare students for the world of work, we need them to be able to communicate their mathematical understanding. To be ready for many workplaces, for example those where spreadsheets are used, students need to understand the concept of a variable and be familiar with simple algebraic manipulation. They also need be proficient and persistent in problem solving.

Research has found that students who study mathematics to an advanced level learn ways of working and thinking – especially learning to reason and be logical – that make them more productive in their jobs. Students learning mathematics at higher levels learn how to approach mathematical situations so that once they are employed, they are promoted to more demanding and more highly paid positions.[9] Mathematics therefore acts as a social discriminant.

# We learn mathematics for its own sake

A thorough knowledge and understanding of mathematics is of academic value in its own right. From the perspective of the individual, this is about the importance of mathematics as a subject for the improvement of the mind.

---

[8] **ACME**, *Mathematical Needs: Mathematics in the Workplace and in Higher Education* (London: Advisory Committee on Mathematics Education, 2011).

[9] **H. Rose and J.R. Betts**, 'The Effect of High School Courses on Earnings', *Review of Economics and Statistics* 86 (2004): pp. 497–513. http://faculty.smu.edu/millimet/classes/eco7321/papers/rose%20betts.pdf accessed 11 August 2017.

The purpose of study for mathematics in the 2014 National Curriculum[10] in England, for example, emphasises this:

> Mathematics is a creative and highly interconnected discipline that has been developed over centuries, providing the solution to some of history's most intriguing problems ... A high-quality mathematics education therefore provides a foundation for understanding the world, the ability to reason mathematically, an appreciation of the beauty and power of mathematics, and a sense of enjoyment and curiosity about the subject.

Mathematics can therefore be viewed as a subject worth studying in its own right, in the absence of any application. Learners can be surprised and intrigued by mathematics. Through mathematics learning they can develop their creativity and curiosity. As Anne Watson states in her 2006 book, 'Mathematics can be terrific fun; knowing that you enjoy it is psychologically and intellectually empowering.'[11]

Viewing the study of mathematics as a means to developing thought is by no means new. As far back as the ancient Greeks, mathematics has been taught with this purpose. Plato described how the study of arithmetic 'draws the mind upwards', though only 'if one studies it for the sake of knowledge and not for commercial ends'.[12]

Through high-quality mathematics education, sufficient people will be inducted into the academic community, including an adequate supply of good teachers at all levels. This guarantees the future development of mathematics and its place within our cultural heritage.

To induct students into the academic mathematics community, we need them to be able to communicate mathematical ideas precisely and efficiently using accepted terminology. School mathematics as a grounding for further study of mathematics might include beginning to develop mathematical models and understand proofs. Students need to be proficient in algebra and mathematical reasoning. They should also be proficient and persistent in problem solving.

Knowledge about mathematics is important, and countries need citizens who can reproduce such knowledge. But they also need people who can

---

[10] **Department for Education**, *Draft National Curriculum Programmes of Study* (London: Department for Education, 2013), p. 40.

[11] **A. Watson**, *Raising Achievement in Secondary Mathematics* (Buckingham: Open University Press, 2006), p.3.

[12] **Plato**, *The Republic*, trans. H. Lee (Harmondsworth: Penguin, 1987), p. 322.

extrapolate from what they have learned and can apply that knowledge in unfamiliar settings. The emphasis, then, must go beyond what people know, to what they can *do* with what they know.

The team behind the PISA study use the term 'mathematical literacy' to describe the purpose of mathematics education. According to them:

> *Mathematical literacy is defined as students' capacity to formulate, employ and interpret mathematics in a variety of contexts. It includes reasoning mathematically and using mathematical concepts, procedures, facts and tools to describe, explain and predict phenomena. It assists individuals in recognising the role that mathematics plays in the world and to make the well-founded judgements and decisions needed by constructive, engaged and reflective citizens.*[13]

The ultimate aim of mathematics education is to ensure that young people are proficient and persistent in problem solving. They should learn to solve problems relating to real-life situations and to the workplace, as well as abstract mathematical problems.

What are the implications of this for classroom practice? Students need to:

- represent mathematical ideas, make connections, use mathematics flexibly, and learn to decompose and recompose numbers

- reason, and communicate their mathematical ideas

- learn to ask mathematical questions, explore patterns and relationships, and think, generalise and problem-solve.

The ultimate aim of mathematics education is to ensure that young people are proficient and persistent in solving mathematical problems.

Problem solving is the purpose of mathematics education. The facts and techniques we teach are absolutely vital as a means to this end, not an end in themselves.

 **Consider**

Remember the question we asked at the start of this chapter – why is learning mathematics important? What if you were to ask the same question of the students you teach, or of your colleagues in other subject departments. Would their answer be the same or different from yours?

---

[13] **OECD**, *PISA 2015 Results (Volume II): Policies and Practices for Successful Schools* (Paris: OECD Publishing, 2016), p. 28. http://dx.doi.org/10.1787/9789264267510-en accessed 14 August 2017.

Often, when justifying the value of learning mathematics to students, teachers – especially those who teach subjects other than mathematics – emphasise how mathematics is used when budgeting, shopping or undertaking other tasks in daily life. Or they make claims – often well evidenced – about the advantage mathematics (or mathematics *qualifications*) gives people in the workplace.

Yes, a mathematics education is useful. In mathematics lessons, students learn skills and knowledge that will be useful in everyday life, and that will equip them for the workplace. But that should not be all they learn, or all they expect to learn. Mathematical scholarship is valuable in its own right.

# Summary

Mathematics is important for everyone. Everyone needs mathematics for their day-to-day life, for the workplace, and for its own sake.

All students should experience the benefits of all three purposes of learning mathematics. All school learners have a right to learn key mathematical ideas. Teaching for mastery means teaching every student to reason mathematically, to use mathematical concepts and techniques to describe, explain and predict phenomena, and to make well-founded judgements and decisions.

## We learn mathematics for our day-to-day life

An important aim in teaching and learning mathematics is as preparation for adult life and as a foundation for understanding the world. People must be equipped to think for themselves and to make judgements on all issues affecting them. A good foundation in mathematics is a key component of this.

## We learn mathematics for the workplace

Mathematics education should provide students with the relevant knowledge and skills they need in the world of work. By teaching mathematics, we enable people to contribute to the development of a productive economy.

## Mathematics is a subject worth studying in its own right

Learners can be surprised and intrigued by mathematics. Through mathematics learning they can develop their creativity and curiosity.

A mathematics education is useful, but mathematical scholarship is also valuable in its own right. It is important that we go beyond the merely useful when designing, teaching and justifying mathematics education.

# Chapter 4

## What mathematics should you teach when?

**A** curriculum designed for mastery reflects high expectations for every learner. As soon as you try to put the belief that everyone can learn mathematics into practice, you are likely to find yourself asking how you can offer every student the appropriate learning experiences. How can a curriculum be mapped out to enable every student to succeed?

A curriculum for mastery is built on the following principles:

- A belief that *every student* is entitled to access key concepts and skills: the key ideas and building blocks are important for everyone, with differentiation through depth.

- Time is spent *understanding* core mathematics content.

- *Connections* between areas of mathematics are emphasised and learning builds over time: future mathematical learning is built on solid foundations that do not need to be re-taught.

In this chapter, we take a look at the theoretical and evidence-based rationale for this approach to curriculum design.

---

### A curriculum for mastery

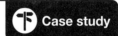 **Case study**

**The school context:** In 2009, only 22 per cent of students at Charter Academy, Portsmouth, UK, achieved five A*–C grades, including English and Mathematics – 78 per cent did not. Adopting a curriculum for mastery, where teachers and students took their time to explore and learn big ideas, was one of the major changes Charter Academy's mathematics team made to transform the school's performance at GCSE (i.e., at 16+).

Students are grouped by prior attainment, but all classes (from the lowest set to the highest) work towards the same aim in each lesson, tackling the same mathematical problems. When chatting between lessons, students are able to talk about the mathematics they are learning. Sometimes students in higher sets find that their peers in other groups have solved a problem that they are still grappling with, giving a positive message about growth mindset for all involved.

**Their impact:** The mathematics team found the new curriculum structure has meant their students are no longer daunted by mathematics. Students talk about mathematics, enjoy their lessons, engage with concepts, and succeed with problems they previously wouldn't have attempted to tackle.

In just five years, the school shifted attainment from 22 per cent successfully achieving five A*–C grades, including English and Mathematics, to 83 per cent of students achieving this.

# One curriculum

The *Mathematics Mastery* programme of study for 11–12-year-olds focuses on additive relationships for a couple of months at the start of secondary school. Rather than hurry higher-attaining students on to cover more content, teachers following the programme stick to addition and subtraction of integers and decimals.

During this time, when focusing on the concept of perimeter, teachers find that some students seem to have grasped the concept. They readily state that the perimeter is the distance around a shape. They accurately and efficiently calculate the perimeter of a rectangle.

There can be a tendency in some Western countries, England included, to conclude that these 'quick graspers' should move on to a new topic. Area, perhaps, or even volume?

It's time to think about things differently.

**Try this in the classroom**

### Upping the challenge with perimeter

The rectangle has a perimeter of 50 cm.
The rectangle is cut into two shapes. The cut is a straight line.

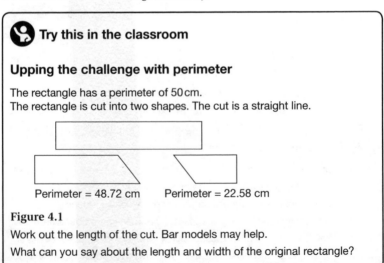

Perimeter = 48.72 cm      Perimeter = 22.58 cm

**Figure 4.1**

Work out the length of the cut. Bar models may help.
What can you say about the length and width of the original rectangle?

**Preparing to teach – do the mathematics!**

In preparing to teach the task above, you might consider the following points:

- How did you refer to the width and length of the rectangle? Did you allocate each of them a letter and, if so, how did this help you to engage with the problem?

- What did you do first? If you set up algebraic equations, now try and solve the problem without formal algebra.

- Adapt the parameters of the question. What if you started with a square, or a pentagon? What information would you need to be able to solve the problem?

All students who have learned how to add and subtract decimal numbers, and understand perimeter, will be able to tackle this task. The problem develops higher-level thinking skills. It provides a more stimulating educational experience than merely skimming over a large quantity of content. This is not at the expense of full curriculum coverage – all content will be taught. Rather, it ensures that students really do learn the full curriculum, in depth.

High-achieving countries insist on *all* students reaching the same high standard. They recognise that some students start secondary school without the necessary foundations in mathematics, and that time is needed to pull them up to this level.

Rather than categorising students by their apparent abilities or attainment, teachers in high-performing East Asian jurisdictions encourage *all* students to achieve adequate understanding in the same topic before moving on to the next topic or area.[1]

In most OECD countries, only a minority of 15-year-olds grasp and can work with core mathematics concepts, according to PISA. On average, less than half of students can work with the concept of a polygon, and less than a third understand the concept of an arithmetic mean.[2]

---

[1] **J.W. Stigler and H.W. Stevenson H.W.**, 'How Asian Teachers Polish Each Lesson to Perfection', *American Educator* (Spring 1991): pp. 12–47.

[2] **OECD**, *Equations and Inequalities: Making Mathematics Accessible to All* (Paris: OECD Publishing, 2016).

### 'One curriculum' in Japan

In Japan's primary and lower secondary schools, there is no streaming or grouping within or between schools. From primary to the end of lower secondary school, the same compulsory programme of mathematics is taught to all students in mixed-attainment classes.

Japan is unusual with respect to grouping students. Within mixed-attainment classes, students are often divided again into mixed-attainment groups. These groups are deliberately designed to enable all learners to assist and encourage each other. The same provision is made for all students, irrespective of attainment.

The introduction of educational 'tracking' tends to increase inequality and is associated with reduced educational achievement.[3] Interestingly, some higher-performing countries do set or stream students but, strikingly, placement in a 'lower' group doesn't seem to limit access and opportunity as significantly as it does elsewhere.

### 'One curriculum' in Singapore

In Singapore, for example, secondary students are 'streamed' into three groups, but as the same content is taught to all three streams, students are able to move between streams when appropriate. Although different secondary schools in Singapore require different minimum scores on the Primary School Leaving Exam, the vast majority of schools include students with a wide range of scores, and provide for all three streams.

Singapore's primary and secondary mathematics curricula consistently emphasise depth over coverage, and a commitment to every student accessing the key concepts and skills. Countries like Singapore push children to understand foundational concepts deeply – and they stretch the most successful students, not by giving them the next set of numbers, but by offering them ways to explore and apply concepts, especially through problem solving.

In Singapore's secondary curriculum, this means that learning of equations, for example, is carefully mapped out across the years:

---

[3] **E.A. Hanushek and L. Woessman**, 'Does Educational Tracking Affect Performance and Inequality? Differences-In-Differences Evidence Across Countries', *Economic Journal* 116(510) (2006): C63–C76.

- Secondary 1 (S1): Linear equations

- Secondary 2 (S2): Simultaneous linear equations. Quadratic equations by factorisation

- Secondary 3 and 4 (S3 and S4): Quadratic equations by using the formula, completing the square and the graphical method.

In their first year of secondary, *all* 12–13-year-old students focus on understanding what an equation is, and formulating and solving linear equations in one variable.

In the second year, *all* 13–14-year-old students learn how to formulate and solve simultaneous linear equations, and to solve quadratics by factorising.

Only in the third and fourth years of secondary do students (now 14–16 years old) study other methods of solving quadratic equations.

Keeping the focus on linear equations in S1 does not slow down the progress of the 'quick graspers'. On the contrary, allowing time to work with linear equations in one variable enables students to explore more complex problems, for example solving fractional equations that can be reduced to linear equations such as $\dfrac{x}{3} + \dfrac{x-2}{4} = 3$ and $\dfrac{3}{x-2} = 6$

Expectations are higher – every student in S1 is expected to succeed with linear equations – and this in itself leads to greater success. By Years 3 and 4 (14–16-year-olds), all students are expected to be able to explain why there are no real solutions to a quadratic equation $ax^2 + bx + c = 0$ when $b^2 - 4ac$ is negative. This puts the onus on teachers to find engaging and accessible approaches that will make this mathematics meaningful for every student.

There is plenty of time on the curriculum for learning about equations. In S2, all students use algebra software to draw a straight-line graph ($ax + by = c$), check that the coordinates of a point on the line satisfy the equation, and explain why the solution of a pair of simultaneous linear equations is the point of intersection of two straight lines. This gives all students the chance to fully explore and understand the concepts involved.

This curriculum structure also gives teachers the time to really think about the concepts and skills, to look at the underlying nature of the mathematics themselves, and to discuss the related pedagogy with colleagues.

'Differentiation' takes place through the way in which students are being taught and the level of support they are given. Every student is entitled to access the same content as their peers, and challenge is provided through increased depth – rather than acceleration through content.

Teachers avoid making assumptions about the amount of scaffolding students in each set will require. Instead they are careful to avoid too much support (which would result in passive learning) or too little support (which would limit success).

## The importance of 'opportunity to learn'

**L. Burstein,** ed., 1992.[4]

**The study:** The Second International Mathematics Study (SIMS) was conducted in schools across 20 education systems. Volume III describes the main findings from analyses of classroom processes and mathematic growth.

The study asked:

- how successful have the national education systems been in providing the opportunity to learn mathematics by the end of the lower secondary school?

- what do students at the lower secondary level know across educational systems and what have they learned during their most recent schooling experiences?

- what teaching practices are used in the mathematics classroom of the various systems and to what extent can these classroom processes explain differences in student achievements?

The SIMS focused on the study of mathematics through three different levels:

- the intended curriculum: the mathematics intended for learning by national and system-level authorities

- the implemented curriculum: the curriculum as interpreted by teachers and presented to students

- the attained curriculum: the curriculum learned by students and determined by their achievement and attitudes.[5]

---

[4] **L. Burstein,** ed., *The IEA Study of Mathematics III: Student Growth and Classroom Processes* (Oxford: Pergamon Press, 1992).

[5] **K.J. Travers and I. Westbury,** *The IEA Study of Mathematics I* (Oxford: Pergamon Press, 1989): pp. 6–7.

**What it tells us:** The study found that the most significant schooling variable that related to test outcome was the curriculum that students had been offered. This was called 'opportunity to learn'. It was also found that countries with 'less differentiation' performed better. Burstein pointed out that the 'opportunity to learn' and the differentiation variables were not independent, because students in lower sets covered reduced curricula.

PISA 2012 found that socio-economic differences among students and schools account for around 9 per cent of the variation in familiarity with mathematics concepts. In some countries, these differences account for as much as 20 per cent of the difference.[6]

Across OECD countries, more than 70 per cent of students attend schools that group students by prior attainment for mathematics.[7] One potential problem with the use of setting – grouping students based on prior attainment – is that it is associated with curriculum polarisation.

In a small-scale study, Jo Boaler and colleagues found that students in lower sets had restricted opportunities to learn and students in top sets were pushed to cover content faster than they could understand it.[8] Often in England, different sets within the same year group experience different teaching and learning approaches,[9] but this is not inevitable.

Different learners do have different needs, but they do not need different content. Teaching for mastery does not need to differentiate through content. Although learners may benefit from learning in different ways, with different amounts of independence, challenge and support, they are all aiming to learn the same core content.

By age 15, students in Shanghai, Singapore, Hong Kong and other high-performing East Asian jurisdictions are less likely to have missed out on accessing key mathematical ideas such as solving a quadratic equation or finding the volume of a box.[10] The complete curriculum content is taught to all students.

---

[6] **OECD** 2016, *op. cit.*

[7] *Ibid.*

[8] **J. Boaler, D. Wiliam and M. Brown**, 'Students' Experiences of Ability Grouping – Disaffection, Polarization and the Construction of Failure', *British Educational Research Journal* 26(5) (2000): pp. 631–648.

[9] **P. Kutnick et al.**, *Pupil Grouping Strategies and Practices at Key Stage 2 and 3: Case Studies of 24 Schools in England*, Report RR796 (London: Department for Education and Skills, 2006).

[10] **OECD**, *PISA 2012 Results: What Students Know and Can Do (Volume I, Revised edition, February 2014): Student Performance in Mathematics, Reading and Science: Measuring Opportunities to Learn Mathematics* (Paris: OECD Publishing, 2013).

It is essential that all students benefit from exposure to mathematics concepts and procedures. Even when they accounted for other factors (such as socio-economic background and the amount of time spent learning mathematics) the PISA study found that greater exposure to pure mathematics tasks and concepts (such as linear and quadratic equations) increased performance.[11]

Every child is entitled to a deep understanding of the whole curriculum. This means ensuring that even learners who find mathematics difficult have access to all key concepts and skills, and allowing all learners to investigate concepts more deeply, rather than rushing to cover new content.

In order for every student to succeed, teachers somehow need to avoid restricting students' progress inadvertently by denying them access to key concepts and skills. When teachers 'differentiate' by teaching different concepts to different children, they limit the achievements of students by making assumptions about their potential. It is therefore important that every student has access to the same curriculum content.

> *Opportunities to learn formal mathematical problems at school and familiarity with fundamental concepts of algebra and geometry have a stronger impact on performance when the entire student population benefits from them.*[12]

Because every student is entitled to master the key mathematical content for their age, the concepts and skills studied by a student are determined by their school year. Every student in a year group studies the same concepts and skills, regardless of prior attainment.

Teaching for mastery means following one curriculum for all, with sufficient time for every student to access and understand age-appropriate concepts and skills. Every student must receive the support and challenge they need. This personalisation can be achieved with all students learning the same concepts and skills.

# Don't some students need to go faster?

A curriculum for mastery offers one set of mathematical concepts and big ideas for all. Students are extended and challenged through deepening

---

[11] **OECD** 2016, *op. cit.*

[12] **OECD**, *PISA 2012 Results: Excellence Through Equity: Giving Every Student the Chance to Succeed (Volume II)* (Paris: OECD Publishing, 2013). www.oecd.org/pisa/keyfindings/pisa-2012-results-volume-II.pdf accessed 14 August 2017.

understanding of and increasing fluency with core content such as fractions, ratio or algebra. For example, fluency with algebraic fractions – a real advantage when studying more advanced mathematics – can be developed throughout lower secondary school without content acceleration.

Where teachers are seeking to provide challenges for students with high prior attainment, it can be tempting to bring forward work from subsequent years. Teachers can feel pressure from parents, from school inspection or elsewhere, to accelerate students who grasp content more quickly on to new content.

Such content acceleration, or 'differentiation by content', might sometimes seem like the only option. The materials needed for teaching the content seem to be easily available, and appear to provide the extra challenge these students are perceived to need. However, this acceleration risks students superficially covering content while their grasp of key ideas remains fragile.

Mathematics educationalists (for example those who participated in a seminar at the Royal Society in London, England on this subject[13]) caution against acceleration, recommending that it is handled with great caution. They argue that major acceleration often has unanticipated disadvantages for students' long-term development.

If and when we choose to expect more of some students than others, it is in their best interests that – in comparison with their peers – they are more fluent, have better understanding, and are better equipped to reflect on the connections between the mathematics they know. Rather than 'accelerate' students by teaching them content intended for older children, it is far better to challenge them to deepen their understanding of the area of content they are currently learning about. This puts them in a much stronger position than if they learn the same mathematics to the same depth, but get there a year or two earlier.

The term 'enrichment for added depth' was used by the UK Mathematics Foundation to describe an approach which routinely aims:

*(i) to lay stronger foundations – including greater fluency in basic technique,*

*(ii) to achieve a deeper understanding of that material, and*

---

[13] **UK Mathematics Foundation**, 'Acceleration or Enrichment. Report of a Seminar Held at the Royal Society on 22 May 2000', *The De Morgan Journal* 2 no. 2 (2012): pp. 97–125. http://education.lms.ac.uk/wp-content/uploads/2012/02/Acceleration_or_Enrichment_15Aug12.pdf accessed 14 August 2017.

*(iii) to cultivate a greater willingness to reflect on connections between different parts of the discipline.*[14]

One great advantage of focusing on depth rather than coverage in this way is that *every* student can benefit from an emphasis on accuracy, understanding and connections. Because it is very difficult to predict future mathematical success, identification of 'able' mathematicians is almost inevitably inaccurate. Better, then, to make provision for the mathematically gifted available to as wide a group of students as possible.

Considering the needs of those with the potential to be exceptionally successful in mathematics (while acknowledging that we are unlikely to be able to accurately identify them), the UK Mathematics Foundation argues that the most important lesson for them to learn is:

> *not to be satisfied with incomplete understanding, to realise that one can (and should) understand the internal connections and reasonings which explain why a method is correct, and to insist on getting things completely right.*[15]

This is both achievable with one curriculum for all, and made impossible if the focus shifts to content coverage.

## 'Differentiation through depth' in East Asia

East Asian countries and economies Singapore, South Korea, Hong Kong, Chinese Taipei and Japan have the largest percentages of students reaching the Advanced International Benchmark.

By aiming to achieve this for all their students, the East Asian countries succeed in educating a high proportion of students to this standard. Rather than 'challenging' their high-attaining students through accelerated content coverage, they spend more time on the fundamental ideas with every student. Far from 'holding the brightest back', this approach results in a much greater proportion of students reaching the highest benchmark, i.e. more students becoming high attainers.

By Year 5, Singapore had 43 per cent of their students reach the Advanced International Benchmark, followed by South Korea (39%), Hong Kong SAR (37%), Chinese Taipei (34%), and Japan (30%). Northern Ireland was next with 24 per cent, then England with 18 per cent.[16]

---

[14] *Ibid.*, p.107.

[15] *Ibid.*, p.108.

[16] **Ina V.S. Mullis et al.**, *TIMSS 2011 International Results in Mathematics* (Amsterdam: International Association for the Evaluation of Educational Achievement, 2012).

By Year 9, the East Asian countries – Chinese Taipei, Singapore and South Korea in particular – are pulling away from the rest of the world in mathematics achievement by a considerable margin.

## What can students at the Advanced International Benchmark do?

At the Advanced International Benchmark students can:

- reason with information, draw conclusions, make generalisations and solve linear equations

- solve a variety of fraction, proportion and per cent problems, and justify their conclusions

- express generalisations algebraically and model situations

- solve a variety of problems involving equations, formulas and functions

- reason with geometric figures to solve problems

- reason with data from several sources or unfamiliar representations to solve multi-step problems.[17]

Instead of progressing by moving on to a new topic, or learning content intended for older students, those who grasp the current concept more quickly than others can be challenged through exploring the same topic in greater depth, so they build a stronger understanding of the main mathematical concepts. A task that questions student understanding or encourages students to approach the topic from a different perspective can be highly challenging. A core concept or procedure, set in the context of a complex and unfamiliar problem, both deepens students' understanding of that core content and develops their reasoning and mathematical thinking skills.

For example, when the *Mathematics Mastery* programme of study focuses on addition and subtraction of integers, higher-attaining students are asked to work in different bases. Challenges include:

- Find the sum of $334_7 + 526_7$

- Explain what is the same and what is different about the column method in base 7 compared to base 10.

- Now find two numbers which sum to $12345_8$. Find three different ways to do this.

---

[17] *Ibid.*

- Find four different numbers which sum to $1000_6$. Find three different ways to do this.

- If 102 is double 31 what base is being used?

 **Preparing to teach – do the mathematics!**

In preparing to teach the challenges above, you might consider the following points:

- In talking about place value in bases other than ten, what do you call them? Does it seem natural to shift from referring to 'ones, tens and hundreds' and instead to talk about 'ones, sevens and forty-nines'?

- Might Cuisenaire or place value counters support you to answer the questions, or to explain your reasoning to others?

- With the final question, is there more than one possible answer? How do you know?

 **Try this in the classroom**

Ask a group of students to tackle the challenges above.

 **Consider**

Were the students reluctant to engage with topics that are not directly assessed on the exam? Where has this reluctance come from, and how might it be reduced over time?

Developing a depth of understanding supports students in building their problem-solving skills, improves flexibility and fluency, and helps make links between topics. This helps students retain their understanding, which is hugely beneficial when they reach high-stakes secondary examinations – and beyond!

To achieve mastery, students can be challenged by developing their depth of understanding of a topic – instead of being accelerated on to (superficially) harder content.

Learning mathematics for mastery should be challenging, so a mastery approach is absolutely not about the highest-attaining students waiting for the rest to catch up. Every single concept in mathematics is infinitely extensible.

In a mastery model, students who grasp an idea more quickly go beyond the stated demands of the national curriculum and work on deep mathematics.

Also, because learners come to understand ideas in different ways, everyone can have a turn at being the one who grasps something more quickly and therefore gets to work on the deep material.

# Take your time – a curriculum for depth

For every learner, whatever their background and prior attainment, there are significant advantages to focusing on depth of understanding over content coverage.

In a mastery classroom, each new concept or skill is given several weeks of learning time when it is first introduced, with a focus on depth of understanding. Deep understanding is promoted by planning for fewer topics in each week and term, with the full curriculum taught across secondary education.

The curriculum is designed in this way in order to promote deep understanding that is:

- flexible and useful in solving real problems

- connected to previous experiences

- sufficiently solid to form the foundations for future mathematical learning.

Many countries adopt a 'spiral' curriculum, where the aim is to cover a topic at an appropriate level which increases in depth with time. Arguably, due to the nature of mathematics, all curricula must be spiral in some sense. All topics introduced to younger children are developed and built on later in their school career. The difference between curricula, then, may lie in the pitch of the spiral.

Some countries adopt a flatter spiral, with a relatively low rate of revisiting topics. Others use an extended spiral, with topics revisited comparatively frequently. Although it is difficult to establish the pitch of the spirals in the taught curriculum, published materials such as textbooks offer some insight.

Textbooks used in England suggest a greater fragmentation of the curriculum and a more frequent return to particular topics than elsewhere. In a study of the curricula of 16 countries, Graham Ruddock found that, in comparison with England, many systems seem to devote a longer period of time to consolidating a topic at a particular level before returning to develop the topic further at a later date.[18]

 **Discuss**

Take a look at the scheme of work your school uses for the first few years of secondary education.

• What principles underpin its design?

• How much overlap is there between years?

• Do you have sufficient time to teach each concept?

Many schools find that they are revisiting many areas taught in one year in the following year. Of course, no mathematical topic is ever taught as a 'one off', never to be returned to. But students should understand key ideas sufficiently well in the first place so that, when they meet them again, they do not need them to be re-introduced as if from scratch. As mathematics is such an interconnected subject, topics will be regularly revisited, but they should not need re-teaching.

I often speak to teachers who tell me they feel that they are rushing to cover concepts quickly. They feel they have insufficient time to embed new concepts when they are first taught. This becomes a vicious circle, as students lack the deep understanding of the concept that they need, so when they revisit it in future years the concept needs to be substantially re-taught.

A curriculum for mastery requires taking the brave step of devoting more time to key concepts and techniques in the first place.

Spending more time on teaching a concept or skill allows for the development of conceptual understanding and sufficient practice to embed learning. Spending sufficient time on key ideas in this way means that future mathematical learning is built on solid foundations that do not need to be re-taught.

A curriculum for mastery focuses on depth of understanding rather than content coverage. All students are given time to understand something before they move on. Students demonstrate progress by making connections between representations, and applying them within and beyond the curriculum. One surprising outcome of this commitment to spending more time is that, when

---

[18] **G. Ruddock**, *Mathematics in the School Curriculum: An International Perspective* (London: National Foundation for Educational Research, 1998). The 16 countries compared were Australia, Canada, England, France, Germany, Hungary, Italy, Japan, South Korea, the Netherlands, New Zealand, Singapore, Spain, Sweden, Switzerland and the United States.

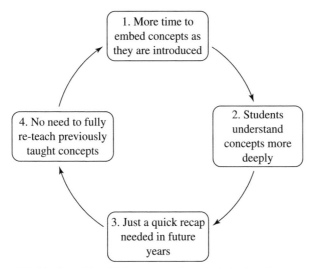

**Figure 4.2:** The benefits of taking more time to introduce key concepts

they do move on, teachers feel their students pick up new concepts more quickly.

At secondary school level, key building blocks such as multiplicative and proportional reasoning are given plenty of time early on, so that multiplication facts and fractions are not a barrier to later work with algebra and geometry.

This is not about holding back students who have higher prior attainment while their lower-attaining peers catch up. This is a curriculum structure that benefits every learner. Multiple experiences over time enable students to develop new ways to work on mathematical tasks, and to develop the ability to choose which earlier learning to apply and how to apply it. In fact, higher-attaining students might particularly benefit from a curriculum structure with more time given to key ideas, as studies[19, 20] have suggested that students in higher sets often feel too rushed to fully understand curriculum content.

### The case of England: a curriculum problem?

Some countries' assessment procedures are based on the notion of level descriptors. Until recently, this has been the case, for example, with the National Curriculum in England. The problem that arises here is that teachers can come to equate progress with knowing new procedures and rules. Many students

---

[19] **J. Boaler**, 'When Even the Winners are Losers: Evaluating the Experiences of "Top Set" Students', *Journal of Curriculum Studies* 29(2) (1997): pp. 165–182.

[20] **J. Boaler**, 'Setting, Social Class and Survival of the Quickest', *British Educational Research Journal* 23(5) (1997): pp. 575–595.

build a superficial knowledge of a large number of techniques, but find that at advanced level (known in British educational systems as 'A-level') or beyond they lack the depth of understanding to apply these skills to new situations.

Many mathematics teachers have witnessed students hitting a 'brick wall' when they reach 16+ examinations, which they struggle to break through when continuing to study the subject at a more advanced level. Even for the very high-attaining students, a lack of deep mathematical understanding can suddenly be a huge inhibitor when studying at A-level.

Some students starting A-level with the top grades in 16+ examinations struggle when they need to tackle coordinate geometry and calculus. They need to apply their previous learning about fractions, indices, surds, quadratics and simultaneous equations – and it's tough. It's not that they weren't successful with these topics at 16+, but more that their knowledge lacks the required understanding to take them to the next level. Many A-level teachers find they have to begin the first year of A-level re-teaching the algebraic and surd work from previous years.

Some students seem to hit this barrier earlier. Their understanding of adding fractions – which served them perfectly well when answering straightforward fraction addition questions – is insufficiently deep to be applied to a new context such as solving equations. Or their grasp of multiplication facts – which they can skip-count or derive from known facts – doesn't serve them well when factorising quadratics.

Before working with a mastery approach, I found that 16+ and A-level students were often impeded in their flexibility with algebra due to limited fluency with multiplication facts and fractions. It's one thing to find the product of 9 and 7 by starting with the known fact that $7 \times 10 = 70$ then subtracting 7 to find 63, and quite another to look at the expression $x^2 - 2x - 63$ and think immediately that 9 and 7 are factors of 63, and thereby factorise the expression to $(x - 9)(x + 7)$.

A key difference between mathematics education in the UK and that of other, more successful, countries is the apparent size of the mathematics curriculum. Rather than attempt to 'cover' a vast number of concepts and skills in each academic year, it seems that teachers in these countries are able to ensure their students have time to really master key mathematical ideas. This relatively 'small' curriculum is a consistent feature of 'high flying' countries and economies, including Shanghai, Singapore and Japan.

There are those who argue that the mathematics curriculum in England is much bigger than that of higher-performing jurisdictions. Even colleagues in

England's Department for Education (DfE) have been heard to affectionately refer to the 2015 Key Stage 4 curriculum as a 'big fat maths GCSE'. But this need not be a reason to despair.

Although, naturally, there is variation between countries, the mathematics to be taught by the end of secondary school (usually by age 16) is fairly consistent.

So why do teachers in England feel that there is so much content to cover? Are teachers really trying to cover more content, or teach more mathematics, than other countries? Or is it that the same content is being covered in a different way?

In fact, careful comparison of the various curricula suggests that much of this difference may be presentational. Where other countries might briefly state 'solving quadratics', the English National Curriculum spells out more detail. To some extent this is a consequence of the relatively high levels of teacher autonomy in England (for example, around textbook and resource selection) and the market system for examination provision – specificity is required to ensure some level of commonality and consistency across the country.

### *'Fewer topics' in Singapore*

A comparison of the algebra requirements for 14–16-year-olds in England and Singapore reveals that the content coverage and pitch are roughly equivalent. For example, here are the algebra requirements related to graphs for secondary Key Stage 4 students in England:

- *Use the form $y = mx + c$ to identify parallel (and perpendicular) lines; find the equation of the line through two given points, or through one point with a given gradient.*

- *Identify and interpret roots, intercepts and turning points of quadratic functions graphically; deduce roots algebraically (and turning points by completing the square).*

- *Recognise, sketch and interpret graphs of linear functions, quadratic functions, simple cubic functions, the reciprocal function $y = \frac{1}{x}$ with $x \neq 0$, (the exponential function $y = k^x$ for positive values of $k$, and the trigonometric functions (with arguments in degrees) $y = \sin x$, $y = \cos x$, and $y = \tan x$ for angles of any size).*

- *Sketch translations and reflections of the graph of a given function.*

- *Plot and interpret graphs (including reciprocal graphs (and exponential graphs)) and graphs of non-standard functions in real contexts, to find approximate solutions to problems such as simple kinematic problems involving distance, speed and acceleration.*

- *Calculate or estimate gradients of graphs and areas under graphs (including quadratic and other non-linear graphs), and interpret results in cases such as distance–time graphs, velocity–time graphs and graphs in financial contexts.*

The corresponding requirements in the Singapore curriculum are considerably briefer. The requirements for Singapore Secondary 3/4 are as follows:

*6.8 Sketching the graphs of quadratic functions given in the form:*

- $y = (x - p)^2 + q$

- $y = -(x - p)^2 + q$

- $y = (x - a)(x - b)$

- $y = -(x - a)(x - b)$

*6.9 graphs of power functions y + ax$^n$, where n = –2, – 1, 0, 1, 2, 3 and simple sums of not more than three of these*

*6.10 graphs of exponential functions y = ka$^x$, where a is a positive integer*

*6.11 estimation of the gradient of a curve by drawing a tangent.*[21]

The English National Curriculum is not, in fact, any bigger or fatter than that in Singapore. Rather, it gives a more detailed description of what each aspect includes. This detail and exemplification is provided in Singapore through state-approved textbooks and the national exams.

The National Curriculum in England[22] attempts to be concise, while needing to stand alone without exam papers or textbooks. In attempting to be both comprehensive and concise, it could well be argued that it fails to be either.

There is a temptation, when presented with a lengthy curriculum document, to see the various statements within it as discrete topics, each demanding significant time.

The Expert Panel for the National Curriculum in England observed:

> *Amongst the international systems which we have examined, there are several that appear to focus on fewer things in greater depth in primary education, and pay particular attention to all pupils having*

---

[21] **Ministry of Education**, *Mathematics Syllabus, Secondary One to Four* (Singapore: Curriculum Planning & Development Division, Ministry of Education, 2012), p. 44.

[22] **Department for Education**, *Mathematics Programmes of Study: Key Stage 4 National Curriculum in England* (London: Department for Education, 2013). www.gov.uk/government/uploads/system/uploads/attachment_data/file/331882/KS4_maths_PoS_FINAL_170714.pdf accessed 14 August 2017.

*an adequate understanding of these key elements prior to moving to the next body of content – they are 'ready to progress'. We judge this approach to be a fundamental rather than surface element of a number of high-performing jurisdictions.*[23]

There is some evidence that, having achieved this solid foundation at primary, high-performing systems do start to cover a significant amount of content in upper secondary.[24] By only beginning to differentiate by speed of content coverage once every student has a solid foundation, these systems significantly reduce the correlation between background and success in mathematics. They ensure that high-attaining students have a depth of understanding in key areas of the subject.

## Take your time – teach topics less frequently, for longer

In a review of relevant literature, Anne Watson concluded:

*Schemes of work and assessment should allow enough time for students to adapt to new meanings and move on from earlier methods and conceptualisations; they should give time for new experiences and mathematical ways of working to become familiar in several representations and contexts before moving on.*[25]

In practice, this means teaching all of an area of mathematics relevant to that age group in one block, for example beginning the year with several months focused on number. Once an area has been covered, it is incorporated into all subsequent areas. For example, when working on algebraic expressions, students can work with fractions and decimals as well as integers.

Focusing on big ideas – blocking together concepts with very close links – leads to greater curriculum coherence. By integrating the teaching of fractions and percentages, for example, the very strong connections between these concepts can be made more explicit. This curricular coherence has been shown to be a consistently important factor across successful countries.[26]

Many people have asked me how a mastery curriculum can make time for each concept or skill to be taught in depth. They wonder whether

---

[23] **Department for Education**, *The Framework for the National Curriculum. A report by the Expert Panel for the National Curriculum review* (London: Department for Education, 2011), p. 45.

[24] *Ibid.*, Annex 5.

[25] **A. Watson**, *Key Understandings in Mathematics Learning. Paper 7: Modelling, Problem-solving and Integrating Concepts* (Nuffield Foundation, 2009), p. 6. www.nuffieldfoundation.org/sites/default/files/P7.pdf accessed 14 August 2017.

[26] **ACME**, *Mathematical Needs: The Mathematical Needs of Learners* (Advisory Committee on Mathematics Education, 2011).

schools adopting a mastery approach have to allocate additional hours to mathematics. I have worked with schools on a mastery curriculum for mathematics in three hours a week, and even five hours across a fortnight. More time is, of course, preferable, but within these time constraints a mastery approach can be adopted, with no curriculum content left out. This is made possible by viewing the learning of mathematics as one coherent long-term endeavour, rather than a multitude of separate, unconnected chunks.

In some curricula, there are substantial overlaps between the various stages: this is the case, for example, with the key stages in the National Curriculum in England. This means that taking more time for teaching and learning key concepts in the earlier stages reduces the need to spend time on the same concepts later on.

## 'Take your time' in Japan

In Japan, expectations of content coverage are, if anything, higher than in the UK. But rather than write long and potentially daunting lists of concepts and skills required by the age of 16, they have arrived at just four key objectives for each year.[27] This is fewer objectives across the whole year than we in the UK tend to have for a single week! In lower secondary, these four objectives are focused on four areas of mathematics:

**1** Numbers and mathematical expressions

**2** Geometric figures

**3** Functions

**4** Data handling.

For 14-year-olds, one of these four objectives is that:

*Students will understand functions in the form of $y = ax^2$ through exploration of concrete phenomena, while extending their ability to represent and analyse functional relationships.*

By taking this approach, it is made clear that mathematical learning takes place over time. It is made explicit that this learning will build on the functions and understanding developed in the first and second years of secondary school:

---

[27] http://ncm.gu.se/media/kursplaner/andralander/Japanese_COS2008Math.pdf accessed 14 August 2017.

Grade 1: Through investigations of actual phenomena, students will deepen their understanding of proportional and inversely proportional relationships.

Grade 2: Students will understand linear functions through exploration of concrete phenomena while developing their ability to identify, represent and utilise functional relationships in inquiries.

Teaching 'big ideas' in this way ensures that students gain a deep and lasting understanding and create foundations they can build on in later years.

We, too, can pull out the key ideas and teach them for longer first time round. A curriculum for mastery can learn a great deal from these different international approaches. Although it is difficult to establish how often specific mathematical topics are revisited in different countries, there is evidence to suggest that there is pressure to move from topic to topic more rapidly in some countries than in others.[28]

The fundamental thing to keep in mind is that, while the Singapore syllabus and Japanese Course of Study present mathematical content very differently from the National Curriculum Programme of Study in England and other Western countries, the actual content varies only in very minor details.

This means that teachers in the West can adopt the curricular philosophy of these higher-performing jurisdictions. This means teaching in the earlier secondary years those concepts and skills that have the most applications in the rest of the mathematics curriculum. For example, teaching most number content (topics such as calculation and decimals) towards the start of the school year means that throughout the rest of the year, those number concepts can be applied when learning other areas of mathematics.

# Mastery over time – a cumulative curriculum

Before I adopted a mastery approach, I would often find myself teaching a topic such as addition and subtraction of decimals, or of fractions, and subsequently teaching perimeter. Due to my own sense of needing to rush through content, I would be aware that many students were not secure with addition and subtraction of rational numbers, so I would stick to integers when teaching 'perimeter'. What a missed opportunity!

---

[28] **G. Ruddock** 1998, *op. cit.*

Once I had committed to teaching with students' long-term learning in mind, rather than lurching from one lesson objective to the next, it seemed obvious that there was an alternative way. By enabling students to spend longer learning to add and subtract rational numbers – not to the point of mastery perhaps, but sufficient time to explore, clarify and practise the key concepts and skills – addition and subtraction of decimals and fractions could quite naturally be 'applied' in a wealth of contexts across the mathematics curriculum. There would no longer be any need to artificially restrict numbers to integers, opening up a wealth of opportunities to practise working with rational numbers.

To maintain this level of familiarity, students need to use the skills frequently over time, so it is important to reduce calculator use to relatively essential areas, such as trigonometry. There can be a temptation, particularly in the later years of secondary education, for calculators to be used in almost every lesson, meaning that opportunities to reinforce essential number skills are reduced.

Teachers necessarily break down mathematical content and offered experience into lesson-size chunks. But mathematics is an interconnected web of ideas and concepts.

If teaching is solely thought of in terms of individual lessons, this can result in fragmentation of topics and ideas. There's a tough job, then, ensuring that mathematical ideas and concepts are presented in an interrelated way; but if we don't do this, there is a risk that mathematics can seem fragmented and incoherent to students.

If topics such as 'fractions' and 'ratio' are taught separately, and treated separately, students may never appreciate the connections between them. If each individual lesson has to have its own distinct 'objective', planning can become rigid, opportunistic learning can be inhibited and trivialised to surface-level behaviours that can be more easily communicated and measured. Research evidence has demonstrated that this is a very real risk.[29]

The effectiveness of teachers who make connections is indicated in a study by Mike Askew and other researchers at King's College London. They found that 'connectionist teachers' saw greater student progress than those who taught in a more fragmented way.

---

[29] **P. John**, 'Lesson Planning and the Student Teacher: Re-thinking the Dominant Model', *Journal of Curriculum Studies* 38(4) (2006): pp. 483–498.

## The importance of connections

**M. Askew et al. 1997.**[30]

**The study:** The researchers compared different teaching approaches that were more and less effective.

**What it tells us:** The teachers whose classes made the greatest gains across the year were those who, whatever pedagogic approach they used, emphasised connections between different mathematical ideas, between mathematics and the real world, and between the new skills and knowledge being introduced and their students' existing ideas and approaches.

Although this study looked at teachers at primary school level, this way of describing teaching has been found useful by many teachers and other researchers.[31] A mastery curriculum is structured to support teachers in making these connections.

Of course, it is not possible for us to map out exactly what will be *learned* when, but it would surely be irresponsible not to carefully map out what will be *taught*. One of the great challenges of teaching mathematics is that, as the concepts are interconnected, the teacher can never be entirely sure which experience will result in precisely what learning. Being immersed in one aspect of mathematics can frequently lead to unexpected learning in another.[32] However, the mastery curriculum takes a long-term perspective, with careful consideration of the concepts and representations that will be introduced at each age, and how these will be adapted and applied in later years.

A focus on long-term orientation when considering the learning of mathematics is one of the main pedagogical principles that characterise the perspective of Hans Freudenthal. Freudenthal's learning theory underpins 'Realistic Mathematics Education' (RME) in the Netherlands, where there

---

[30] **M. Askew et al.**, *Effective Teachers of Numeracy* (London: King's College, 1997).

[31] For example, **M. Swan and J. Swain**, 'The Impact of a Professional Development Programme on the Practices and Beliefs of Numeracy Teachers', *Journal of Further and Higher Education* 34:2 (2010): pp. 165–177.

[32] **B. Denvir and M. Brown**, 'Understanding of Number Concepts in Low Attaining 7–9 Year Olds: Parts i and ii', *Educational Studies in Mathematics* 17 (1986): pp. 15–36, 143–164.

is a strong focus on the relation between what has been learned earlier and what will be learned later – longitudinal coherence.[33]

One example of such a 'longitudinal' model in RME is the number line. It begins in the first year of school as a bead string on which the students can practise a variety of counting activities. In later years, this bead string successively becomes:

- an empty number line for supporting additions and subtractions

- a double number line for supporting problems on ratios

- a fraction/percentage bar for supporting working with fractions and percentages.

Focusing on depth enables us to carefully consider how new concepts will be represented (using concrete manipulatives and pictures or diagrams) and when abstract notation will be introduced. The concepts and skills that are taught earliest are not 'the easiest', but the ones that will be most foundational for future learning.

Mathematics learning is essentially about building connections between concepts and procedures. Students must be supported to organise their mathematical knowledge into schemas. If students' knowledge of fractions is secure when they are introduced to the concept of percentages, they are well placed to connect the new information with their existing knowledge.

It is important that, as teachers, we know what the students have already mastered when we are teaching each specific topic area.

 **Discuss**

Some concepts and skills are important precursors to others. Getting the sequencing of these right is an important skill in planning and teaching for mastery. Has your school's current scheme of work got this right?

For example, to confidently tackle the task below, students need to be relatively fluent with converting between metric units.

---

[33] **H. Freudenthal**, *Revisiting Mathematics Education: China Lectures* (Dordrecht, The Netherlands: Kluwer Academic Publishers, 1991).

## 🔖 Try this in the classroom

Which of these shapes has a perimeter closest to 1 metre?

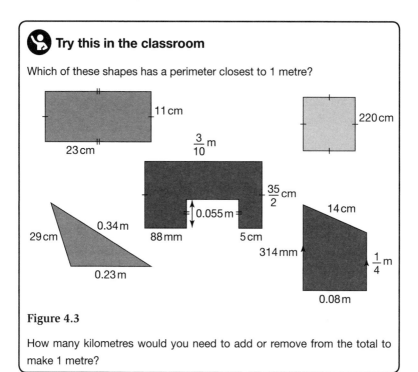

**Figure 4.3**

How many kilometres would you need to add or remove from the total to make 1 metre?

## 💬 Consider

What other concepts and techniques would students need to be familiar with in order to successfully tackle this task?

For this reason, effective formative assessment is both vital *in*, and facilitated *by*, teaching for mastery. To teach students in a way that builds connections requires frequent effective questioning to gain as complete a picture as possible of their current understanding.

Many teachers I have worked with have observed that a significant proportion of students seem to lack a solid understanding of key skills in mathematics. They find that students often find aspects of geometry and statistics relatively easy, but have gaps in their understanding of the number system.

Many teachers have taught 13- or 14-year-old students who are still using repeated addition to find the product of seven and eight, rather than recalling the multiplication fact. Without quick recall of these facts, such students find problem solving more challenging due to the extra cognitive load of searching for the relevant facts. Quick recall of such number facts is a tool that supports understanding, rather than in any way replacing it.

In solving the equation $x^2 + 14x + 48 = 0$, for example, students will be significantly hampered if they have to *work out* all the factors of 48 (by dividing 48 by various integers on a calculator, for example, to see whether they give integer answers). To solve this quadratic equation fluently, a student needs the knowledge that:

$1 \times 48 = 48$

$2 \times 24 = 48$

$3 \times 16 = 48$

$4 \times 12 = 48$

$6 \times 8 = 48$

With this knowledge, they will be able to consider which of the factor pairs sums to 14, without placing undue demand on their working memory.

Students' capacity to solve problems can be significantly hampered by lack of fluency. For example, think how much calculation is required to multiply mixed numbers.

Following a cumulative curriculum addresses this by 'creating' extra time to practise and apply number skills. The skills build up over time, with teachers able to really embed a concept and build on it.

Many basic skills can be practised in the context of more advanced skills. As cognitive scientist Daniel Willingham points out:

> *A competent bridge player needs to be able to count the points in a hand as a guide to bidding, but if I were a bridge instructor I wouldn't have my students do nothing but count points until they could do so automatically. Automaticity takes lots of practice. The smart way to go is to distribute practice not only across time but also across activities. Think of as many creative ways as you can to practice the really crucial skills, but remember that students can still get practice in the basics while they are working on more advanced skills.*[34]

Because a mastery curriculum is cumulative, once a concept or skill has been learned, it is built on and applied in the learning that follows. As well as helping previously lower-attaining students to keep up, this enables all students to gain a much deeper foundation in key concepts and skills, which better prepares them for the study of mathematics and mathematical subjects in further education and beyond.

---

[34] **D. Willingham**, *Why Don't Students Like School?* (San Francisco, CA: Jossey-Bass, 2009): p. 125.

For example, in the *Mathematics Mastery* programme of study 'square numbers' are not seen as an isolated topic, taught on two or three separate occasions every year and then revised in the run-up to the external examination. Rather, once the core concept has been studied in depth, it is continually applied in new contexts. Such opportunities are abundant as soon as you begin to look for them: perimeter and area, Pythagoras' theorem, algebraic equations …. In this way students have the opportunity both to understand the concept in depth, and to learn how square numbers crop up in successively more complex mathematical contexts.

A true fluency with square numbers will make examination questions such as this one[35] the work of moments:

Solve: $3x^2 = 75$

Rather than considering this to be a two-step process of dividing 75 by 3, then finding the square roots of 25, a student who has mastered square numbers might spot by inspection that 5 or –5 squared fits the requirement, so $x = 5$ or $x = -5$.

Teachers find that spending longer on each topic enables them to think carefully about how students can experience connections. Sequencing the concepts and methods so that previously learned ideas can be connected to new learning, supports students in understanding the coherent and connected nature of the subject. This ensures that they consolidate learning by continually using and applying it in a variety of contexts.

---

 **Consider**

Pick a topic – look back: when will students explore ideas that will connect with the topic? Where can you plant seeds? Where are the vital foundation stones laid?

Now look forward: where are the opportunities to apply this topic in future topics? If a while is going to go by without revisiting key ideas (without forcing them), consider a quick quiz to keep the ideas alive.

---

Deep understanding cannot be achieved in an hour. Teachers must be clear on the purpose of each task, in each lesson, but this is very different from expecting that a particular, specified learning objective will be 'mastered' by every learner. Every moment of every lesson *is* extremely important, but important as part of a coherent long-term learning experience.

---

[35] OCR Foundation Specimen Question Paper 3, Question 18(b).

It is conventional that the unit of teaching is the lesson – a period of time of, say, 30 to 120 minutes, where teacher and students are together in a classroom. But while lessons are conventionally the unit of *teaching*, there is no such unit of *learning*.

Learning does not necessarily occur only in the presence of a teacher. It can occur at any time. For each key concept or skill in mathematics, students must have opportunities to explore, clarify, practise and apply the concept. Many of these opportunities arise outside the mathematics classroom, or within the classroom unplanned by the teacher.

Take the example of a 13-year-old, Sam, learning about dividing quantities in a given ratio.

### ❶ Learners *explore* mathematical concepts and techniques

Cycling up hills, Sam becomes aware of how much harder it is to ascend a road with a slope of 1:4 than one of 1:8. He understands that these signs show how many parts run (distance along) there are for every one part rise (distance up), and appreciates that the smaller the second number, the steeper the hill.

On Saturdays, Sam works in people's gardens. When mixing up cement Sam uses one shovel of cement to three shovels of sand. If three shovels more cement are put in the mixer, they have to put in nine shovels more sand.

In mathematics lessons, Sam uses Cuisenaire rods to model the comparative size of two quantities and find fractions of amounts. Sam explores how the relationship between the red rod and the dark green rod is 'the same' as the relationship between the light green rod and the blue rod – in each case the longer rod is three times as long as the shorter rod.

### ❷ Learners *clarify* meanings and methods

Sam's Year 8 mathematics teacher introduces the term 'ratio' as the relationship between two numbers, indicating how many times the first number contains the second.

He learns that the ratio of numbers *A* and *B* can be written as A:B, and that this is read, 'the ratio of A to B'.

Sam finds that ratio is a way of comparing amounts of something. He learns that when the two quantities have the same units, their ratio is a dimensionless number.

In mathematics lessons, Sam works on questions such as this one:

*X and Y share a cash prize in the ratio 5:3. X receives £20 more than Y. Calculate the total value of the cash prize.*

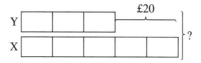

**Figure 4.4**

On a school trip, Sam hears that the ratio of staff to students has to be 1:7. There are three teachers and 19 students on the trip, and Sam is initially confused by this. A teacher explains that the maximum number of students on the trip, given that there are three teachers, would be 21, but that having two fewer students doesn't mean the number of teachers can reduce. That's because the number of teachers and the number of students are *discrete* quantities.

**3** Learners *practise* techniques

Sam develops fluency in sharing a quantity in a given ratio through experiencing it on numerous occasions.

These include sharing quantities in a given ratio, as in the following:

- Share £75 in the ratio 2:3.

- Abe and Ban share £45 in the ratio 2:3. How much more money does Ban receive than Abe?

- Abe and Ban share some money in the ratio 3:5. Ban gets £24 more than Abe. How much money do they share in total between them?

**4** Learners *apply* concepts and techniques to solve non-routine problems

Working with the Fibonacci sequence, Sam finds and simplifies the ratio of 1 to 2, 2 to 3, 3 to 5, 5 to 8 … etc. As he simplifies 34:55, 55:89, he finds that the ratios tend towards the golden ratio – 1.6180339…

Making a scale drawing of the garden plot at the Youth Centre, Sam wonders how he can represent the plot on a piece of A4 paper (210 mm × 297 mm). The plot is 6 m by 7 m. He realises that he can use his understanding of ratio to help him out, with a ratio of 2 m:7 mm or 2000:7. As well as applying his understanding of ratio here, Sam is applying his fluency with multiplicative relationships more broadly. For each measurement on the plot, Sam divides the measurement in metres by 2 and multiplies it by 7 to find the length in millimetres. Once he's completed the diagram, he uses it to find the actual dimensions of the raised beds he's planned, by dividing each measurement in millimetres by 7, and doubling it, to find the real-life length in metres.

Over time, students need a wealth of opportunities to explore mathematical ideas, to have these ideas clarified, to practise using skills and concepts, and to apply them to new contexts. This cannot all happen in a single task or lesson. It is therefore helpful to be explicit about lesson purpose when planning, teaching, and reflecting on learning.

In my experience, a lack of agreement about the success of a task or lesson often comes down to lack of clarity about purpose, for example the observer thinks the teacher should have clarified a point, but the teacher wanted to leave learners to discover and resolve the misunderstanding for themselves. Or the observer thinks there was insufficient practice, but the teacher believed it was important to let the students figure out what mathematics to use for themselves.

 **Discuss**

Think of a time you have given or received feedback about an observed lesson and disagreed about the appropriateness of a task.

- What made you think the task was or wasn't appropriate?
- Were you both clear about what the intended purpose of the task was?
- Was there a different task that would have better met the intended purpose?

## Learning takes time

Exploration, clarification, practice and application take time. Mastery does not happen in one individual lesson. Clarification and practice of mathematical concepts and skills are most effective when they take place over time. Sustained opportunities to practise help every student to become secure enough to be able to apply concepts and skills to unfamiliar problems in new contexts.

A curriculum for mastery is designed so that concepts and skills with many connections to other areas of mathematics are taught earlier in the academic year. This affords opportunities for plenty of practice and application of earlier topics when later topics are being studied.

It makes sense to start the year looking at place value and the base ten system, for example, because the representations and language used when studying place value can then be regularly revisited throughout the year. When we study addition and subtraction, we can use ones, tens and hundreds blocks to represent the numbers (the power of these base ten blocks – made popular by and named after Zoltan Dienes – is discussed further in Chapter 7). When we multiply, say, 700 by 30, we can use our knowledge that $700 = 7 \times 100$ and $30 = 3 \times 10$. Place value ceases to be 'a topic' and becomes an integral part of mathematics.

The rate of student progress should be evaluated over the longer term. Initially, it might seem that students are progressing more slowly through key concepts than previously, but the strong foundations they are building mean that progress in future years will be more rapid.

---

 **Consider**

When you teach Pythagoras' theorem for the first time, what connections can be made with the mathematics that students have previously learned?

What mathematics is:

- a vital prerequisite?

- strongly connected?

- possible to connect?

The topic of Pythagoras' theorem is an opportunity for students to apply what they have learned about angles in a triangle, square numbers and square roots, classifying triangles (e.g. isosceles), ratios, calculating area and much more.

By making time for students to solve associated problems in other shapes where right-angled triangles arise, connections can be made with the properties of different types of triangle.

For example, students can be challenged to find the area of an isosceles triangle where the lengths of the three sides are given, but not the perpendicular height.

---

In planning for and teaching each topic, it is (of course) important to consider what concepts and skills students need to learn about. But consideration of the focus topic does not end here. Teachers might also reflect on when, in studying previous topics, their students might have explored these concepts and skills. Once this topic is taught, in what future topics will the topics and skills be applied?

Reflecting on these questions increases the likelihood that teachers will help students connect this learning with their previous learning, and 'signpost' forwards to when students will use these concepts again in mathematics lessons.

The figure below offers a framework for considering how a topic coheres with students' learning over time.

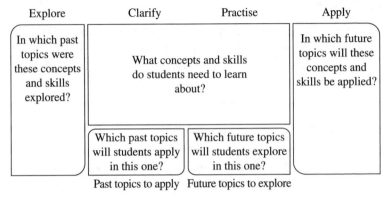

**Figure 4.5:** A framework for students' learning

Almost every topic taught will be applied when studying another aspect of mathematics. For example, when finding volumes of prisms, learners apply their knowledge of areas of cross-sections; when solving quadratic equations, learners apply knowledge of solving linear equations.

Of course, some concepts and techniques will reappear much more frequently than others. Those handy facts for angle chasing, for example, find themselves somewhat isolated. There are a few applications of angle facts – for example, the angle sum around a point is useful when working with pie charts. And there are also a few opportunities to shoe-horn them in. When studying fractions, why not include questions involving the fraction of the angle sum? But teaching angle facts in a block, and relying only on the cumulative and connected nature of the curriculum for their ongoing reinforcement, is insufficient.

For these potentially isolated topics, it makes sense to use a little time here and there to keep students' knowledge fresh in their minds. Perhaps pose a quick question at the start of a lesson, or maybe set a short quiz including questions on a few such topics.

## Putting it into practice

A mastery curriculum is one in which:

- students in the same year group study the same concepts and skills at the same time (one curriculum)

- there is sufficient time for each concept or skill to be understood in depth (take your time)

- students apply learning and make connections, and the most similar topics are blocked together (cumulative curriculum).

Starting with high expectations for every student, the *Mathematics Mastery* team set out to design a curriculum with more time for all learners to really explore key concepts in mathematics, with fewer topics, in greater depth.[36]

In their first year of secondary school, 11–12-year-old students in *Mathematics Mastery* partner schools focus on the content in table 4.1.

This core content underpins the cumulative curriculum and is developed and built on across academic years. The table shows when they are explicitly focused on for the first time. At the end of the year, all students are expected to know, understand and be able to do *all* core content studied during the year. Objectives specified for a particular half term are explicitly taught during this time, and then applied in future lessons.

**Table 4.1:** A timetable for the core content of the Mathematics Mastery programme

| | |
|---|---|
| Autumn 1 | Understand place value to compare and order numbers including decimals. |
| | Use approximation and rounding in problem solving. |
| | Understand and solve problems involving addition and subtraction including perimeter. |
| Autumn 2 | Multiply and divide multi-digit numbers, including decimals. |
| | Find and understand factors and multiples, including lowest common multiples and highest common factors. |
| | Understand and apply the formulae for area of a rectangle and triangle. |
| Spring 1 | Accurately draw, measure, and identify types of angle. |
| | Use facts to solve problems involving unknown angles on a line and at a point. |
| | Understand and use properties of triangles and quadrilaterals. |
| Spring 2 | Understand and use fraction notation in a variety of contexts. |
| | Compare and order fractions, decimals and mixed numbers. |
| | Multiply and divide with fractions. |
| Summer 1 | Carry out combined calculations using all four operations with brackets. |
| | Represent unknowns with letters forming and manipulating algebraic expressions. |
| | Evaluate algebraic expressions through substitution. |
| Summer 2 | Read and interpret statistical diagrams, including pie charts. |
| | Interpret percentage and percentage change as a fraction or a decimal. |

---

[36] **H. Drury**, 'Joining the Dots: Transforming Mathematics Education with a Coherent Whole School Approach', *Mathematics Teaching* (Association of Teachers of Mathematics, 2014): p. 15.

**Discuss**

- What are the similarities and differences between this yearly overview and the Year 7 mathematics curriculum your school currently follows?

- What might be the benefits of adopting a mastery curriculum such as this one?

- What might be the challenges of adopting a mastery curriculum such as this one?

What is important are the underlying principles, not the specifics. You may want to design your own curriculum map, use your department's existing map, or design a new map with your department. As I have advocated elsewhere,[37] collaboration between schools can be more profound if they use a common curriculum structure. Many organisations and school groups have developed curriculum maps that follow the principles explored in this chapter. For more guidance on selecting or designing a scheme of work, see Chapter 10.

 **Discuss**

Take a look at a curriculum for mastery.[38]

- On the scheme of work, identify where students study conversion between fractions and decimals. Identify opportunities to practise and apply this topic in subsequent topics.

- Why might scatter graphs be taught relatively late in secondary school (say age 13+)? Identify the concepts and skills learned in the preceding years that might be applied when learning about scatter graphs.

## Isn't 'one curriculum' too hard for some?

There's an undeniable challenge here. Secondary students in East Asian countries achieve great things, but their teachers have one big advantage – their intake. It's not that the East Asian population is innately more intelligent than the population of the West – it isn't – but East Asian students' primary education does seem to prepare them better for meeting high expectations and accessing one curriculum at secondary.

---

[37] *Ibid.*

[38] For example, you can find the full and most up-to-date Mathematics Mastery curriculum map at www.mathematicsmastery.org.

Where children benefit from a high-quality learning environment in the early years, average achievement is higher and variation is reduced.[39] Children who can count, identify written numbers, recognise shapes and have some sense of number before starting school have an important head start. High-performing systems make sure that their primary education overcomes these initial differences between learners. Teaching for mastery at primary is intended to reduce variance and raise achievement for all.

A well-established mastery approach in all feeder primary schools would narrow the gap between students' attainment on entry and deepen all students' understanding of the Key Stage 2 mathematics content. Of course, any activity in the primary phase will take some time to demonstrate impact.

This situation forces each secondary school to make an important decision – to wait to adopt teaching for mastery until the students joining them demonstrate higher and less varied understanding on entry, or to adopt teaching for mastery for the first few years of secondary school.

It can be argued that the present situation for secondary teachers in England and comparable countries has key aspects in common with the primary, rather than the secondary, schools in high-performing systems. Like the primary schools in these jurisdictions, secondary schools in England take students with a wide range of achievement. To choose to adopt a mastery approach given this intake is to choose to take on a significant challenge with the aspiration of achieving success for all students, regardless of background.

Differences in students' attainment and understanding at the start of secondary school are due, for the most part, to different experiences in early years, different parental expectations, and different experiences of primary mathematics. If these students are to catch up, they need to have full access to mathematics learning from the start of secondary school, as well as being supported to learn any key concepts from primary school that are not yet sufficiently secure.

As soon as you offer opportunities to learn to some students but not others – you teach only 'higher-attaining' 12-year-olds to multiply and

---

[39] **K. McCartney et al.,** 'Quality Child Care Supports the Achievement of Low-Income Children: Direct and Indirect Pathways through Caregiving and the Home Environment', *Journal of Applied Developmental Psychology* 28 (2007): pp. 411–426.

**B.K. Hamre and R.C. Pianta**, 'Academic and Social Advantages for At-Risk Students Placed in High Quality First Grade Classrooms', *Child Development* 76(5) (2005): pp. 949–967.

divide fractions, say – you are placing limits on learning. If we have high expectations for every student, we must offer one curriculum for all.

This is not about holding back students with higher previous attainment in order to enable their peers to catch up. It is about an ambitious and rich curriculum offer for all students at the start of secondary school, with additional provision, as required, for students who would be otherwise unable to access this content.

The mastery approach follows a cumulative curriculum, with sufficient time for every student to access age-appropriate concepts and skills. So, what can be done to support students who do not have the concepts and skills appropriate for an earlier age group?

If you go less slowly – if an 11–12-year-old student does not spend time exploring, clarifying, practising and applying all the concepts specified in the relevant programme of study, for example – it becomes very unlikely that the student will be able to learn all the mathematics that they are entitled to by the age of 16. When and how will they catch up?

In other words, students who are operating significantly below age expectation in the short term need more time to learn. There are a number of different forms this might take, such as increased lesson time, same-day-intervention or pre-teaching. Whichever you pursue, the role of intervention is vital here.

As teachers' approach to intervention beyond the lesson tends to be determined and implemented on a school-wide basis, Chapter 10 looks at this important subject in more detail.

# Differentiation through depth

In Chapters 6 to 9, we take a detailed look at the implications and possibilities of this curriculum structure relating to what takes place inside classrooms.

Teaching for mastery means one curriculum: all students working towards mastery of the same core content at the same time. Here, we begin to consider how the individual learning needs of students can best be met within this structure. How do teachers differentiate if all students are working towards the same aim?

Differentiation should not mean students are given fundamentally different work; rather, they should be supported in accessing the same content as their peers.

Differentiation need not be achieved by accelerating through the curriculum or by task modification in the traditional sense (such as making numbers smaller or bigger, providing a different number of questions, or making calculations 'easier' or 'harder'). Instead, differentiation can be carefully planned and designed around one of these three intentions:

- deepening mathematical understanding – being able to move between representations of concepts and skills

- deepening mathematical thinking – being able to question, sort, compare and see patterns in mathematics

- deepening mathematical language – being able to explain, justify and prove using mathematical language.

All students can work on the same mathematical tasks, as Tracey Hall, Nicole Strangman and Anne Meyer have emphasised. They state that 'differentiated instruction allows all students to access the same classroom task by providing entry points, learning tasks, and outcomes that are tailored to students' needs'.[40]

Ultimately, the learning intention – the goal of the lesson – must be the same for all students. Peter Sullivan, Judith Mousley and Robyn Zevenbergen, researching classroom practice in Australia, find that:

> Many lessons seem to either ignore the diversity of students' backgrounds and needs, or address them in ways that exacerbate differences by having alternative goals for particular groups of students. Our intention is that all students engage sufficiently in a lesson to allow them to participate fully in a whole-class review of their work on the goal task. Students may follow different pathways to the ultimate task, being supported or detoured along the way, but all will feel part of the classroom community. All will know they are expected to master the content.[41]

Where an exercise is being offered, careful use of variation (which will be explored in Chapter 6) ensures that all students can access the same set of questions. These questions can be carefully ordered to deepen understanding and provide increasing challenge. Wherever possible, students should be offered the same mathematical tasks.

---

[40] **T. Hall, N. Strangman and A. Meyer**, *Differentiated Instruction and Implications for UDL Implementation* (Wakefield, MA: National Center on Accessing the General Curriculum, 2003). Retrieved 22 August 2007 from the National Center on Accessible Instructional Materials.

[41] **P. Sullivan, J. Mousley and R. Zevenbergen**, 'Describing Elements of Mathematics Lessons that Accommodate Diversity in Student Background', in *Proceedings of the 28th Conference of the International Group for the Psychology of Mathematics Education*, edited by M. Johnsen Hoines and A. Fuglestad (Vol. 4, pp. 265–272) (Bergen: PME, 2004).

A task like the one below offers opportunities for students to practise expanding brackets, might include representations of the expressions using area models, and offers an opportunity to develop and apply problem-solving strategies.

A teacher working with a class on this task might have many aims for students' learning. They might want students to know and use the terms 'term' and 'coefficient' in algebraic expressions. They might want students to know and understand how linear expressions can be represented using bar models.

---

 **Try this in the classroom**

**Equivalent expressions**

$10n + 20$

Which expressions are not the same as $10n + 20$?

$5(2n + 15)$

$5(n + 4) + 5n$

$2(4n + 10 + n)$

$\frac{1}{2}(40 + 20n)$

$3(7n + 17)$

$2(\frac{1}{2}n + 1)$

$12(n + 2) - 2(n + 2)$

---

 **Preparing to teach – do the mathematics!**

In preparing to teach the task above, you might consider the following points:

- How will you use the terms 'coefficient' and 'term' when facilitating class discussion around this task?

- How will you ensure that students correctly use these terms?

- What concrete or pictorial representations might you use to deepen students' understanding?

- How might you adapt this task for use in the classroom if you wanted to increase opportunities for practice?

A possible adaptation, to encourage students to appreciate how and when we use letters to represent numbers, would be to ask students to choose a value for $n$ and check whether the expressions they have identified as the same as $10n + 20$ have the same value.

This could be an exploration task, offered to students with limited, if any, experience of either substitution or expanding brackets.

Students could be offered this area model representation of $10n + 20$:

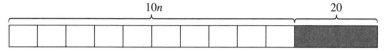

**Figure 4.6**

They could then be asked to represent the other expressions using area models.

For example, $5(2n + 15)$ might be represented as:

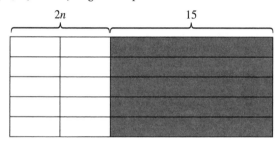

**Figure 4.7**

$2(4n + 10 + n)$ as:

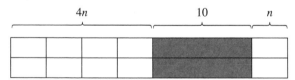

**Figure 4.8**

$5(n + 4) + 5n$ might look like this:

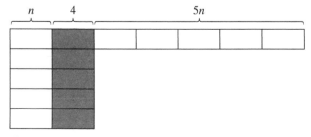

**Figure 4.9**

**Consider**

If you intended the purpose of this task to be clarification of multiplying out brackets, how might you adapt or present it?

*Students could be asked to explain why someone might wrongly conclude that $5(2n + 15) = 10n + 20$. What mistake is being made? Why is this incorrect?*

*They could be challenged to create a plausible but incorrect answer (such as $10(n + 20)$) and to write an explanation as to why it is not equivalent to $10n + 20$.*

The task might also be presented for the purposes of application. One such purpose might be applying calculation with decimals. Students could be offered decimal values for $n$, such as 3.7 or 57.84, and asked to substitute this value for $n$ in each expression. This task has the advantage of potential for self-checking, as many of the expressions have the same value as $10n + 20$.

The purpose here is not contained *within* the task – the same task can be used for a variety of different purposes with different groups of students.

Students could be asked to design their own, similar, task, such as one that asks, 'Which expressions are not the same as $16x - 10$?'

Students might be challenged (by themselves, by a peer, or by the teacher) to create as many such expressions as possible that are equivalent to the expression $16x - 10$.

$10x + 6x - 10$

$10(x - 1) + 6x$

$16(x - 1) + 6$

Once students are used to taking ownership of and responsibility for their learning in this way, an element of ambiguity or choice about the purpose of a set task can be advantageous. Students can work purposefully on the task in the way that maximises their own learning.

Occasionally, it is reasonable to assume that a task that is appropriately challenging for most students will be found to be too challenging by some. In this case, these students might not engage with the task, or might rely too heavily on prompts from the teacher.

What do we do when we anticipate that some students will find a task we are setting very difficult to access? Research suggests that previously lower-attaining students are often required to listen to additional explanations, or to pursue substantially different learning goals from more successful students.[42] This is unlikely to result in mastery for all, as these learners are being denied access to the key concepts and skills they're entitled to.

As an alternative, all students can be offered the same task, with enabling prompts provided for those students who would otherwise find the task too challenging. Enabling prompts can involve slightly lowering an aspect of the task demand, such as the form of representation, the size of the numbers, or the number of steps, so that a student experiencing difficulty can proceed at that new level, and can go on to proceed with the original task.

Sometimes we need to do more than offer the same task to all – we may ask students who experience difficulty to work on differentiated tasks. These will be similar to the ones undertaken by their peers, with increased accessibility and, crucially, no reduction in conceptual content. Sometimes the original designer of the task will have suggested alternative tasks, sometimes we plan them in anticipation, and sometimes we adapt a task in the classroom as we teach.

Students are, of course, aware when they are being offered enabling prompts or more accessible tasks than their peers. It helps if we can make it really clear to them that the differentiation is to enable them to pursue the same learning goals as other students. This gives them confidence in the guidance or task, as well as communicating the expectation that all can succeed.

The key message for students is that they are all working towards deepening their understanding of the same curriculum aims.

# Grouping students

Where setting increases the tail of underachievement in mathematics, it does so because it leads teachers to expect less of students in lower sets and to provide higher-attaining students with challenge by teaching them content from higher year groups, rather than exploring the appropriate year's content in greater depth.

Setting can exacerbate disadvantage due to self-fulfilling prophecy effects and poor modelling and mentoring for students who really need it.[43]

---

[42] **P. Sullivan, L. Knott and Y. Yang**, 'The Relationship between Task Design, Anticipated Pedagogies, and Student Learning', in *Task Design in Mathematics Education*, edited by A. Watson and M. Ohtani. New ICMI Study Series (Springer, 2015).

[43] **J.E. Brophy**, 'Research on the Self-Fulfilling Prophecy and Teacher Expectations', *Journal of Educational Psychology* 75(5) (1983): pp. 631–661.

However, how we choose to group students is not the most important factor in determining their success. Much more influential are questions such as:

- What do we believe students with lower attainment by the end of primary are capable of, given appropriate opportunities to learn?

- Are all teachers of mathematics developing their know-how as to effective pedagogy?

- How do we challenge students who seem to more quickly grasp the key ideas and skills?

Setting can undermine student confidence and 'discourage the belief that attainment can be improved through effort'.[44] Students' sense of self-worth and engagement have been found to vary according to the set that they are in.[45] A student might excel in one area of mathematics, but be challenged in other areas. Those who appear to struggle, may not necessarily struggle with all concepts.

> ### Preparing task variations to meet diverse student needs
>
>
>
> **P. Sullivan, J. Mousley and R. Zevenbergen** (2004) *op. cit.*[46]
>
> **The study:** Peter Sullivan, Judith Mousley and Robyn Zevenbergen researched effective actions that teachers can take to improve mathematics learning for all students. The model they developed has four key elements: the type of task; the building of mathematical community; enabling prompts that can be used to support students experiencing difficulty in learning; and extending prompts that can be used to challenge students who have completed the set work.
>
> **What it tells us:** The study emphasised the importance of preparing variations to set tasks in order to address differences in students' backgrounds.

Regardless of whether teachers are working with students grouped according to their prior attainment, or students grouped with mixed prior attainment, these four recommendations still stand. Teachers differentiate through depth when they teach a common problem, with scaffolding that uses enabling

---

[44] The Sutton Trust EEF Teaching and Learning Toolkit Summer 2013.

[45] For example, **M. Arnot and D. Reay**, 'The Social Dynamics of Classroom Learning', in *Consultation in the Classroom: Developing Dialogue about Teaching and Learning*, edited by M. Arnot *et al.* (Cambridge: Pearson Publishing, 2004).

[46] **P. Sullivan, J. Mousley and R. Zevenbergen**, 'Teacher Actions to Maximise Mathematics Learning Opportunities in Heterogeneous Classrooms', *International Journal of Science and Mathematics Education* 4 (2006): pp. 117–143.

prompts to support those whose mathematical background might be an issue, and plans to extend the thinking of students who require a further challenge.

A mastery approach can be successful whether you choose to set students according to prior attainment or to teach them in mixed groups. Where expectations are high, and differentiation is through depth rather than content coverage, either structure can result in success for every student, regardless of their background.

This is particularly true if your department teaches using predominantly the same tasks, problems and exercise sets for each year group. Students are surprisingly quick to realise that they are being given equal curriculum access – they do seem to talk about their mathematics lessons! – which reduces the impact of being in a different set.

# Summary

A curriculum for mastery has three vital components – full curriculum access for all with differentiation through depth, taking your time, and cumulative learning over time.

*Full curriculum access for all:* a curriculum for mastery is one where every student is entitled to access key concepts and skills, where connections between areas of mathematics are made explicit, and where learning builds over time.

*Take your time:* a mastery approach to curriculum design means reducing the number of key ideas introduced over a period of time, but taking longer over each one, so that deep and sustainable understanding is fostered. Future mathematical learning can then be built on solid foundations, which need not be retaught.

*Cumulative learning over time:* teaching for mastery emphasises connections between different mathematical ideas, so that students appreciate the rich connections between core content. When introducing new concepts and skills, it is important to make connections with earlier content that has already been understood.

Differentiation takes place through the way in which students are being taught and the level of support they are given. Every learner is entitled to access the same content as their peers, and challenge is provided through increased depth, rather than acceleration of content.

# Chapter 5

## Is testing a help or a hindrance?

**A**ssessment is integral to the process of teaching and learning. It is one of the most powerful tools we have as teachers. Awareness of students' current skills, knowledge and understanding is the key – for both teacher and student alike – to planning the next step in their learning.

When we teach mathematics for mastery, our priority is long-term learning, not short-term performance. Long-term mastery of mathematics is immeasurably more valuable than the short-term ability to answer questions in tests or exams. Such tests are an inevitably imperfect tool that we can use to try and measure what students have learned.

There is no question (or answer) that shows a student has 'mastered' a concept. However deeply we understand a concept, there is always more depth and always more to learn. There are always new connections or ways of looking at a concept.

A better question to ask, then, in preference to whether students have 'mastered' a concept, is: 'Have my students learned what I wanted them to learn?'

We begin this chapter with a focus on the role and impact of high-stakes national exams. We then look at those aspects of assessment that are within the control of the school or school group. Having clarified the key differences, and the relationship, between summative and formative assessment, we move on to look at each in more detail. This includes consideration of the role of summative assessment, then of formative assessment: both formative use of timed written tests and responsive teaching more broadly, including effective feedback.

# High-stakes national exams

National tests, such as the GCSEs taken by 16-year-olds in England, Wales and Northern Ireland, are not the ultimate aim of teaching secondary mathematics. Students who have been taught mathematics for mastery should experience success in these national tests, but this is a by-product (albeit a very important and high-stakes by-product) of students enjoying and achieving in mathematics, not the sole objective.

The pressure that some education systems – including England's – currently place on teachers and students is reducing students' enjoyment of and achievement in mathematics. Highly committed, intelligent and inspirational mathematics teachers openly talk and write about how time pressures and exam focus distort the way they teach.

Although governments and assessment authorities often aspire to incorporate all aspects of mathematical proficiency in national examinations, in practice some types of proficiency are easier to test than others. National exams can consequently become dominated by routine procedures and familiar applications.

In England, ACME found strong agreement among teachers, educationalists and Ofsted inspectors that, unless all aspects of mathematics are assessed, schools will not give them the teaching time and resources they need.[1]

Of course, national exams can assess only a small part of students' learning. Their role is to provide a summary of that learning, by assessing a sample from the domain. If this truly were a random sample from the full domain we expect students to study, this would work pretty well. If a student performed well on the exam, we could reasonably conclude they had a good grasp of the wider domain.

Unfortunately, timed written assessments can only assess limited forms of competence. National exams do not, in fact, assess a random sample from the domain of interests. They assess a particular subset from the domain – and teachers are able to predict which aspects of competence will be assessed.

Because it is possible to predict which aspects of mathematical competence will be assessed, and because of the high-stakes nature of national exam results, there is an incentive for teachers and students to concentrate on only the content that is likely to appear in the exam.

---

[1] **ACME,** *Mathematical Needs: The Mathematical Needs of Learners* (Advisory Committee on Mathematics Education, 2011). www.acme-uk.org/media/7627/acme_theme_b_final.pdf accessed 11 August.

In making critical decisions about what and how to teach mathematics, teachers will naturally focus on those areas they expect to feature in high-stakes tests.

Though the intention behind national testing is to make the important measurable, unfortunately their impact is to make what's measurable important.

Because teachers are so incentivised to teach to the test, correlation between attainment in national exams and the wider domain of mathematics achievement weakens over time. National exams are therefore a less and less adequate proxy for achievement in mathematics.

There have certainly been times when students have asked me, 'But why do we have to learn this?' and I have felt the only possible response was, 'Because it's on the exam syllabus.' The approach to teaching mathematics described in this book does not eradicate such interactions, but it should at least constrain them to a period of six months or so in the run-up to high-stakes national exams.

Students only ask 'why' they have to learn something when they are struggling to make sense of it, struggling to engage with it. The more teachers can do to ensure that mathematics is taught in ways that have meaning, and that are accessible to every learner, the less students question the value of learning it.

If the pressure of high-stakes exams becomes so high that they really *are* the only purpose the teacher has in mind when planning and teaching a topic, then sadly we are no longer talking about mathematics education, merely exam preparation.

This concern was expressed by the Expert Panel for the National Curriculum in England, which wrote:

> ... *we are concerned that an instrumental attitude, which values test and examination results and certificates as ends in themselves, has become increasingly evident in the English system. This diminishes the priority that should be given to ensuring that the underlying learning being accredited is deep and secure.*[2]

---

[2] **Department for Education,** *The Framework for the National Curriculum. A report by the Expert Panel for the National Curriculum review* (London: Department for Education, 2011): p. 27.

## The risk of 'teaching to the test'

 **Evidence**

**OECD** 2013.[3]

**The study:** Over three years, the OECD reviewed the evaluation and assessment policies in 28 countries, which resulted in the *Review on Evaluation and Assessment Frameworks for Improving School Outcomes.* While emphasising that each country context is unique, the review identified several common policy challenges.

**What it tells us:** The study found that many countries demonstrated a lack of alignment between central curricula, standards and assessment approaches.

*Because of their role in providing accountability, evaluation and assessment systems can distort how and what students are taught. For example, if teachers are judged largely on results from standardised student tests, they may 'teach to the test', focusing solely on skills that are tested and giving less attention to students' wider developmental and educational needs. It is important to minimise these unwanted side-effects by, for example, using a broader range of approaches to evaluate the performance of schools and teachers.*[4]

This is felt to be a particular issue in the West. Some feel that students in England have become the most tested students in the world.[5] Teachers and school leaders are operating in a culture of accountability with constant comparison of test scores.

American professor Daniel Koretz cautions about the need to be more realistic about the use of tests for educational accountability.

*Systems that simply pressure teachers to raise scores on one test (or one set of tests...) are not likely to work as advertised, particularly if the increases demanded are large and inexorable. Instead, they are likely to produce substantial inflation of scores and a variety of undesirable*

---

[3] **OECD,** *Synergies for Better Learning: An International Perspective on Evaluation and Assessment* (Paris: OECD Publishing, 2013). www.oecd.org/edu/school/Synergies%20for%20Better%20Learning_Summary.pdf accessed 15 August 2017.

[4] *Ibid.,* pp. 2–3.

[5] **W. Mansell,** *Education by Numbers: The Tyranny of Testing* (London: Politico's Publishing, 2007).

*changes in instruction, such as an excessive focus on old tests, an inappropriate narrowing of instruction, and a reliance on teaching test-taking tricks.*[6]

---

 **Discuss**

What are the implications of this distorting effect of high-stakes exams? What action can the teachers working within these systems take to mitigate this? A couple of possibilities are:

- Stay aware of the decisions you are making to narrow the curriculum or focus on some skills above others.

- Consider whether a broader, less exam-focused offer, particularly in the early years of secondary education, might actually result in improved exam performance.

---

# Purposeful assessment

Assessment is a vital part of learning. We can view assessment as running on a spectrum from high-stakes national assessment, through timed written summative and formative tests, through to responsive teaching. Each of these is intrinsically linked with the curriculum, teaching and learning.

Assessment systems the world over puzzle over the relationship between formative and summative assessment.[7] Summative assessment is about measuring what learning has taken place, while formative assessment is about informing and improving teaching and learning. Formative assessment involves measuring prior learning so that any misconceptions can be clarified, any gaps filled.

Formative assessment helps teachers and students alike to adjust their teaching and learning strategies. It enables teachers to diagnose learning needs and differentiate teaching, and also to provide timely feedback to students. Formative assessment also strengthens students' self-monitoring and engages them in their own learning.

---

[6] **D. Koretz,** *Measuring Up: What Educational Testing Really Tells Us* (Cambridge, MA: Harvard University Press, 2008): p. 330.

[7] **OECD,** *op. cit.*

The role of summative assessment is very different. Sometimes summative assessment is intended to certify learning and award qualifications. Even where this is not the intention, summative assessments are usually designed to provide information about performance to students, parents and others. Importantly, summative assessment can be used to signal high standards and expected performance. This can motivate students to increase effort and achievement.

The relationship between formative and summative assessment is a puzzling one. Both are important, and time-consuming, and it can be tempting to think that – to save potentially over-assessing students – the same assessment can be used for both purposes.

However, summative assessment is effective only if it provides an accurate shared meaning. For assessment to offer a shared meaning in this way, it has to consist of standard tasks taken in standard conditions, to sample from a large domain of content and to distinguish between students. Tests that are designed with these three features – which are vital for summative purposes – are unfit for formative use. As Daisy Christodoulou emphasises in her book, *Making Good Progress?*, 'We need different scales and different types of assessment for the different elements we want to assess.'[8]

Too often, assessments are used to provide snapshots of comparative performance, rather than providing information that can be used by students or their teachers to improve future teaching and learning. Most current assessments provide minimal feedback. They tend to emphasise performance on recently taught content and are used for external accountability measures, rather than as feedback devices that are integral to the teaching and learning process. In other words, although we may think we're using tests both summatively and formatively, in fact, their formative use is very limited.

# The role of summative assessment

Students, teachers and school leaders are judged by results in national examinations. It is in everyone's interests to track and monitor students' progress towards success in these tests.

However, because high-stakes exams often skew the curriculum towards short-term goals, a school's own assessment tracking system can often get in the way of students' learning.

---

[8] **D. Christodoulou**, *Making Good Progress? The Future of Assessment for Learning* (Oxford: Oxford University Press, 2016): p. 159.

Counter-intuitive as it may seem, continually preparing for summative assessments in the style of high-stakes national tests is not the best way to prepare students for success in these examinations.

In 2009, England's Expert Group on Assessment admitted that:

> *We cannot ignore the risk that tests whose results are used for high-stakes accountability purposes can adversely lead to narrowing of the curriculum, 'teaching to the test' and undue pupil stress. We do not support drilling or narrow test preparation. The best way to prepare for ... tests is through a varied programme of high-quality teaching throughout the year, not through repeatedly sitting practice test papers.*[9]

Simply practising assessments will generally improve students' performance in the short term, but this short-term performance gain does not indicate that the test practice has helped them with their learning. In practising tests, students often aren't learning anything new or meaningfully deepening their understanding.

As we saw earlier in this chapter, there are significant negative consequences of teaching to the test. It is not possible for a test, however competently it is designed, to measure everything we want students to know, understand and be able to do. This is especially true of timed, written tests. Any assessment method has to select a sample of the desired knowledge and skills and test that. The result is used to make an inference about the wider domain.

---

 **Discuss**

Are there any year groups or classes where you feel pressure to teach to the test? What are the advantages and disadvantages of this approach for the students?

---

The danger with high-stakes testing is that teachers may narrow the curriculum that they teach to match the test. If we teach to the test, we stop teaching important things that aren't on the test.

Teaching must focus on students' conceptual development rather than merely prepare them for the next test. But where schools implement frequent high-stakes summative assessment, teachers are inevitably tempted to teach only what is required for the next test rather than laying the foundations for understanding overarching mathematical ideas.

---

[9] **Department for Children, Schools and Families,** *Report of the Expert Group on Assessment* (London: Department for Children, Schools and Families, 2009): p. 26.

Teachers often feel they do not have time to teach the full breadth and depth of the curriculum because of pressure for coverage and test results. This makes mathematics harder to learn for many students, because they do not have the opportunity or the required knowledge to make sense of fragments of mathematical information within the broader context of mathematics and its applications.

The Commission on Assessment without Levels, a government body set up in England to help schools improve approaches to assessment, emphasised that 'In-school summative assessment should not be driven by nationally collected forms of statutory summative assessment. What works best for national accountability purposes does not necessarily work best for supporting teaching and learning or for monitoring pupil progress.'[10]

Ofsted, England's school inspectorate, found that 'Too much teaching concentrates on the acquisition of sets of disparate skills needed to pass examinations.'[11] Based on observational evidence from 192 schools, it found that classroom practice focused on what was to be tested next. This resulted in teaching predominantly factual and procedural knowledge and predictable problem-solving techniques.

Teaching to the test – focusing on the contents of the next summative assessment, which mirrors the content and style of high-stakes national exams – can result in excessive focus on facts and procedures at the expense of deep understanding. It also forces teachers to rush through content, so that everything has been 'covered' before the test. For these reasons, teaching that prioritises test preparation results in students being less equipped than they could be to face the challenges presented in high-stakes national exams.

In too many cases, testing is used by teachers and school leaders as the measure to judge whether change has occurred rather than as a tool to further improve teaching and learning. The costs of these accountability tests are high, and the returns are minimal.[12]

Assessment that is too frequent can distort the taught curriculum, as teachers rush to introduce or re-introduce concepts and skills in advance of the test.

---

[10] **J. McIntosh,** *Final Report of the Commission on Assessment without Levels* (London: Department for Education, 2015): p. 24.

[11] **Ofsted,** *Mathematics: Understanding the Score – Messages from Inspection Evidence,* Report Number 070063 (London: Ofsted, 2008).

[12] **L.A. Shepard et al.,** 'Effects of Introducing Classroom Performance Assessments on Student Learning', *Educational Measurement Issues and Practice* 15 (1996): pp. 7–18.

Tests that are not curriculum aligned can lead to greater distortions, as time is wasted introducing topics out of sequence. Such assessments are arguably more important for school or teacher accountability than for learning, and as such their use should be minimised.

Frequent summative tests and assessments can also have a negative impact on students' views of mathematics and of themselves as learners. This happens where the emphasis in mathematics lessons shifts from learning and understanding to feeling judged or measured.

 **Consider**

Could a training session on the perils of teaching to the test, and the negative effects on students' mathematics education, help colleagues, including the senior leadership team, understand the importance of teaching for mastery?

However, summative assessment is an important way in which schools track and monitor student progress. Feedback from summative assessment activities can also provide information for students to plan their subsequent phase of study.

Information gained in the summative assessment activities can be used as a basis for the planning of the teaching sequence and the breadth and depth of the learning units in the subsequent term or year. This information can be very useful for the mathematics department to adjust the aims and strategies of their offer.

There is clearly a compromise to be made here. Anything more frequent than termly testing for summative purposes places too great a distortion on teaching and learning. This is recognised in England by the Commission on Assessment without Levels:

> Measuring pupils' progress over a short period is unlikely to be helpful or reliable and it should, therefore, not be necessary to conduct and record in-school summative assessment for monitoring progress more than once a term. Ofsted does not require progress to be recorded with any particular frequency.[13]

Schools successfully teaching for mastery schedule between one and three summative assessment points in the year. They take care to ensure that the tests do not include too many concepts or skills that the students are both unfamiliar with and do not have the tools to figure out for themselves.

---

[13] **J. McIntosh,** *op. cit.,* p. 24.

**Discuss**

How many summative assessment points does your senior leadership team currently require you to have? If more than three, could you encourage them to reduce these, in light of the recommendations of the Commission on Assessment without Levels, which recommends a maximum of three?[14]

# The role of formative assessment

Assessment is used formatively where the evidence collected from assessment activities is used as important feedback for teachers to adjust teaching strategies and pace, and for students to improve their learning.

A useful definition of assessment for learning is given by Paul Black and his colleagues:

> Assessment for Learning is any assessment for which the first priority in its design is to serve the purpose of promoting pupils' learning. It thus differs from assessment designed to primarily serve the purposes of accountability, or of ranking or of certifying competence. An assessment activity can help learning if it provides information to be used as feedback, by teachers, and by their students in assessing themselves, to modify the teaching and learning activities in which they are engaged. Such assessment becomes 'formative assessment' when the evidence is actually used to adapt the teaching work to meet learning needs.[15]

The most important part of this is the last – we are not using assessment for learning unless the evidence we gather about student understanding really does have an impact on what we do in the classroom.

What matters from formative assessments is not numbers or grades, it is the feedback they provide – what they can tell teachers and students about the students' learning.

Day-to-day, in-school formative assessment includes question and answer during class, scanning and marking students' work, observing students while they work, and regular short quizzes to recap information.

---

[14] *Ibid.*

[15] **P.J. Black et al.**, *Working Inside the Black Box: Assessment for Learning in the Classroom* (London: nferNelson, 2002).

One effective method of assessing formatively is to offer students a short set of questions to complete every few lessons. These questions can relate to topics studied relatively recently, as well as topics studied less recently. Following analysis of students' responses to these questions, teachers might repeat lesson content, clarify definitions, or offer additional opportunities for practice.

Regular quizzes such as these also directly support student learning. The act of retrieving the relevant knowledge helps to fix it in students' long-term memory. Somewhat counter-intuitively, these quizzes are valuable even for those students who consistently score full marks.

 **Consider**

Do your students retrieve their mathematical knowledge frequently enough to embed it in long-term memory? Would they benefit from more regular quizzes?

Practising skills that students appear to have fully learned is surprisingly valuable. As cognitive scientist Daniel Willingham explains:

> Odd as it may seem, that sort of practice is essential to schooling. It yields three important benefits: it reinforces the basic skills that are required for the learning of more advanced skills, it protects against forgetting, and it improves transfer.[16]

Assessment for formative purposes need not take the form of timed written tests. Students and teachers can use assessment formatively as part of their usual classroom practice. This form of assessment is often called 'responsive teaching'.

Responsive teaching involves being active and purposeful in the classroom. Teachers can use the information collected in ongoing assessment activities such as observation and questioning to adjust teaching strategies, decide whether to include further consolidation activities or introduce enrichment topics in the subsequent day-to-day teaching.

For example, when working on the area and perimeter of rectangles, a teacher might ask students what is the same and different about these three shapes:

Rectangle A measures 4 cm by 10 cm

Rectangle B measures 5 cm by 8 cm

Rectangle C measures 3 cm by 11 cm

---

[16] **D. Willingham,** *Why Don't Students Like School?* (San Francisco, CA: Jossey-Bass, 2009).

Students' responses to this question might indicate to the teacher:

- whether or not students correctly use the terms 'perimeter' and 'area'
- the extent to which students are able to move between the two concepts and make comparisons
- whether any students expect rectangles with equal area to have equal perimeter.

Immediate feedback from ongoing assessment activities can be provided to students during class time or in delivering their assignments. This can be in verbal or in written form. Students with this immediate feedback can clarify their mistaken concepts before building further knowledge on them. They can make additional effort to improve areas of weakness.

## Responsive teaching in Hong Kong

The Hong Kong Education Bureau recommends the use of diverse assessment methods to collect information on student learning. Moreover, it emphasises that formative assessment should be ongoing as well as carried out through timed written tests. It encourages the following ongoing assessment activities in mathematics: classroom discussion and oral presentations; observation of student performance in class; classwork, homework and project work; and short quizzes.[17]

Hong Kong's syllabus emphasises that assessment is 'a process of gathering information to find out students' achievements related to the set objectives *so as to enhance the teaching and learning processes*'.[18] [author's italics]

The Hong Kong Curriculum Development Centre makes a point of emphasising that the purpose of assessment is as an integral part of the teaching and learning cycle. It explicitly recognises that assessment can also be used for summative purposes, such as to evaluate the effectiveness of teachers, or to screen students or set them in different groups. However, it cautions against over-use of tests for these purposes, rather than to improve learning.

---

[17] **Curriculum Development Council,** *Mathematics Education: Key Learning Curriculum Guide (primary 1–secondary 3)* (Hong Kong: CDC, 2002). Retrieved from http://www.edb.gov.hk/en/curriculum-development/kla/ma/curr/basic-education-2002.html accessed 15 August 2017.

[18] **Curriculum Development Council,** *Syllabuses for Secondary Schools, Mathematics, Secondary 1–5* (Hong Kong: CDC, 1999). www.edb.gov.hk/en/curriculum-development/kla/ma/curr/sec-math-1999.html accessed 15 August 2017.

Its secondary school syllabus advises that:

*Information collected in assessment helps*

*1. teachers to*

- *understand how students are progressing;*
- *recognise students' strengths and areas for improvement in learning;*
- *work out ways of helping students;*
- *plan their lessons.*

*2. students to*

- *understand their own progress;*
- *recognise areas and ways for improvements in learning.*[19]

# Designing and selecting test questions

How might we use test questions to gather evidence about students' understanding? American educator John Holt described what it felt like to him when he could understand something.[20]

England's National Centre for Excellence in Teaching Mathematics has adapted and added to Holt's checklist for assessing students' understanding of mathematical concepts, ideas or techniques. For 'recognise it in various guises and circumstances', it suggests the use of concrete, pictorial and symbolic representations.

The resulting list provides a helpful checklist:

- *describe it in his or her own words;*
- *represent it in a variety of ways (e.g. using concrete materials, pictures and symbols – the CPA approach);*
- *explain it to someone else;*
- *make up his or her own examples (and non-examples) of it;*
- *see connections between it and other facts or ideas;*

---

[19] *Ibid.*

[20] **J. Holt,** *How Children Fail* (New York: Pitman Publishing Corp, 1964): p. 176.

- *recognise it in new situations and contexts;*

- *make use of it in various ways, including in new situations.*[21]

Teaching mathematics for mastery means emphasising the deep structure – that is, promoting understanding and sense-making. Because the questions teachers ask – orally and in tests – send messages to students about what is important, it is essential that some of these questions demand deep understanding.

As far as students are concerned, if it's not on the test, it's not important. If it is possible to complete tests with just a surface knowledge of the material, students will conclude that deep understanding is not really of value.

That said, if a student is unsuccessful on a question that demands deep understanding, it can be less informative than if they had tackled a more surface-level question. Their teacher may be unable to tell which of many possible barriers prevented the student from success with the question, limiting the formative use of the assessment.

Retrieval of surface knowledge is also an effective way to fix it in students' long-term memory. Efficient recall of surface knowledge will support students in accessing deeper understanding.

 **Consider**

Have a go at questions A and B below. Why might you use each question?

*Question A: 85% of the students in Year 8 study Spanish. 54 students do not study Spanish. How many students are in Year 8?*

*Question B: Calculate 15% of 360.*

Although both questions are about percentages (in fact, in one way or another, both questions are concerned with 15% of 360), they offer different affordances and constraints.

Question A asks students to connect their work on calculating a percentage of an amount with other facts and ideas. In their discussion or written workings, students might draw on some or all of the following mathematical ideas:

- One whole is 100%

- 85 and 15 are complements to 100

---

[21] **A. Askew et al.,** *Teaching for Mastery: Questions, Tasks and Activities to Support Assessment* (Buckingham: Open University Press, 2015).

- 5% is a third of 15%

- 54 is equal to 30 plus 24

- A third of 30 is equal to 10; a third of 24 is equal to 8

- A third of 54 is equal to 18

- If 5% of the whole is equal to 18, then 10% of the whole is equal to 36

- If 10% of the whole is equal to 36, then 100% of the whole is equal to 360.

### 🗨 Consider

- Which, if any, of the above ideas should students draw on to answer the question? Should they use any additional ideas?

- How would you expect your students to tackle this question?

- What action could you take to support your students in making their thinking more accessible to you and to each other?

Including a question of this style in infrequent (termly or biannual) summative assessment sends an important message to students that deep understanding of percentages has value. However, the formative use of this question on a written test is relatively limited, as any incorrect student responses may not make the barrier or barriers to success clear.

If the question is intended to be used for formative assessment, it may be best to ask students to work on it in pairs or small groups, discussing their reasoning. Through circulating, the teacher can gain an insight into student understanding. Students can then be guided as much or as little as is necessary to achieve success.

Question B lends itself to inclusion in 'five quick questions' or a weekly mental mathematics test. This will also require students to retrieve their knowledge about calculating percentages, and thus improve their long-term memory.

# Effective feedback

The route to better learning is more effective teaching. A key component of this is feedback, which keeps teaching and learning on track to achieve its goals.

Carefully considered teacher responses can encourage students as mathematical thinkers. Effective feedback lessens students' dependence on the teacher and gives them the sense that they can do mathematics. However, teacher responses that provide too much assistance can stifle students' thinking and make them too reliant on the teacher.

---

 **Discuss**

Look at a piece of student work together. Identify an error the student has made. What possible feedback might you give? List as many different responses as you can.

Sort and classify the responses. Which responses most encourage mathematical thinking?

For example, say a student attempts to subtract 39 from 55 using the standard written algorithm, and obtains the solution 24.

$$
\begin{array}{r}
55 \\
- \underline{39} \\
24
\end{array}
$$

What feedback could you give?

Here are some possibilities:

- 'You forgot to carry.'

- 'Can you model this subtraction using concrete manipulatives?'

- 'How did you work it out?'

- 'Is that a reasonable answer?'

- 'How could you check?'

- 'What happens if you subtract 9 from 5?'

- 'What do you have to do when the number you are subtracting is bigger?'

- 'Could you work it out another way?'

From the list above, five items could be considered to encourage mathematical thinking, in that they are questions that students can ask themselves when working on questions. These are 'Can you model this … ?', 'How did you work it out?', 'Is that a reasonable answer?', 'How could you check?' and 'Could you work it out another way?'

---

Students receive feedback about their performance or understanding from teachers, peers, or through their engagement with a task. Feedback can increase effort, motivation, or engagement to learn, or it can prompt actions that lead to understanding. Feedback is among the most critical influences on student learning.

**Effective feedback is positive, specific, and focused on challenging tasks**

 Evidence

**J. Hattie and H. Timperley** 2007.[22]

**The study:** John Hattie and Helen Timperley systematically investigated the impact of different types of teacher feedback to students.

**What it tells us:** Their work identifies four different levels of feedback. These are feedback about the task itself, about the process of learning, about students' management of their own learning, and about the students as individuals. They argue that the level at which feedback is directed influences its effectiveness. Research suggests that feedback is best directed at the first three levels – task, process and self-management.

In addition, they suggest that:

- feedback should be about challenging tasks, not easy ones
- feedback about what is right is more important than feedback about what is wrong
- feedback should be as specific as possible.

Consideration of these four different levels of feedback, and efforts to direct feedback at task, process and self-management, can take us a long way on our journey to raise achievement in mathematics.

Let's look at what this research means for feedback in the mathematics classroom. We'll look at this task involving graphical representations of direct proportion.

---

[22] **J. Hattie and H. Timperley,** 'The Power of Feedback', *Review of Educational Research* 77(1) (2007): pp. 81–112.

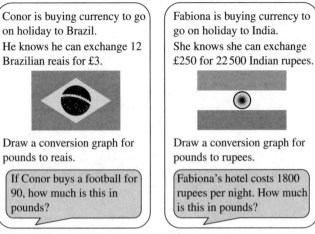

Find an equation for each graph

**Figure 5.1:** Bureau de change

---

 **Consider**

As the students work on this task, what might teacher feedback look like at each of the four levels:

- task

- process

- self-regulation

- personal?

---

Task-based feedback might focus on whether work is correct or incorrect. If a student had drawn a graph which didn't pass through the origin, the teacher might ask, 'What could £0 be exchanged for?' and 'What does this tell you about the coordinates?' As well as improving their work on this specific task, such questions are intended to remind the student, or to help them realise, that all conversion (and all direct proportion) graphs will pass through the origin.

Process-focused feedback would be aimed at the process used to complete the task. This kind of feedback is more directly aimed at the processing of information, or learning processes requiring understanding or completion of the task. For example, to a student whose conversion graph for pounds to Brazilian raeis has a raeis axis from 0 to 60 (and a pounds axis from 0 to £15) and so struggles to find the conversion of 90 raeis, a teacher may say,

'You need to look at all the information in the question when planning your answer.'

Feedback to students might be focused at the self-regulation level, including greater skill in self-evaluation or confidence to engage further on a task. For example, 'You know the important features of a graph. Check to see whether you have included them all.'

Also focusing on self-regulation, students could be asked to come up with more possible questions that could be answered using their graphs, perhaps reversing the conversions. 'Can you create a question that gives the amount in pounds and asks for a conversion to Brazilian reais?'

Creating your own similar questions is an effective strategy for learning mathematics.[23] Prompting students to do this increases the likelihood that they will use this learning strategy in future. Feedback of this type can have a big influence on students' self-efficacy and beliefs about themselves as learners. It can encourage or inform students so that they are able to continue more effortlessly with the task.

The fourth level at which feedback can be directed is personal and unrelated to performance on the task. Examples of such feedback include, 'You are a great student' and 'That's a really good graph, well done.'

Unfortunately, although it has the least impact, it is this fourth level of feedback that tends to dominate in classrooms, accompanied by some task-based feedback. Despite its high potential, feedback focused on purpose and self-regulation is much less common. This may be because, when we were learners, we didn't benefit from much purpose- and self-regulation-focused feedback ourselves.

 **Consider**

In planning to teach your next topic, anticipate possible student responses to one of the key tasks. What feedback would you give to students giving these responses? Plan the exact words you would use.

---

[23] **A. Watson and J. Mason,** *Mathematics as a Constructive Activity: Learners Generating Examples* (Mahwah, NJ: Lawrence Erlbaum Publishers, 2005).

# Summary

*Mastery* is not a state that learners either have or haven't achieved. However deeply we understand a concept, there is always more depth and always more to learn. There are always new connections or ways of looking at a concept.

*High-stakes national exams* can become dominated by routine procedures and familiar applications. Teaching that focuses on exam preparation can narrow the curriculum, rush through content coverage, and ultimately reduce students' chances of exam success.

*Summative assessment* should be infrequent:

- Between one and three summative assessment points should be scheduled in the school year.
- High-stakes exams often skew the curriculum towards short-term goals.
- Frequent summative assessment places too great an emphasis on teaching and learning.

*Formative assessment* should be frequent:

- Assessment is formative only if the evidence gathered about student understanding has an impact on teaching and learning.
- In addition to observation and questioning, one effective method of assessing formatively is to offer students a short set of questions to complete every few lessons.
- It is important to assess both surface understanding and deep understanding.

*Feedback* is most effective when it is positive, specific and encourages students to manage their own learning.

# Chapter 6

## What's the point of practice?

**W**e're getting used to being told convincingly that it takes around 10000 hours of quality practice to be good at almost anything.[1] Practising is vital to memory and learning. But what kind of practice?

When I think of practising in mathematics, what first comes to mind are exercise sets with 20, 50 or 100 questions asking pretty much the same thing. My own experience of 'practice questions', when learning mathematics, was often one of ploughing mindlessly through question after question, applying a procedure that had very recently been modelled by my teacher. This – which researchers term 'blocked practice' – has been shown to be about the least effective way to learn.

This may seem surprising. There is something vaguely therapeutic about factorising page after page of quadratic expressions, converting lists of improper fractions into mixed numbers, or solving set after set of simultaneous equations. It certainly feels in the moment as if it is increasing fluency. And, of course, it does all help a bit – but it is far from the most efficient way to learn. This is because:

- *spaced out practice is more effective.* The benefit of spacing repetitions is well established. Studies have shown that practice is more effective when it's broken into separate periods of training that are spaced out.

- *for students to learn, they have to think!* Students are more likely to retain knowledge that they have had to grapple with.

- *practice can deepen understanding.* Practice that focuses exclusively on fluency, at the expense of understanding, misses an important opportunity to develop fluency and conceptual understanding.

---

[1] **M. Gladwell,** *Outliers: The Story of Success* (London: Little, Brown, 2008). **A. Ericsson, R. Krampe and C. Tesch-Romer,** 'The role of deliberate practice in the acquisition of expert performance', *Psychological Review* 100 (1993): pp. 363–406.

# Spacing out practice makes it more effective

Students do not develop fluency in key topics in a single lesson. Students' performance analysing the properties of two-dimensional and three-dimensional shapes is likely to be strong immediately after a series of lessons that focus on precisely that. While teaching probability and statistics, a teacher would naturally expect all students to use related language precisely, but this short-term performance may not translate into correct use of 'mode', 'range' or 'relative frequency' in a different context at another time.

When teaching students to substitute values in expressions, to rearrange and simplify expressions, or to solve equations, there is a risk that teachers over-focus on short-term performance in each of these skills, rather than sustained fluency in a range of important content over time. While learning about algebraic expressions, for example, students can be asked to apply and practise prior learning concerning decimals, fractions, powers and roots.

Studies have shown that distributing practice over time improves retention,[2] as Daniel Willingham explains:

> If you pack lots of learning into a short period, you'll do ok on an immediate test, but you will forget the material quickly. If, on the other hand, you study in several sessions with delays between them, you may not do quite as well on the immediate test but, unlike the crammer, you'll remember the material longer after the test.[3]

We therefore need to carefully plan students' practice over time, maximising the opportunities to practise some skills in the context of learning about others. By building a cumulative curriculum, as we saw in Chapter 4, we can provide practice activities for previously taught topics across the year and key stage.

---

[2] **D. Rohrer and H. Pashler,** 'Increasing Retention without Increasing Study Time', *Current Directions in Psychological Science* 16 (2007): pp. 183–186.

[3] **D. Willingham,** *Why Don't Students Like School?* (San Francisco, CA: Jossey-Bass, 2009), p. 119.

# For students to learn, they have to think!

'Memory is the residue of thought', as Dan Willingham has put it.[4] We remember what we think about, so it's important that the tasks we set students have them thinking about – and so remembering – the right things.

As teachers, we need to provide students with just the right amount of challenge. This requires them to engage in high-order thinking rather than passively receiving and regurgitating knowledge.

This does not mean that the greater the challenge, the greater the thought and engagement. As we all know from first-hand experience, if the work is too hard, students switch off.

Students are more likely to retain knowledge that they have had to grapple with.[5]

> *Wrestling with the question, you rack your brain for something that might give you an idea. You may get curious, even stumped or frustrated and acutely aware of the hole in your knowledge that needs filling. When you're then shown the solution, a light goes on.*[6]

### A bit of struggle is a positive thing

**L.L. Jacoby** 1978.[5]

**The study:** Larry Jacoby investigated the difference in performance between learners who are shown a solution to a problem and those who attempt to solve it.

**What it tells us:** The means of obtaining the solution is shown to influence subsequent retention performance; retention of the solution suffers if it has been obtained by remembering rather than by solving the problem.

---

[4] *Ibid.*, p.41.

[5] **L.L. Jacoby,** 'On Interpreting the Effects of Repetition: Solving a Problem Versus Remembering a Solution', *Journal of Verbal Learning and Verbal Behavior* 17 (1978): pp. 649–667.

[6] **P.C. Brown, H.L. Roediger and M.A. McDaniel,** *Make It Stick: The Science of Successful Learning* (Cambridge, MA: Harvard University Press, 2014), p. 88.

Attempting to figure something out before being taught how to do it has been shown to enhance learning.[7]

> *Unsuccessful attempts to solve a problem encourage deep processing of the answer when it is later supplied, creating fertile ground for its encoding, in a way that simply reading the answer cannot. It's better to solve a problem than to memorise a solution. It's better to attempt a solution and supply the incorrect answer than not to make the attempt.*[8]

## Expert teachers offer more challenge

 Evidence

**T.W. Smith *et al.* 2008.[9]**

**The study:** The researchers identified five dimensions of expert teachers from a literature review involving thousands of studies. For each of these five dimensions, they devised a series of student tasks, class observation schedules, interviews with the teacher and students, and surveys. They also collected artefacts from the lessons they observed. They compared the teaching of 65 teachers who scored just above ('expert teachers') or just below ('experienced teachers') the pass score for National Board certification.

**What it tells us:** The more accomplished teachers set tasks that had a greater degree of challenge. Seventy-four per cent of the work samples of students in the classes of 'expert teachers' were judged to reflect a deep level of understanding, compared with 29 per cent of the work samples of other experienced, non-expert teachers. While the experienced non-experts were as adept as the experts at teaching for surface learning, they were much less effective at teaching for deep learning.

Students who were taught by expert teachers exhibited more integrated, more coherent understanding of the concepts taught, at a higher level of abstraction. Expert teachers were found to present a greater degree of challenge to students, resulting in students learning to process information in greater depth.

---

[7] **L.E. Richland, N. Kornel and L.S. Kao**, 'The Pretesting Effect: Do Unsuccessful Retrieval Attempts Enhance Learning?', *Journal of Experimental Psychology: Applied* 15 (2009): pp. 243–257.

[8] **P.C. Brown, H.L. Roediger and M.A. McDaniel** 2014, *op. cit.*

[9] **T.W. Smith *et al*.**, 'A Validity Study of the Certification System of the National Board for Professional Teaching Standards', in *Assessing Teachers for Professional Certification: The First Decade of the National Board for Professional Teaching Standards*, edited by L. Ingvarson and J.A.C. Hattie. Advances in Program Evaluation Series #11 (Oxford: Elsevier, 2008), pp. 345–380.

Keeping the level of challenge high does not equate to making lessons more 'difficult'. While it may be usual for questions to become more difficult as they become more complex, this is not always the case. For example, the cognitive depth of a student's thinking is not necessarily increased by asking them to answer questions with bigger numbers, with fractions or decimals, or with more steps.

Altering questions in this way may make them more difficult, but it does not shift student understanding from surface to deep. Depth is not the same as difficulty – perhaps it is this confusion that explains why so many questions posed by teachers do not require students to use higher-order thinking skills but instead require a greater attention to detail.[10]

Practice is therefore most effective when it is intelligent practice, i.e. where the teacher avoids mechanical repetition and creates an appropriate path for practising the thinking process with increasing creativity.[11]

## 🗨 Consider

Consider this practice exercise aimed at students beginning to add and subtract positive and negative numbers.

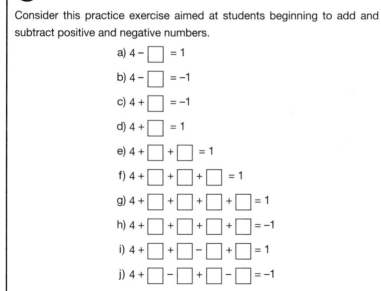

**Figure 6.1:** Adding and subtracting positive and negative numbers

---

[10] **J.H. McMillan**, *Classroom Assessment: Principles and Practice for Effective Instruction* (2nd ed.) (Boston, MA: Allyn & Bacon, 2001).

[11] **L. Gu, R. Huang and F. Marton**, 'Teaching with Variation: A Chinese Way of Promoting Effective Mathematics Learning', in *How Chinese Learn Mathematics: Perspectives from Insiders*, edited by L. Fan *et al.* (Singapore: World Scientific Publishing, 2004), p. 315.

Intelligent practice is a term used to describe practice exercises that integrate the development of fluency with the deepening of conceptual understanding.

When practice is 'intelligent', attention is drawn to the mathematical structures and relationships to assist in the deepening of conceptual understanding, while at the same time developing fluency through practice. Exercises are structured with great care to build deep conceptual knowledge alongside developing procedural fluency. This helps to develop deep and sustainable knowledge.

# Practice can deepen understanding

Fluency can – indeed must – be developed in tandem with understanding. Students need a holistic overall grasp of the concept and its connections with other concepts. They need this as well as (not instead of) the ability to carry out a succession of mathematical processes.

In the West, there's a tendency to hold up teaching through problem solving and teaching through rote learning and memorisation as opposites. A tension has been set up between repetition and understanding. But Chinese teachers see repetition and understanding as complementary, as part of an interconnected process.[12]

In designing and selecting examples, tasks and exercises for students, there need not be any tension between promoting the use of efficient algorithms and deepening mathematical understanding.

**Teachers' conceptual understanding of algorithms**

**L. Ma** 1999.[13]

**The study:** Liping Ma interviewed 23 teachers from elementary schools in the USA and 72 teachers from Chinese schools. The American teachers were classed as above average, but the Chinese teachers were of more varied ability. They came from urban and rural schools that ranged from high to low performing.

---

[12] **D.A. Watkins and J.B. Biggs**, 'The Paradox of the Chinese Learner and Beyond', in *Teaching the Chinese Learner: Psychological and Pedagogical Perspectives*, edited by D.A. Watkins and J.B. Biggs (Melbourne, Australia: ACER, 2001).

[13] **L. Ma,** *Knowing and Teaching Elementary Mathematics: Teachers' Understanding of Fundamental Mathematics in China and the United States* (Mahwah, NJ: Lawrence Erlbaum Publishers, 1999).

**What it tells us:** Chinese teachers had a deeper understanding of fraction division than American teachers. In comparison with their American colleagues, the Chinese teachers had:

- a deeper understanding of the rationale of the algorithm
- more solid knowledge of abundant connections
- more flexibility in solving problems.

Quick recall of number bonds, tables and key formulas is vital for problem solving. Students need to spot links, patterns and have an idea of what could be done to tackle a problem. We need students to have rapid recall of certain key number facts, and to be able to use these to calculate efficiently. Speed and memorisation are therefore essential for high-level mathematics but they are not the only very important skill.

While acknowledging the significant impact of East Asia's orientation towards academic success, researchers have found the synthesis of memorisation and understanding to be a key contributor to East Asian students' high achievement.[14]

There is a tendency in the West to regard those who memorise and calculate well as strong mathematics learners. But recent PISA evidence tells us that those students who approach mathematics with a memorisation approach are the lowest-achieving students in the world.[15] Strong mathematics learners are those who think deeply, make connections and visualise.

What makes things confusing is that learners who think deeply, make connections and visualise, are in a stronger position to commit facts to memory – so many strong memorisers and calculators *are* strong mathematical learners. The point is that they are fast calculators because they are strong mathematics learners, and not the other way round.

The myth of the Chinese learner as prone to rote memorisation is being dispelled. The role of repetition and memorisation has been linked to developing understanding of the subject content.

---

[14] **F.K.S. Leung**, 'The Traditional Chinese Views of Mathematics and Education: Implications for Mathematics Education in the New Millennium', in *Mathematics Education in the 21st Century*, edited by C. Hoyles, C. Morgan and G. Woodhouse (London: Falmer Press Ltd, 1999), pp. 240–247. **J. Biggs**, What are effective schools? Lessons from East and West (The Radford Memorial Lecture), *Australian Educational Researcher* 21 (1994): pp. 19–39.

[15] **OECD**, *Learning by Heart May Not be Best for Your Mind* (2016). http://oecdeducationtoday.blogspot.fr/2016/03/learning-by-heart-may-not-be-best-for.html accessed 15 August 2017.

## Hong Kong students memorise prior to understanding

**F. Marton, D. Watkins and C. Tang** 1997.[16]

**The study:** Ference Marton, David Watkins and Catherine Tang interviewed 43 high-school students in Hong Kong. They investigated the nature of the relationship between memorisation and understanding as experienced by Chinese learners.

**What it tells us:** Over time, the students began by 'acquiring', then 'knowing' and, ultimately, 'making use of' new content. They also saw learning as a continuum from 'committing words to memory', through 'committing meaning to memory' and 'understanding meaning' to 'understanding phenomena'.

The study's findings point to the possibility of the experience of understanding being developmentally preceded by, and differentiated from, the experience of committing to memory.

Emphasising the idea of repetition rather than rote, researchers argue that the emphasis is on the 'intention to both memorise and to understand'.[17]

Daniel Willingham recounts how he was not required by his teachers to memorise the multiplication table for many years:

> *Instead I practiced using different materials and techniques that emphasised what multiplication actually means. These techniques were effective, and I readily grasped the concept. But by about fifth grade, not knowing the multiplication table by heart really slowed me down because the new things I was trying to learn had multiplication embedded in them. So every time I saw 8 × 7 within a problem I had to stop and figure out the product.*[18]

There is increasing interest in the West in the importance of practice. It is vital that this does not result in erroneously equating repetitive learning with

---

[16] **F. Marton, D. Watkins and C. Tang**, 'Discontinuities and Continuities in the Experience of Learning: An Interview Study of High-School Students in Hong Kong', *Learning and Instruction* 7 (1997): pp. 21–48.

[17] **B. Dahlin and D. Watkins**, 'The Role of Repetition in the Processes of Memorising and Understanding: A Comparison of the Views of German and Chinese Secondary School Students in Hong Kong', *British Journal of Educational Psychology* 70 (2000).

[18] **D. Willingham**, *op. cit.*, p. 84.

surface learning without understanding. There is a risk that practitioners in the West over-simplify and misinterpret the meaning of practice as understood in China.

When students are repeatedly experiencing mathematical facts – when repetition and practice are being employed to help students commit something to memory – mathematical thinking is an important dimension of depth to develop.

In learning from Shanghai, the National College for School Leadership in England saw the importance of repetition and practice:

> *Unlike rote learning, this process supports deep learning and is a necessary factor in meaningful pupil progress. Practice and repetition should be deemed features of good teaching and time devoted to them.*[19]

The difficulty here is in distinguishing between rote learning and practising. Worthwhile tasks and exercises deepen conceptual understanding and embed procedural fluency.

The perspective of variation theory is useful here. If students are offered too much scaffolding, or are offered an insufficiently rich variety of experiences, learners become passive and the practice becomes rote learning.

As Ference Marton points out, in East Asian culture, repetitive learning is 'continuous practice with increasing variation'.[20]

It seems that, when Chinese students are practising mathematics, they are deepening their conceptual understanding and strengthening their mathematical thinking. What might seem to the uninformed observer to be a series of repetitive exercises, actually makes use of careful variation.

Variation theory was developed inductively by observing cases of good practice.[21] When designing a series of examples or tasks for students, with the intention that they experience and grasp some key concept or skill, teachers practise 'variation theory' if they focus on what varies and what

---

[19] **National College for School Leadership**, *Report on research into maths and science teaching in the Shanghai region*. Research by National Leaders of Education and Subject Specialists in Shanghai and Ningbo, China 11–18 January 2013. www.gov.uk/government/uploads/system/uploads/attachment_data/file/340021/report-on-research-into-maths-and-science-teaching-in-theshanghai-region.pdf accessed 15 August.

[20] **F. Marton**, 'Student Learning: East and West', public lecture delivered at the Chinese University of Hong Kong, 18 March 1997.

[21] **F. Marton and A.B.M. Tsui**, *Classroom Discourse and the Space of Learning* (Mahwah, NJ: Lawrence Erlbaum Publishing, 2004), p. 56.

stays the same.[22] To do this, they need to analyse the possible variations so that students have opportunities to 'observe regularities and differences, develop expectations, make comparisons, have surprises, test, adapt and confirm their conjectures within the exercise'.[23]

The key to variation is to decide which things to keep the same and which things to vary. Successful variation requires teachers to make careful decisions about:

- what to keep the same (the invariant)
- what to change (the variant)
- by how much to vary it.

Following Gu,[24] there are generally thought to be two major types of variations in mathematics teaching:

- *Procedural variation* – this aims to systematically vary problems to support students in forming concepts stage by stage.
- *Conceptual variation* – this aims to provide students with multiple perspectives and experiences of mathematical concepts.[25]

# Procedural variation

What is procedural variation? Procedural variation can be found in a well-designed sequence of tasks that invites learners to reflect on the effect of their actions so that they recognise key relationships.[26]

In creating and sequencing tasks and exercises, it is important to expose the underlying structure of concepts and the mathematical relationships between students' current and prior learning.

---

[22] **U. Runesson**, 'Beyond Discourse and Interaction. Variation: A Critical Aspect for Teaching and Learning Mathematics', *The Cambridge Journal of Education* 35(1) (2005): pp. 69–87.

[23] **A. Watson and J. Mason**, 'Seeing an Exercise as a Single Mathematical Object: Using Variation to Structure Sense-making', *Mathematical Thinking and Learning* 8(2) (2006): p. 109.

[24] **L. Gu**, 'The visual effect and psychological implication of transformation of figures in geometry', paper presented at annual conference of Shanghai Mathematics Association, Shanghai, China (1981).

[25] **L. Gu, R. Huang and F. Marton**, *op. cit.*

[26] **M. Simon and R. Tzur**, 'Explicating the Role of Mathematical Tasks in Conceptual Learning: An Elaborating of the Hypothetical Learning Trajectory', *Mathematical Thinking and Learning* 6 (2004): pp. 91–104.

Some practice exercises over-simplify the mathematics. They need to be carefully crafted to provide the appropriate level of challenge.

Chinese textbooks use systematic variation in the choice and structure of problems.[27] Chinese teachers use variation problems with the aim of students discerning and comparing the invariant feature of the relationship among concepts and solutions, according to Xuhua Sun.[28]

There is certainly repetition in Western textbook exercises[29] but does it amount to procedural variation? Not according to researchers Yeap Ban-Har, Beverly Ferrucci and Jack Carter, who found that American textbooks did not use variation in a systematic way to enhance students' capacity to generalise.[30]

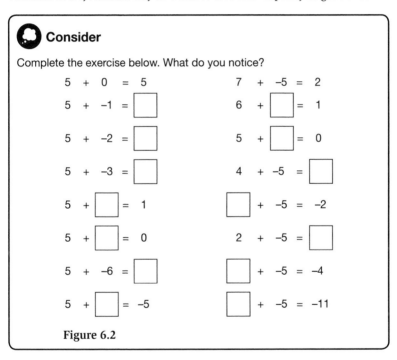

**Figure 6.2**

---

[27] **L. Gu, R. Huang and F. Marton**, *op. cit.*, p. 315.

[28] **X. Sun**, '"Variation Problems" and Their Roles in the Topic of Fraction Division in Chinese Mathematics Textbook Examples', *Educational Studies in Mathematics* 76 (2011): pp. 65–85.

[29] **J. Vincent and K. Stacey**, 'Do Mathematics Textbooks Cultivate Shallow Teaching? Applying the TIMSS Video Study Criteria to Australian Eighth-grade Mathematics Textbooks', *Mathematics Education Research Journal* 20(1) (2008): pp. 82–107.

[30] **B-H. Yeap, B. Ferrucci and J. Carter**, 'Comparative Study of Arithmetic Problems in Singaporean and American Mathematics Textbooks', in *Mathematics Education in Different Cultural Traditions: A Comparative Study of East Asia and the West*, edited by F.K.S. Leung, K. Graf and F.J. Lopez-Real (USA: Springer, 2006).

Variation can be used to scaffold the construction of different tasks that are conceptually related.[31] In giving students a series of three or four problems to solve, there may be an advantage to offering problems that have something in common. The solution method, for example.

Of course, if students are asked to repeat a similar group of problems using similar methods or strategies, the problems will quickly become routine. There is a risk that this will become rote learning, resulting in surface-level understanding where the intention is something much deeper. As long as there is sufficient difference between tasks, by organising separate but interrelated tasks into an integration, students can be supported to connect interrelated concepts.[32] Anne Watson and John Mason describe how the structure of the tasks as a whole, not the individual items, can promote common mathematical sense making.[33]

---

 **Consider**

Complete the sentences below:

- −2 is halfway between ……………….. and 0.
- −2 is halfway between ……………….. and 2.
- −2 is halfway between ……………….. and −5.
- −2 is halfway between ……………….. and −20.

What do you notice?

---

Procedural variation is derived from three forms of problem solving:[34]

**1** Varying a problem: extending the original problem by varying the conditions, changing the results and generalisation.

**2** Multiple methods of solving a problem by varying the different processes of solving a problem and associating different methods of solving a problem.

**3** Multiple applications of a method by applying the same method to a group of similar problems.

---

[31] **J. Zawojewski and E. Silver**, 'Assessing Conceptual Understanding', in *Classroom Assessment in Mathematics: Views from a National Science Foundation Working Conference*, edited by G. Bright and J. Joyner (New York, NY: University Press of America, 1998), pp. 287–294.

[32] **L. Gu, R. Huang and F. Marton**, *op. cit.*

[33] **A. Watson and J. Mason**, *op. cit.*, pp. 91–111.

[34] **L. Gu, R. Huang and F. Marton**, *op. cit.*

Teachers in the *Mathematics Mastery* partnership have adopted a neat way of incorporating the second category of procedural variation above – asking students to 'find three ways'.

## Find three ways

While working on using angle facts to find missing angles, we ask students to find three ways to carry out each of these calculations mentally.

- $180 - 67$
- $180 - 2 \times 47$
- $180 - 97$
- $(180 - 88) \div 2$
- $180 - 36 - 44$

# Conceptual variation

Students can be helped to understand the essential features of a mathematical concept by carefully structuring examples and questions.

Ference Marton argues that learning can be seen in terms of extending the awareness of dimensions of possible variation associated with tasks, techniques, concepts and contexts, as well as the awareness of the range of permissible change within each of those dimensions.[35] To appreciate and be able to use a concept, students have to know what is allowed to change so that an object still meets the definition or criteria for that concept, which features of situations the concept is most usefully applied to, and what techniques are usually associated with it.

Mathematical examples always point beyond their own particularity. Anne Watson and John Mason define the process of 'exemplification' as '... any situation in which something specific is offered to represent a general class with which the learner is to become familiar – a particular case of a generality'.[36]

In recent years, studies on exemplification have attracted growing attention in mathematics education.[37] When we experience an example, both essential

---

[35] **F. Marton and S. Booth**, *Learning and Awareness* (Mahwah, NJ: Lawrence Erlbaum Associates, 1997).

[36] **A. Watson and J. Mason**, *Mathematics as a Constructive Activity: Learners Generating Examples* (Mahwah, NJ: Lawrence Erlbaum Publishers, 2005), pp. 3–4.

[37] **L. Bills *et al.***, 'Exemplification in Mathematics Education', in *Proceedings of the 30th Conference of the International Group for the Psychology of Mathematics Education Vol. 1*, edited by J. Novotn. *et al*. (Prague, Czech Republic: PME, 2006), pp. 126–154.

and non-essential aspects of that example naturally affect our awareness. Ideally, essential aspects should be the focus of our awareness, while non-essential aspects should be overlooked.

To teach the meaning of 'chair', for example, you might offer a learner several examples of chairs. You would hope that they would attend to the essential aspects of these chairs – their purpose, say, or their approximate height – and ignore the non-essential aspects, such as colour or number of legs.

To teach the meaning of 'percentage', similarly, you might offer a learner several examples of percentages. The essential aspects of these percentages would be your focus. But learners could be attending to non-essential aspects of the examples they experience. They might generalise from these non-essential aspects and form conclusions such as 'percentages must be less than 100' or 'percentages must be whole numbers'.

This kind of experience – the perception of deep structures – is regarded as a deep approach to learning. However, certain non-essential aspects frequently come to the fore while essential aspects are neglected, leading to a superficial approach to learning.

Ference Marton and his colleagues distinguished between deep and surface approaches to learning.[38] They further identified varying activities that are helpful to distinguish between essential and non-essential features.

These notions have been further expanded for mathematics by Watson and Mason. They emphasise that simply providing examples is rarely sufficient for most learners to detect essential aspects.[39]

In using examples, they emphasise that it is important to be aware of two important parameters of mathematics structure: the dimensions of possible variation and the associated ranges of permissible change.[40] In other words, what can be changed, and by how much?

Watson and Mason introduce the notion of an 'example space'. In the preface to *Mathematics as a Constructive Activity: Learners Generating Examples*, they introduce this theoretical construct as '… examples learners produce arise from a small pool of ideas that simply appear in response to particular tasks in particular situations. We call these pools example spaces.'[41]

---

[38] **F. Marton and S. Booth**, *op. cit.*

[39] **A. Watson and J. Mason** 2005, *op. cit.*

[40] **A. Watson and J. Mason** 2006, *op. cit.*, pp. 91–111.

[41] **A. Watson and J. Mason** 2005, *op. cit.*, p. ix.

The structure and sequencing of examples and exercises varies considerably from country to country and from textbook to textbook.[42]

To provide students with opportunities to compare and contrast, examples of concepts are presented alongside 'non-examples'. For example, students might be asked to distinguish between functions that are or aren't linear, or polygons that are and aren't quadraliterals.

To enable students to perceive and discern the critical aspects of a specific object of learning, the teacher carefully organises a set of specific patterns of variation. In other words, 'variation with repetition' is the key to good teaching.[43]

Teachers extend students' understanding of the concepts by considering both non-routine examples and 'non-concepts'. For example, they show how the concept of 'opposite angles' is illuminated by the consideration of near opposite angles. The diagrams below give concept and non-concept examples for discerning the essence of concepts.[44]

Concept figure          Non-concept figure

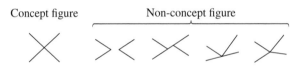

**Figure 6.3**

Through comparison, we can perceive and highlight the structures, dependencies, and relationships that define a particular concept. Comparison is therefore a necessary prerequisite to mathematical abstraction, as Xuhua Sun emphasises.[45]

 **Discuss**

Where in the curriculum do you already make use of non-examples? Are there topics in which you could make more use of non-examples?

---

[42] **T. Rowland**, 'The Purpose, Design, and Use of Examples in the Teaching of Elementary Mathematics', *Educational Studies in Mathematics* 69 (2008): pp. 149–163.

[43] **F. Marton and A.B.M. Tsui**, *op. cit.*

[44] **L. Gu**, *op. cit.*

[45] **X. Sun**, *op. cit..*

# Is variation the solution to the Chinese paradox?

Students in East Asia tend to outperform their peers in the West, both in international tests of academic achievement, and on measures of deep approaches to learning.[46] The Chinese team has been placed in the top three in the International Mathematical Olympiad since 1988.[47] However, their mathematics learning environment – large class sizes, an exam-oriented curriculum and teacher-centred teaching methods with a focus on memorisation – runs counter to what is considered to be conducive to learning by Western researchers.[48]

This puzzling phenomenon of how Chinese students can be both rote learners and high achievers has been called the 'paradox of the Chinese learner'.[49] This paradox has attracted many researchers to explore the reasons for the East Asian students' superior performance in mathematics from various perspectives.[50]

Ference Marton relates this so-called Chinese paradoxical phenomenon to the use of variation in Chinese teaching. Drawing on his cross-cultural research of more than 25 years, he explains that, in the Chinese mathematics classroom, careful use of exemplification means that students learn to pay attention to certain features. Rather than 'rote learning', students are learning to discern the critical features of concepts and problems.

[46] **D.A. Watkins**, 'Learning Theories and Approaches to Research: A Cross-Cultural Perspective', in *The Chinese Learner: Cultural, Psychological and Contextual Influences*, edited by D.A. Watkins and J.B. Biggs (Hong Kong/Melbourne: Comparative Education Research Centre, The University of Hong Kong/Australian Council for Educational Research, 1996), pp. 3–24.

[47] www.imo-official.org/results.aspx accessed 16 August.

[48] **J. Biggs**, *op. cit.*

**F.K.S. Leung**, 'Why East Asian Students Excel in Mathematics? Characteristics of High Achieving Classroom', in *Proceedings of the Second East Asia Regional Conference on Mathematics Education and Ninth Southeast Asian Conference on Mathematics Education* Vol. 1, May, edited by D. Edge and Y.B. Har (Singapore Association of Mathematics Educators & National Institute of Education, NTU, 2002), pp. 127–131.

[49] **J. Biggs**, 'Approaches to Learning of Asian Students: A Multiple Paradox', in *Asian Contributions to Cross-Cultural Psychology*, edited by J. Pandy, D. Sinha and P.S. Bhawuk (New Delhi: Sage, 1996), pp. 180–199.

[50] **A.E. Lapointe, N.A. Mead and J.M. Askew**, *Learning Mathematics* (Princeton NJ: Educational Testing Service, 1992). http://files.eric.ed.gov/fulltext/ED347081.pdf accessed 15 August.

**S.Y. Lee**, 'Mathematics Learning and Teaching in the School Context: Reflections from Cross-Cultural Comparisons', in *Global Prospects for Education: Development, Culture, and Schooling*, edited by S.G. Garis and H.M. Wellman (Washington, DC: American Psychological Association, 1998), pp. 45–77.

# Practice versus problem solving – a false dichotomy

The central role of solving problems in the teaching and learning of mathematics is long established. As long ago as the 1960s, mathematician and teacher educator George Polya asked:

> What is know-how in mathematics? The ability to solve problems – not merely routine problems but problems requiring some degree of independence, judgment, originality, creativity. Therefore, the first and foremost duty of the high school in teaching mathematics is to emphasize methodical … problem solving. [51]

The research literature around problem solving risks setting up a false dichotomy. Teachers do not need to choose between teaching *for* and teaching *through* problem solving. This is not to say that consideration of the affordances and constraints of each approach is unproductive. On the contrary: by reflecting on the potential advantages of these two approaches we can gain clarity as to what mathematics teachers are trying to achieve, and the methods that might be most likely to help them achieve it.

Over three decades ago, a robust and wide-ranging report was carried out into mathematics education in England, chaired by Sir Wilfrid Cockcroft. His report claimed that problem-solving ability lies 'at the heart of mathematics'[52] because it is the means by which mathematics can be applied to a variety of unfamiliar situations.

There's not much controversy in this. There is very little divergence from the view that preparing students to solve problems is the ultimate goal of teaching mathematics. However, originality, independence, judgement and creativity cannot be exercised in a vacuum. Students need to be fluent with a wide mathematical knowledge base in order to use that knowledge to solve problems.

For example, let's consider an angle-chasing problem. The challenge is to find the value of $a + b$ in as many different ways as possible.

---

[51] **G. Polya**, *Mathematical Discovery: On Understanding, Learning and Teaching Problem Solving*. Combined edition (New York, NY: Wiley, 1962), pp. xi–xii.

[52] **W.H. Cockcroft**, ed., *Mathematics Counts*. Report of the Committee of Inquiry into the Teaching of Mathematics in Schools (London: Her Majesty's Stationery Office, 1982), p. 73.

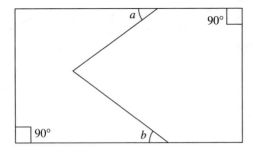

**Figure 6.4**

This problem certainly offers opportunities for originality, independence, judgement and creativity. But if the problem solver is not familiar with the basic angle facts – for example, the interior angles of a triangle sum to 180°, angles on parallel lines are equal – they are unlikely to demonstrate any of these traits.

The need for students to benefit from exposition, consolidation and practice, as well as problem solving, application and investigation, has long been appreciated. The 1982 Cockcroft report stated that:

> *Mathematics teaching at all levels should include opportunities for:*
>
> - *exposition by the teacher;*
> - *discussion between teacher and pupils, and between pupils themselves;*
> - *appropriate practical work;*
> - *consolidation and practice of fundamental skills and routines;*
> - *problem solving, including the application of mathematics to everyday situations;*
> - *investigation work.*[53]

# Deliberate practice of small steps

To be effective, a progression model for learning mathematics must keep a clear focus on the end goal – problem solving – while carefully planning the small steps that build to this goal. Some of these small steps will involve exposition, consolidation and deliberate practice. Other small steps involve investigation and problem solving.

---

[53] *Ibid.*, p. 71.

The best way to achieve the ultimate aim of mathematics education – the ability to solve problems – is not to provide a diet that consists mostly of classroom problem solving. In particular, devoting substantial lesson time to students attempting past examination questions is, perhaps counter-intuitively, not an efficient approach.

The activities that help you to get better at a skill often don't look like the skill itself. Becoming a better problem solver doesn't involve solving problems all the time.

When it comes to the crunch, common sense tends to prevail. If you try to shoe-horn every important concept or skill into an enquiry-based approach – trying to teach every single thing via problems – you set yourself an enormous challenge of finding relevant, stimulating and appropriate problems. To teach purely through problem solving would take an inordinate amount of time, both in the planning and in the learning. And even then, students might be insecure in fundamental concepts and skills that just don't lend themselves so well to teaching via problems.

Mere experience and hours logged don't matter. This is not just any old practice. Practice isn't about doing the final thing – although it's hard to imagine getting a footballer to do drills and never play a game (or watch a game!) or getting a young musician to practise scales and never play a full piece of music (or hear one!).

The constituent knowledge that's needed for problem solving doesn't look like problem solving. There's a benefit to doing things that don't look like the final thing, but get you better at it. Problem solving is the ultimate aim – but that doesn't make it the best route.

In order to improve their ability to solve problems, students need experience in solving problems, but they also need to practise other types of task.

When you break a complex activity down into a series of components, what you end up with often doesn't look much like the final activity. Dylan Wiliam uses the analogy of coaching baseball players:

> The coach has to design a series of activities that will move athletes from their current state to the goal state. Often coaches will take a complex activity, such as the double play in baseball, and break it down into a series of components, each of which needs to be practised until fluency is reached, and then the components are assembled together. Not only does the coach have a clear notion of quality (the well-executed double play), he also understands the anatomy of quality; he is able to see the high-quality performance as being

*composed of a series of elements that can be broken down into a developmental sequence for the athlete.*[54]

All the complex skills we want to teach can be broken down into small chunks that can be practised independently. This 'small steps' approach has been noted as a key factor in the success of mathematics teaching in Shanghai.[55]

*All that there is to intelligence is the simple accrual and tuning of many small units of knowledge that in total produce complex cognition. The whole is no more than the sum of its parts, but it has a lot of parts.*[56]

Of course, as well as teaching students all these small steps, we must also give them the opportunity to learn how to combine them together to solve complex problems.

Deliberate practice is important, but it's vital that we don't overstate its significance. We mustn't ignore the final outcome altogether!

---

[54] **D. Wiliam**, *Embedded Formative Assessment* (Bloomington, I: Solution Tree Press, 2011), p. 122.

[55] **NCETM**, *Shanghai Teachers: Mid exchange report* (2014). www.ncetm.org.uk/public/files/20660892/Shanghai_teachers_special_report_Nov_2014.pdf accessed 16 August.

[56] **J.R. Anderson**, 'ACT: A Simple Theory of Complex Cognition', *American Psychologist* 51 (1996): pp. 355–365.

# Summary

Practice is most effective when it is:

- *spaced out* – the benefit of spacing repetitions is well established; studies have shown that practice is more effective when it's broken into separate periods of training that are spaced out

- *sufficiently challenging* – students are more likely to retain knowledge that they have had to grapple with

- *designed to deepen understanding as well as develop fluency* – fluency and understanding can grow together. Practice that focuses exclusively on fluency, at the expense of understanding, misses an important opportunity to develop fluency and conceptual understanding.

The key to variation is to decide which things to keep the same, and which things to vary.

- *Procedural variation* – uses systematic variation in the choice and structure of problems.

- *Conceptual variation* – makes considered use of variation in examples, including use of non-examples.

There is often a *false dichotomy* in the research literature between practice and problem solving.

To be effective, a progression model for learning mathematics must keep a clear focus on the end goal – problem solving – while carefully planning the *small steps* that build to this goal.

# Chapter 7

## How can you teach for deep understanding?

I s it just me, or have we all been there? You've been working with a class on equivalent fractions, say, for a good while, and you're pretty happy with their progress. They've engaged in a wealth of deliberate practice involving completing the blanks in pairs of equivalent fractions. They've identified missing numerators and denominators. Give them a fraction, and they can give you five or ten that are equivalent.

You're approaching the end of the time you've allocated to teach the topic and are asking students some quick-fire questions as an additional check for understanding.

You're a few questions in, and feeling positive. Students' responses, offered on mini-whiteboards, to $\frac{3}{5} = \frac{?}{10}$ and $\frac{2}{?} = \frac{6}{21}$ are all spot on. These students seem to have achieved fluency with equivalent fractions! Asking them to write fractions equivalent to $\frac{1}{7}$ produces a wealth of correct responses. A similarly impressive range of accurate fractions equivalent to $\frac{6}{8}$ is readily offered.

Feeling confident, you ask the students to write down a fraction that comes between $\frac{2}{5}$ and $\frac{3}{5}$. The atmosphere is immediately transformed as a sea of teenage faces looks back at you with incredulity. 'It can't be done.' 'There aren't any – there are no numbers between two and three.'

Thankfully, at times like these, cognitive science can offer some much-needed reassurance. As Daniel Willingham puts it:

> Of course deep knowledge is better than shallow knowledge. But we're not going to have deep knowledge of everything, and shallow knowledge is certainly better than no knowledge at all.[1]

It's important to value and celebrate the progress these students have made with equivalent fractions. But what can teachers do to develop students' conceptual understanding of fractions beyond this limited, surface appreciation?

---

[1] **D. Willingham**, *Why Don't Students Like School?* (San Francisco, CA: Jossey-Bass, 2009), p. 49.

When we talk about 'deep understanding', in essence it's conceptual understanding we mean. In Chapter 1, I introduced the idea that mathematical reasoning and problem solving require depth of understanding in three dimensions: conceptual understanding, mathematical thinking and communication. The curricular principles introduced in Chapter 4 – that all students should access the full curriculum in all its complexity, and that time should be taken to explore key ideas in depth – lay the foundations for this. In this chapter, we'll focus on conceptual understanding.

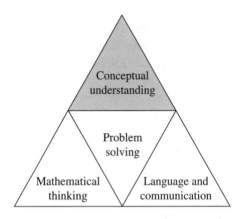

**Figure 7.1:** The three dimensions of depth – conceptual understanding

The three dimensions of depth are, of course, intrinsically linked. In focusing on each in turn, the intention is to take a considered look at all three, as well as to give serious consideration to the connections between them.

In the next two chapters, as we go on to look at mathematical thinking and communication, we'll be thinking about how each of these can contribute to deepening students' conceptual understanding.

# Why is conceptual understanding important?

## Understanding is motivational

I am often asked about the use of 'real-life contexts' in teaching mathematics. Perhaps I'm just unconvincing when I attempt to shoe-horn the mathematics I'm teaching into the context of planning a party, decorating a bedroom or playing football, but I have found these are often singularly *un*motivating for many students.

Real 'wow' moments – lessons with high levels of excitement and engagement – have often come about when my students were learning about the more abstract areas of mathematics, such as trigonometry or simultaneous equations. What do these motivational experiences have in common? They are times when students have really made sense of the mathematics, truly got to grips with the subject.

Understanding is itself the great motivator.

## Understanding of key concepts provides the foundation for future learning

Every student should have the opportunity to develop a deep and meaningful understanding of mathematical ideas. Students need to know more than isolated facts and methods. They should understand why a mathematical idea is important and the kinds of context in which it is useful.

To be able to be a successful mathematician requires more than the ability to carry out a succession of mechanistic steps, be they steps in a numerical calculation, solving a linear equation, differentiating a composite function, or writing down a mathematical proof. What is also required is an overall picture of the task at hand, so that the appropriate solution path can be selected and any errors that occur are more likely to be sensed and corrected.

High-performing education systems typically have three things in common, according to Andreas Schleicher of the Organisation for Economic Co-operation and Development. These are rigour, focus and coherence. He observes that rigour is lacking in the UK curriculum; it has a relatively low level of cognitive demand. Learning in mathematics can be somewhat superficial, due to a curriculum that is 'a mile wide and an inch deep'.[2]

We have seen that East Asian education systems – which traditionally top international league tables – teach fewer topics in more depth and emphasise understanding. Here we consider what a focus on depth and understanding might mean in practice.

---

[2] **Independent**, 'Maths teaching in the UK is "superficial", says education expert' (2016). www.independent.co.uk/news/education/education-news/maths-teaching-in-the-uk-is-superficial-says-education-expert-a6929236.html accessed 16 August 2017.

Write the correct operation $(+, -, \div, \times)$ in these statements to make them true.

$$x \boxed{\phantom{x}} x \equiv 2x$$

$$x \boxed{\phantom{x}} x \equiv 1$$

$$x \boxed{\phantom{x}} x \equiv 0$$

$$x \boxed{\phantom{x}} x \equiv x^2$$

**Figure 7.2**

This exercise contains fundamental principles that underpin students' work with algebraic expressions and equations. There can be a temptation to 'save time' by avoiding such tasks. However, it is deep engagement with key concepts such as this that facilitates efficient learning in later years. Spending time in the early stages of working with a core concept will save significant time in later stages.

## Mathematics makes sense

Rules without meaning discourage students from seeking meaning.

To be successful learners of mathematics, students need to make sense of formal symbols and rules. The vast majority of these are expressions of fundamental regularities and relationships among quantities and physical entities. There is a risk that these are taught as if they are arbitrary conventions.

Strong mathematics learners engage in more sense-making and knowledge-extending activities. Successful learners understand mathematical tasks to be about constructing meaning. They see mathematics as interpretive work rather than as routine manipulations. For example, they figure out alternative strategies for attacking problems and generating solvable sub-problems. [3]

Students are more successful if they have a fluent repertoire of conceptual knowledge and methods, including representations, on which to draw.

A report published by Ofsted, the school inspectorate in England, highlighted this:

> *The fundamental issue for teachers is how better to develop pupils' mathematical understanding. Too often, pupils are expected to remember methods, rules and facts without grasping the underpinning concepts, making connections with earlier learning and other*

---

[3] **C.S. Dweck**, 'Motivation', in *The Handbook of Psychology and Education Vol. 1*, edited by R. Glaser and A. Lesgold (Hillsdale, NJ: Erlbaum, 1988).

*topics, and making sense of the mathematics so that they can use it independently.*[4]

Calculating with fractions, ratio and proportion is a good example of this. Rather than rush to introduce techniques such as 'cross-multiplying', we need to give students an opportunity to make sense of fractions. In fact, more than that, we need to help students to make sense of multiplicative relationships.

Students often struggle with fractions. Part of the problem is that most of the mathematics they studied in primary school focused on additive relationships – addition and subtraction. Even when multiplying and dividing, students are often encouraged to relate this to repeated addition or repeated subtraction.

Students who are familiar with area models to represent fractions can use (and deepen) their conceptual understanding of fractions to consider what it means to find the product of two fractions.

For example, asked to find the value of the expression $\frac{3}{4} \times \frac{4}{5}$, they could represent both fractions as area models:

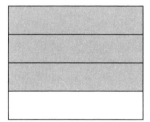 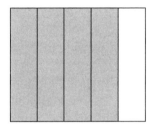

**Figure 7.3**

By overlaying these two models, they can represent the product of the two fractions:

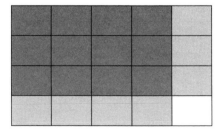

**Figure 7.4**

[4] **Ofsted** (Office for Standards in Education), *Mathematics: Understanding the Score* (London: Ofsted, 2008), p. 5.

The area that is double shaded above represents $\frac{3}{4}$ of $\frac{4}{5}$ or $\frac{4}{5}$ of $\frac{3}{4}$. Through working with this representation over time, students become aware that they are multiplying the numerator by the numerator and the denominator by the denominator.

Of course, we want students to fluently multiply algebraic (as well as numeric) fractions and we certainly don't want area models to act as a 'method' for fraction multiplication.

Students need to be able to do the mathematics without the representation. The representation is not a tool to achieving an answer or solving a problem. The representation is there to help students understand the structure of the concept.

Students possess a wealth of informal knowledge about fractions. Those who are taught rote procedures struggle to connect these with their existing knowledge of fractions.[5]

Students need to grasp the concepts that underpin methods, rules and facts. They need to make connections with earlier learning and other topics. Students need to make sense of the mathematics.

Some 'tricks' or 'shortcuts' can go so far as to lead students to use incorrect methods and arrive at incorrect answers. The rule 'two minuses make a plus', often used to guide students' work multiplying and dividing positive and negative numbers, becomes a real problem when students are evaluating an expression such as:

$-7 - 6$.

There is a real risk here that many students will (mis)apply the 'two minuses make a plus' rule and arrive at the answer 13.

## Understanding structure and making connections improves achievement

Understanding is about making connections, about seeing one concept in another. Understanding involves recognising analogies and subtle similarities and distinctions.

Successful mathematics learners have organised their knowledge into a coherent whole, which enables them to learn new ideas by connecting those ideas to what they already know.

---

[5] **N.K. Mack**, 'Learning Fractions with Understanding: Building on Informal Knowledge', *Journal for Research in Mathematics Education* 21(1) (1990): pp. 16–32.

Teachers who make connections – 'connectionist teachers' – see greater student progress than those who teach in a more fragmented way, [6] as we saw in Chapter 4. Connectionist teaching involves making connections not only *between* topics, but also *within* them; connections between representations; connections between contexts. Students need to understand how mathematical ideas interconnect and build on one another to produce a coherent whole.

Teachers in the highest-achieving nations tend to focus on relationships, connections and complexities within mathematics. In 2003, a study of seven nations[7] looked at those nations that were particularly high-performing in TIMSS 1999. When new concepts are introduced, these are related to key concepts with which students are already familiar, and explicit connections are made to prior learning.

In Japan, lessons often focus on one problem only. This is usually a rich problem that involves students making connections.[8]

Conceptual understanding involves embracing the inherent ambiguity within mathematics that many concepts are also processes (and vice versa).[9]

When lower-attaining students struggle to work, for example, with algebraic expressions, their poorer performance might be a result of them seeing the symbol as representing only a process, not a concept. For example, they see $2 + 3x$ as representing a process of adding two to three lots of $x$. Where the value of $x$ is unknown or variable, students who are yet to appreciate that an algebraic expression can also be a concept, view $2 + 3x$ as a process that – as they do not know the value of $x$ – they are unable to carry out.[10]

Students can likewise struggle with trigonometry as a result of conceiving a trigonometric ratio only as a process of calculation – of dividing the opposite by the hypotenuse – and not a flexible precept.[11]

---

[6] **M. Askew et al.**, *Effective Teachers of Numeracy: Report of a study carried out for the Teacher Training Agency* (London: King's College, University of London, 1997).

[7] **J. Hiebert et al.**, *Teaching Mathematics in Seven Countries: Results from the TIMSS 1999 Video Study* (NCES 2003-013) (Washington, DC: National Center for Education Statistics, US Department of Education, 2003).

[8] *Ibid.*

[9] **E. Gray and D. Tall**, 'Duality, Ambiguity, and Flexibility: a "Proceptual" View of Simple Arithmetic', *Journal for Research in Mathematics Education* (1994): pp. 116–140.

[10] **D. Tall and T. Michael**, 'Encouraging Versatile Thinking in Algebra Using the Computer', *Educational Studies in Mathematics* Vol. 22 (No. 2) (1991): pp. 125–147.

[11] **N. Blackett**, 'Developing Understanding of Trigonometry in Boys and Girls using a Computer to Link Numerical and Visual Representations', unpublished PhD Thesis, University of Warwick (1990).

Number sense is the most important foundation learners can have for all higher mathematics.[12]

In a comparison of mathematics teaching in China and the United States, the Chinese teachers seemed to place greater emphasis on the importance of understanding concepts from multiple perspectives.[13] Evidence suggests that stressing multiple methods and different understandings is an important feature of Chinese mathematics teaching.[14]

---

## High performance in mathematics comes from deep thinking about mathematical concepts and interrelationships

 Evidence

**Askew *et al.* 2010.[15]**

**The study:** In 2010, the Nuffield Foundation, a charitable trust based in London, UK, commissioned a report to address two questions:

- What is the range and type of research evidence from countries with high performance in mathematics that gives insights into the reasons for their relatively high position?

- What constitutes high performance in mathematics learning and what factors appear to contribute most to achieving it?

**What it tells us:** The authors recommended that 'investigation is needed into how teachers can develop classroom tasks that encourage understanding through deeper thinking about mathematical concepts and interrelationships as well as procedural fluency'.

---

A comparison of the national teaching patterns and the cultural beliefs concerning real-life connections indicate that Japanese teachers place a strong emphasis on mathematising and structures.

---

[12] **E. Gray and D. Tall,** *op. cit.*

[13] **L. Ma,** *Knowing and Teaching Elementary Mathematics: Teachers' Understanding of Fundamental Mathematics in China and the United States* (Mahwah, NJ: Lawrence Erlbaum Associates, 1999).

[14] **Y. Zheng,** *Mathematics Education: From Theory to Practice* (Shanghai: Shanghai Educational Press, 2001).

[15] **Askew et al.,** *Values and Variables: Mathematics Education in High-Performing Countries* (London: Nuffield Foundation, 2010), pp. 34–35.

## Different task, different teacher: different demands

**J. Neubrand** 2006.[16]

**The study:** This looked in particular at the idea that cross-national differences are 'deeply rooted in different mathematical demands on the posed problems'. But the analysis raises the question of whether or not 'mathematical demands' are similar across different content.

Looking beyond the types of problem posed to examine how students are actually expected to solve them shows that looking at a problem and judging the type of mathematical demand it might provoke cannot be done in isolation from how the problem plays out in practice.

**What it tells us:** How the teacher develops the problem is the key to the type of mathematical demand students ultimately become engaged in.

The study found that lessons based on problems coded as 'making connections' problems tended to retain this focus in the course of the teaching. However, between 20 and 55 per cent of lessons initially classified as 'using procedures' shifted to emphasising 'making connections' or 'stating concepts'. The author suggests that using 'making connections' could be a central distinctive issue of teaching in high achieving countries (p.315), and that simply looking at the nature of problems posed cannot reveal this.

The TIMSS 1999 Video Study revealed that, of the seven participating countries, Japan had the lowest proportion of problems set up with the use of real-life connections. When comparing average percentage of problems per eighth-grade mathematics lesson that were set up with the use of real-life connections, there were some interesting differences.

In the Netherlands, 42 per cent of the lessons were set up using real-life connections, whereas only 40 per cent used mathematical language and symbols only. This was distinctive, as the other six countries differed between 9 and 27 per cent real-life connections. It is also interesting to see that only 9 per cent of the Japanese lessons had real-life connections.

---

[16] **J. Neubrand**, 'The TIMSS 1995 and 1999 Video Studies', in *Mathematics Education in Different Cultural Traditions – A Comparative Study of East Asia and the West*, edited by F.K.S. Leung, K.D. Graf and F.J. Lopez-Real (New York, NY: Springer, 2006), pp. 290–318.

## Mathematisation and guided reinvention in Japanese classrooms

 **Evidence**

**R. Mosvold** 2008.[17]

**The study:** Reidar Mosvold re-analysed the TIMSS classroom footage to examine more closely how these ideas were actually implemented by teachers in Japan and the Netherlands. The report from the TIMSS Video Study looked only at the number of real-life connections. Mosvold's analysis focused more on the nature of those connections.

**What it tells us:** Although the Dutch lessons were originally coded as displaying more real-life connections, in examining the way teachers developed the problems within the lesson, Mosvold concludes the Japanese lessons actually involved a greater emphasis on guided reinvention and mathematisation. In the Dutch lessons, despite the contexts of the problems, problem solving was much more routine and procedural.

In a comparative study of primary school mathematics teachers in China and the United States,[18] teachers were interviewed on their approaches to teaching selected school mathematics topics. They were presented with some classroom scenarios and were asked how they would react to those scenarios. The study found that teachers in Shanghai were conceptually directed, whereas the teachers in the United States were procedurally directed.

## Procedural fluency and understanding in tandem

 **Evidence**

**F. Leung and K. Park** 2002.[19]

**The study:** A small-scale exploratory study was carried out in Hong Kong and South Korea by Frederick Leung and Kyungmee Park to compare the extent to which teachers focused on teaching procedures or concepts.

[17] **R. Mosvold,** 'Real-life Connections in Japan and the Netherlands: National Teaching Patterns and Cultural Beliefs', *International Journal for Mathematics Teaching and Learning* (July 2008): pp. 1–18.

[18] **L. Ma,** *op. cit.*

[19] **F. Leung and K. Park,** 'Competent Students, Competent Teachers?', *International Journal of Educational Research* 37(2) (2002): pp. 113–129.

Nine teachers from Hong Kong and nine from South Korea were interviewed using the four Teacher Education and Learning to Teach Study (TELT)[20] tasks that Liping Ma had used in her study.[21]

One of the questions used, for example, was:

*Division by fractions is often a little confusing for students. People have different approaches to solving problems involving division with fractions. How would you solve this one?*

$$1\frac{3}{4} \div \frac{1}{2}$$

**What it tells us:** In their examination of teaching in Hong Kong and South Korea, Leung and Park found that although Hong Kong and South Korean teachers possessed conceptual as well as procedural understanding of mathematics, the majority of their reported teaching strategies were procedurally rather than conceptually directed.

That said, these procedures were more coherent, more developed and more mathematically based than those commonly used in the West. For example, while the common procedure for the division of fractions in some countries is 'turn the divisor over and multiply', the teachers in Leung and Park's study refer to the use of the associative and commutative laws in the explanation of the algorithm.

How the teacher develops the problem is the key to the type of mathematical demand students ultimately become engaged in.

Emphasis on procedures can contribute to students seeing mathematics as a set of unconnected rules to be memorised, as researcher Richard Skemp observed. He described how a 'relational' understanding of mathematics is much more powerful, long-lasting and useful than an 'instrumental' understanding.[22]

The students referred to at the start of the chapter had an instrumental understanding of fractions. They had remembered rules for finding equivalent fractions, but had not made connections between the techniques and processes and the meaning of the numbers involved.

---

[20] **D. Ball**, 'Knowledge and Reasoning in Mathematical Pedagogy: Examining What Prospective Teachers Bring to Teacher Education', unpublished doctoral dissertation (Michigan State University, East Lansing, 1988). https://static1.squarespace.com/static/577fc4e2440243084a67dc49/t/579a38e6ebbd1a621986ed6a/1469724904244/Knowledge+and+reasoning+in+mathematical+pedagogy.pdf accessed 16 August 2017.

[21] **L. Ma**, *op. cit.*

[22] **R.R. Skemp**, 'Relational Understanding and Instrumental Understanding', *Mathematics Teaching* No 77 (1976): pp. 20–26.

What can be problematic here is the tendency for some academics to make a distinction between teaching for procedural fluency and teaching for conceptual understanding, in a way that suggests they are 'either/or'.

 **Consider**

Might conceptual understanding be a barrier to reasoning and problem solving for some of the students you teach?

# Why use multiple representations?

Using representations helps students to understand mathematics rather than just 'do' it. This is not about devaluing symbolic representations or discouraging students from thinking and recording in the abstract. Because the modelling methods and tools are chosen to help build understanding of the concepts, they allow students to move to working in the abstract.

Mathematics is an abstract subject. It might be expected that teachers in high-performing jurisdictions, where the students ultimately excel in abstract algebraic manipulation, make less use of concrete and pictorial representations.

However, James Stigler and Michelle Perry found that, in classes observed in China and Japan, teachers did make extensive use of manipulatives and real-world materials or scenarios, more so in fact than the American teachers in the same study.[23]

As mathematical concepts are abstract, we can come to understand them only through experiencing representations of them. Language and notation are perhaps the most prominent means of representing mathematical concepts, which is one reason why language and communication constitutes one of the three dimensions of depth.

Language is itself a representation. Supporting students to use accurate terminology and grammatically correct sentences to describe a representation of a concept helps them move to working in the abstract. We explore the role of language in representing mathematical concepts in Chapter 9.

Use of representations can transform students' mathematical experiences. 'Representing' mathematics – using objects, diagrams, symbols and words

---

[23] **J.W. Stigler and M. Perry**, 'Cross-Cultural Studies of Mathematics Teaching and Learning: Recent Findings and New Directions', in *Perspectives on Research on Effective Mathematics Teaching* (Vol. 1), edited by D.A. Grouws, T.J. Cooney and D. Jones (Reston, VA: National Council of Teachers of Mathematics/Lawrence Erlbaum Associates, 1988), pp. 194–223.

to represent abstract concepts – is essential for deepening understanding. Making non-arbitrary and substantive connections between different representations helps to develop meaning.

The use of concrete or virtual manipulatives shapes the way students think and build mathematical relationships and connections towards conceptual understanding.

In order to achieve success with abstract mathematics, concepts and techniques need to be represented in ways that provide students with an insight into their underlying structure.

Teaching for deep understanding involves using clear and appropriate representations of mathematics that provide insight into and understanding of the concepts being taught. For example, the bar model, used in Singapore and other high-performing countries, is a powerful model that exposes the mathematical structure of a word problem, enabling students to see more clearly the concepts and procedures needed to solve the problem.

From her review of research literature, Anne Watson makes the recommendation that 'schemes of work should allow for students to have multiple experiences, with multiple representations over time'.[24]

Representations of the mathematics in the form of pictures and diagrams can be used to help students make sense of mathematical ideas. They do this by revealing underlying structures.

Students need to be able to do the mathematics without the representation. The representation is not a tool to achieving an answer or solving a problem. The representation is there to help students understand the structure of the concept.

Some secondary mathematics teachers are initially sceptical about increasing the use of diagrams and manipulatives. Mathematics, particularly for older students, is often seen as being mostly about numbers and symbols. 'Real' mathematics is so often taken to be abstract, while pictures and diagrams are seen as being suitable for, as Thomas West quite rightly laments, 'the lay public and children'.[25]

There is a big job to do in changing people's perceptions so that they value mathematical diagrams as highly as they do mathematical symbols. As well as an issue about how mathematics is viewed in wider society, there is an

---

[24] **A. Watson**, 'Paper 7: Modelling, Problem-Solving and Integrating Concepts', in *Key Understandings in Mathematics Learning: A Report to the Nuffield Foundation*, edited by T. Nuñes, P. Bryant and A. Watson (London: Nuffield Foundation, 2009), p. 33.

[25] **T. West**, *Thinking like Einstein: Returning to our Visual Roots with the Emerging Revolution in Computer Information Visualization* (New York, NY: Prometheus Books, 2014).

urgent need for teachers to embrace diagrams and manipulatives as a tool to develop students' understanding.

One important theorist in this area is Jean Piaget. He describes how learning comes about through trying to make connections between our existing understanding of a concept and alternative representations for that concept.[26] The process of attempting to make these connections results in either assimilation of the new representation (if it is compatible with our existing understanding) or restructuring of our understanding to accommodate the new representation.

It is essential that mathematics learning is experiential, offering students the opportunity to engage with models and representations. This resonates with the learning theory of Hans Freudenthal, who stated that 'in mathematics education, the focal point should not be on mathematics as a closed system but on the activity, on the process of mathematization, going from the world of life into the world of symbols'.[27]

The use of manipulatives, visuals and 'people mathematics' is by no means a new idea. Good mathematics teachers use these regularly to enhance students' understanding of mathematical concepts and skills.

Mathematics subject associations have long advocated the use of multiple representations in students' learning of mathematics. Indeed, the UK's Association of Teachers of Mathematics was originally named the 'Association for Teaching Aids in Mathematics', and its journals and conferences are a great source of inspiration for using multiple representations in teaching and learning mathematics.

A teacher might ask students to 'show me …' or to 'describe what you see …'. They might ask students to 'show me this using a diagram, or letters, or numbers, or a graph …' to prompt flexible use of representations.

Over the next few pages, we take a closer look at how visual representations, computer-supported representations and concrete manipulatives can deepen students' understanding.

# Visual representations

The role of visualisation in learning and doing mathematics seems to be increasingly understood. Visual aids can be used to illustrate key concepts. They can also facilitate reasoning, problem solving and proof.

---

[26] **J. Piaget**, *Six Psychological Studies* (New York, NY: Norton, 1968).

[27] **H. Freudenthal**, 'Why to Teach Mathematics so as to be Useful', *Educational Studies in Mathematics* 1 (1968): pp. 3–8.

In recent years, scientists have begun to develop a more nuanced understanding of the ways our brains work when we study and learn mathematics. Our brains are made up of distributed networks. As we think, different areas of the brain are activated and connected. When we think mathematically, our thinking is underpinned by a particularly widely distributed brain network.[28]

## Even arithmetic is visuospatial

 Evidence

**V. Menon** 2014.[29]

**The study:** Neuroscientist Vinod Menon reviewed the four neurocognitive processes involved in arithmetic.

**What it tells us:** Even relatively simple arithmetic requires the integration of multiple cognitive processes, which rely on the engagement and connection of distributed brain areas. Menon describes studies using neuroimaging that have shown how visuospatial areas of the brain are activated.[29] When we work on arithmetic, we use and connect four distinct areas of the brain, of which one area involves the dorsal parietal and ventral cortex systems from which we construct number form and quantity representations.

This visual and spatial area of the brain is particularly activated when people pay attention to representations of quantity, such as a number line. Students learn numerical knowledge through linear representations and visuals. The number line is the central conceptual structure underlying early numerical understanding.[30] A linear representation of number quantity has been shown in cognitive studies to be particularly important

---

[28] **V. Menon**, 'Arithmetic in Child and Adult Brain', in *The Oxford Handbook of Numerical Cognition*, edited by K.R. Cohen and A. Dowker (Published online: Oxford University Press, 2014).

[29] **O. Gruber *et al.*,** 'Dissociating Neural Correlates of Cognitive Components in Mental Calculation', *Cerebral Cortex* 11(4) (2001): pp. 350–359.

**O. Simon *et al.*,** 'Topographical Layout of Hand, Eye, Calculation, and Language-Related Areas in the Human Parietal Lobe', *Neuron* 33(3) (2002): pp. 475–487.

**V. Venkatraman, D. Ansari and M.W. Chee**, 'Neural Correlates of Symbolic and Non-Symbolic Arithmetic', *Neuropsychologia* 43(5) (2005): pp. 744–753.

[30] **R. Case and S. Griffin**, 'Child Cognitive Development: The Role of Central Conceptual Structures in the Development of Scientific and Social Thought', in *Developmental Psychology: Cognitive, Perceptuo-motor, and Neuropsychological Perspectives*, edited by C.A. Hauert (Amsterdam: Elsevier Science, 1990), pp. 193–230.

for the development of numerical knowledge and a precursor of students' academic success.[31]

Researchers have found that after four 15-minute sessions of playing a game with a number line, differences in knowledge between students from low-income backgrounds and those from middle-income backgrounds were eliminated.[32]

## Number line representations

 Evidence

**G. Ramani and R.S. Siegler** 2008.[33]

**The study:** American psychologists Geetha Ramani and Robert Siegler studied the effect of playing numerical board games.

**What it tells us:** The study showed that the positive effects of playing numerical board games are not limited to improved number line estimation. Playing the game also improved the counting, number identification and numerical magnitude comparison skills of pre-schoolers from low-income families.

Board games with consecutively numbered, linearly arranged, equal-size spaces, such as Snakes and Ladders, provide multiple cues to both the order of numbers and the numbers' magnitudes. When a child moves a token in such a game, the greater the number that the token reaches, the greater: a) the distance that the child has moved the token; b) the number of discrete moves the child has made; c) the number of number names the child has spoken and heard; and d) the amount of time the moves have taken.

[31] **K. Kucian et al.,** 'Mental Number Line Training in Children with Developmental Dyscalculia', *NeuroImage* 57(3) (2011): pp. 782–795. doi:10.1016/j.neuroimage.2011.01.070.

**E.M. Hubbard et al.,** 'Interactions Between Number and Space in Parietal Cortex', *Nature Reviews Neuroscience* 6(6) (2005): pp. 435–448. doi:10.1038/nrn1684.

**M. Schneider, R.H. Grabner and J. Paetsch,** 'Mental Number Line, Number Line Estimation, and Mathematical Achievement: Their Interrelations in Grades 5 and 6', *Journal of Educational Psychology* 101(2) (2009): p. 359.

[32] **R.S. Siegler and G.B. Ramani,** 'Playing Linear Numerical Board Games Promotes Low-Income Children's Numerical Development', *Developmental Science* 11(5) (2008): pp. 655–661. doi:10.1111/j.1467-7687.2008.00714.x.

www.psy.cmu.edu/~ siegler/sief-ram08.pdf accessed 16 August 2017.

[33] **G. Ramani and R.S. Siegler,** 'Promoting Broad and Stable Improvements in Low-Income Children's Numerical Knowledge Through Playing Number Board Games', *Child Development* 79 (2008): pp. 375–394.

Abraham Arcavi analyses, exemplifies and reflects on the role of visual representations in the learning and doing of mathematics.[34] He describes how, although the potential of such images in learning mathematics is increasingly well established, there are several challenges to implementation.

One such difficulty is that wider society holds beliefs and values about what it is to do mathematics or to learn mathematics and that these tend to favour the abstract and the symbolic. The impact of this is that visualisation tends not to be valued as an integral part of doing mathematics.[35]

However, diagrams and pictorial representations already have a central role in the secondary mathematics classroom. The number line representation supports work with positive and negative integers. Graphical representations are used when working both algebraically and geometrically.

In the next section, we will consider a pictorial representation which – perhaps due to its relative novelty in the West and high use in Singapore – has become closely associated with teaching for mastery.

# Bar models

Solving word problems involves more than conceptual understanding and procedural skills such as performing computations. The ability to represent problems is critical.

The bar model method was introduced in Singapore as a problem-solving heuristic in 1983 to solve word problems involving whole numbers, fractions, ratios and percentages.[36] Bar modelling involves students drawing diagrams in the form of rectangular bars to represent known and unknown quantities, as well as the relationships between the quantities.

Bar modelling helps students visualise the situations involved so that they are able to decide what calculations to carry out. In drawing the models, students are translating information from words into diagrams. As well as helping students comprehend the word problem, bar models are a form of problem representation that helps students gain a deeper understanding of the operations they may use to solve problems.

[34] **A. Arcavi**, 'The Role of Visual Representations in the Learning of Mathematics', *Educational Studies in Mathematics* 52 (2003): pp. 215–241.

[35] **N. Presmeg**, 'Generalization Using Imagery in Mathematics', in *Mathematical Reasoning. Analogies, Metaphors and Images*, edited by L. English (Mahwah, NJ: Erlbaum, 1997), pp. 299–312.

[36] **T.H. Kho**, 'Mathematical Models for Solving Arithmetic Problems', in *Proceedings of the Fourth Southeast Asian Conference on Mathematical Education (ICMI-SEAMS): Mathematical Education in the 1990s* (Singapore: Institute of Education, 1987), pp 345–351.

Instead of relying on key words and superficial features of a word problem, bar modelling helps students see and understand the relationships between and among the variables in the problem.

Even by working with a very simple bar model such as this one, students come to appreciate that $a + b = c$ implies that $c - a = b$ and $c - b = a$.

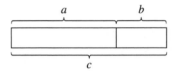

**Figure 7.5**

Bar models are useful for representing, and hence solving, two large classes of mathematical problem: firstly, arithmetic and proportional reasoning problems, and secondly, algebraic problems. In working with these representations, students deepen their understanding of conceptual relationships.

Let's take this 16+ (GCSE) exam question:

*Pierre has 36 sweets. He gives $\frac{2}{3}$ of his sweets to his sister.*

*How many sweets does Pierre give to his sister?*

Students tackling this question might have memorised an algorithm for finding a fraction of an amount. Something like 'multiply by the numerator, divide by the denominator' perhaps. But such a rule is unlikely to be retained for long beyond the exams (and is far from guaranteed to be retained during them!). The rule does little to deepen students' understanding of proportional reasoning.

Let's imagine, instead, that the student's teacher has encouraged them to represent proportional reasoning problems using bar models.

They might first draw a bar that represents Pierre's 36 sweets:

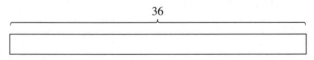

**Figure 7.6**

They could then divide the bar into thirds, and mark $\frac{2}{3}$:

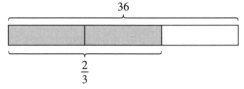

**Figure 7.7**

In the exam, candidates who found this difficult tended to attempt to divide 36 by 2, or to half repeatedly, showing 18 then 9.[37] By representing the fraction $\frac{2}{3}$ on a bar model, students would be much less likely to fall into these errors, and considerably better placed to divide 36 by 3 and gain a mark by showing 12.

Have a go at the following GCSE question using bar models. Consider possible errors students might make. Does representing the problems in this way help mitigate against such mistakes?

*Charlie, Mo and Andrzej share a flat.*

- *Charlie pays 25% of the rent.*

- *Mo pays $\frac{1}{2}$ of the rent.*

- *Andrzej pays £450.*

*How much do they pay altogether for the rent?*[38]

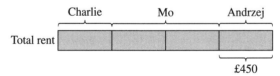

**Figure 7.8**

## Algebraic problems

Bar modelling can also be used to support students with algebraic problems. Algebraic problem solving can be hard for students who struggle to understand the meaning of the letters used and have difficulty translating information in text form into algebraic situations.

---

[37] OCR Report to Centres June 2015. www.ocr.org.uk/Images/251636-examiners report-june.pdf accessed 16 August 2017.

[38] OCR Foundation Specimen Papers, Paper 2 Question 4.

Bar models can lay the foundations for students learning formal algebra. They help students derive, construct and simplify algebraic expressions and equations.

## GCSE exam question

*Kieran, Jermaine and Chris play football.*

- *Kieran has scored 8 more goals than Chris.*

- *Jermaine has scored 5 more goals than Kieran.*

- *Altogether they have scored 72 goals.*

*How many goals did they each score?*[39]

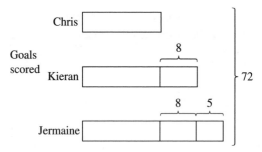

**Figure 7.9**

Many of the topics on the secondary mathematics curriculum lend themselves to representation with bar models.

To demonstrate this, here's a sample of one or two of the ways bar models are used early in *Mathematics Mastery*'s secondary teaching programme.

 **Try this in the classroom**

**Alicia and Bobby**

*Alicia had £6 more than Bobby. If Bobby had £10, how much did they have altogether?*

*Alicia had £6 more than Bobby. If they had £10 altogether, how much did each person have?*

---

[39] OCR Foundation Specimen Papers, Paper 1 Question 15.

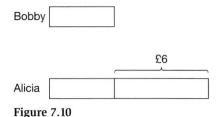

Bobby

£6

Alicia

**Figure 7.10**

**Jack's cupcakes**

*Jack ran a stall selling cupcakes at a summer fair.*

*On the first day, he sold 25 cupcakes.*

*On the second day, he sold 18 more than on the first day.*

*On the third day, he sold double what he sold on the first day.*

*How many cupcakes did he sell altogether?*

*Draw a bar model to show this information and work out how many he sold.*

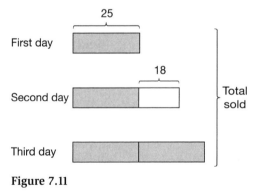

**Figure 7.11**

## Deepening conceptual understanding through bar modelling

 **Case study**

**The school context:** As one of the top achieving schools in the country, Middleton Technology School, Rochdale, UK, had over 85 per cent of students already achieving 'good' GCSE (i.e., 16+) mathematics grades when they initially began to explore teaching for mastery.

The school works with a significantly greater proportion of disadvantaged students than the national average and it looked to teaching for mastery to deepen the understanding of the minority of students still falling behind, and to increase conceptual understanding for all. The staff explicitly aim for

100 per cent of students to make exceptional progress. First steps included 'decluttering' the curriculum and giving more time to developing number sense and big ideas.

The school then protected one teaching period per week for all Year 7 and Year 8 teachers to deepen their own conceptual understanding and that of their students, with a particular focus on pictorial representations. The team have adopted bar modelling of word problems consistently across classes.

Students' books show that bar models are used frequently. In order to ensure there are no split classes – that each class has the same teacher for all mathematics lessons – two non-specialist teachers have joined the teaching team. The team collaborate to ensure they use a consistent conceptual approach. For example, they have developed a way of using bar models of fact families to deepen understanding when solving equations.

**Their impact:** This consistency of conceptual approach across the team and across the year is building students' resilience as problem solvers. Where students were previously reluctant to tackle challenging problems, they are becoming more confident in getting started and trying new approaches.

# Dynamic visual representations

Students who work with computer-supported multiple representations over time can better understand and use graphs, variables and functions. For students to understand the syntax and the concept of functions, they need to be able to switch between representations, and to compare images with symbolic expression.

Many of the basic features of a dynamic geometry environment correspond to important principles in the theory of variation.[40] There is a high potential for partnership between variation theory and the dynamic geometry environment.[41]

---

[40] **A. Leung,** 'Dynamic Geometry and the Theory of Variation', in *Proceedings of the 27th Conference of the International Group for the Psychology of Mathematics Education held jointly with the 25th Conference of PME-NA,* edited by N. Pateman, B. Dougherty and J. Zilliox (Vol. 3) (Honolulu: University of Hawaii, 2003), pp. 197–204.

[41] *Ibid.*

Students can build geometric constructions interactively with points, lines, polygons, circles and other basic objects. By altering geometric figures, students can visualise and extend patterns, make generalisations, and arrive at conclusions.

Students' understanding of graphs, variables, functions and the modelling process can also be aided by ICT-supported multiple representations.

ICT enables the learning environment to be structured to draw students' attention to key characteristics and variation. Students' understanding of quadratics functions can be enhanced by using graphical software.[42] Such software has also been shown to help students understand representations of quantities, and relationships among quantities.[43]

When it comes to learning skills, procedures and concepts related to graphing and functions, students who experience ICT-supported multiple representations gain a deeper understanding than students taught only through pencil-and-paper methods.[44]

# Hands-on experience of mathematical concepts

*I hear and I forget. I see and I remember. I do and I understand.*
Confucius (551–479 BC)

Deep understanding and the ability to apply learning to new situations are increased through direct experience with concrete objects.

The history of manipulatives for teaching mathematics extends at least 200 years. More recent important influences have included Jean Piaget (1896–1980), Zoltan Dienes (1916–2014), and Jerome Bruner (1915–2016). Each of these innovators and researchers has emphasised the importance of

---

[42] **S. Godwin and R. Beswetherick**, 'Reflections on the Role of Task Structure in Learning the Properties of Quadratic Functions with ICT – A Design Initiative', in *Proceedings of the British Society for Research into Learning Mathematics day conference*, edited by S. Pope, 16 November (Nottingham University, British Society for Research into Learning Mathematics, 2002), pp. 43–48.

[43] **M. Yerushalmy**, 'Designing Representations; Reasoning about Functions of Two Variables', *Journal of Research in Mathematics Education* 27(4) (1997): pp. 239–278.

[44] **M. Heid**, 'Resequencing Skills and Concepts in Applied Calculus Using the Computer as a Tool', *Journal for Research in Mathematics Education* 19(1) (1988): pp. 3–25. **J. Ainley**, 'Building on Children's Intuitions about Line Graphs', in *Proceedings of the 18th annual conference of the International Group for the Psychology of Mathematics Education* vol. 1, edited by J. da Ponte and J. Matos (University of Lisbon, Portugal, 1994), pp. 1–8.

authentic learning experiences and the use of concrete tools as an important stage in development of understanding.

Jean Piaget argued that children begin to understand symbols and abstract concepts only after experiencing the ideas on a concrete level.[45]

Zoltan Dienes also promoted the idea that learners whose mathematical learning is firmly grounded in manipulative experiences are more likely to bridge the gap between the world in which they live and the abstract world of mathematics.[46] Jerome Bruner defined three modes or systems of representation: enactive (actions), iconic (pictures) and symbolic (words, numbers and letters).[47]

Several studies have found that the long-term use of manipulatives (enactive learning) has a positive effect on student achievement, as the use of concrete objects allows students to visualise, model and internalise abstract mathematical concepts.[48]

---

### The Concrete Pictorial Abstract approach in Singapore

The Singapore Ministry of Education has emphasised the 'Concrete – Pictorial – Abstract' or 'CPA' approach for several decades. The approach is based on Bruner's conception of the enactive, iconic and symbolic modes of representation and has informed Singapore's textbook and resource design since the 1980s.

Singapore's schools are provided with funds to purchase various teaching aids and manipulatives to support the teaching and learning of mathematics. Each school has a mathematics room, which serves as a focal point for mathematics activities and innovation, where these manipulatives are often stored. Some are stored and made available within each classroom.

---

[45] **J. Piaget**, *The Child's Concept of Number* (New York, NY: Humanities Press, 1952).

[46] **Z.P. Dienes**, *Building Up Mathematics* (London: Hutchinson Educational Ltd, 1960).

[47] **J.S. Bruner**, *Toward a Theory of Instruction* (Cambridge, MA: The Belknap Press of Harvard University Press, 1966).

[48] **E. Sowell**, 'Effects of Manipulative Materials in Mathematics Instruction', *Journal for Research in Mathematics Education* 20 (1989): pp. 498–505.

**R. Ruzic and K. O'Connell**, 'Manipulatives', *Enhancement Literature Review* (2001).

**J. Heddens**, 'Bridging the Gap between the Concrete and the Abstract', *Arithmetic Teacher* 33 (1986): pp. 14–17.

## Dienes blocks

Once students are familiar with Dienes equipment, it provides a practical and accessible representation of many features of our base ten system.

 **Consider**

The Dienes equipment below represents the product 12 × 34.

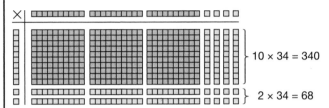

**Figure 7.12**

- How is the written method of multiplication linked to the Dienes representation?
- What were the steps in the written method?
- How does the Dienes model explain them?

```
    3 4
  × 1 2
  -----
    6 8
  3 4 0
  -----
  4 0 8
```

**Figure 7.13**

## Dienes blocks

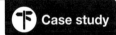 **Case study**

**The school context:** At Weatherhead, in the Wirral, Merseyside, UK, the use of manipulatives is clearly well embedded in most classes, with students regularly using them. A particularly strong example of their use was seen in a Band D lesson, in which lower-attaining students were asked to represent 0.349 using Dienes blocks, given that a 'hundred square' represented 1. Students considered the size of the '9' in 0.349, thinking about it flexibly – both as the decimal 0.009 and as the fraction $\frac{9}{1000}$. They then discussed the difficulties with representing 0.009 given that the smallest Dienes cube they had represented $\frac{1}{100}$, and so came to an understanding of how small $\frac{1}{1000}$ would be. In another lesson, the teacher linked complements to 1 with a concrete representation, by asking students to show the decimal number 0.52 on a bead string, and then show the number 0.48, before asking them whether they could have shown 0.48 without moving any beads.

The work in students' books demonstrates that they are regularly experiencing a variety of activities in their lessons and are using concrete and pictorial representations.

**Their impact:** The Head of Mathematics reports that overall student motivation and engagement is high in lessons, and that they are gaining a deeper understanding. For example, students who could procedurally use a column method for written addition and subtraction (but could not explain how it worked) were able to work through an explanation using Dienes blocks.

Use of concrete and pictorial representations increases student understanding of mathematical concepts and skills.[49] Research has demonstrated that students who use concrete materials develop more precise and more comprehensive mental representations, often show more motivation, understand mathematical ideas, and are better able to apply mathematics to real situations.[50]

When looking to deepen students' understanding of mathematics, the use of manipulatives to represent mathematical concepts and skills is a vital dimension. Students are expected to manipulate the same concepts in a variety of ways, for example using cubes and beads, as well as writing and symbols. Representing ideas in multiple ways both supports students to get a sense of the meaning of the abstract concept, and challenges them to see a concept differently, gaining a more complete and connected perspective. Use of concrete manipulatives can make mathematics lessons practical, engaging and fun.

Manipulatives not only allow students to construct their own cognitive models for abstract mathematical ideas and processes, they also provide a common language with which to communicate these models to the teacher and other students.

For example, understanding the connections between ratio and fractions is a complex area of mathematics. The task 'Ruth and Jo' offers a tactile way to experience how, with two parts, there is a certain relationship between the ratio and the fraction notation, but with more than two parts this relationship becomes less obvious.

---

[49] **A. Baroody**, *Children's Mathematical Thinking* (New York: Teachers College Press, 1987).

**L.M. Kennedy and S. Tipps**, *Guiding Children's Learning of Mathematics* (8th ed.) (Belmont, CA: Wadsworth, 1998).

[50] **M.N. Suydam**, 'Research report: Manipulative materials', *Arithmetic Teacher*, 37 (1984): p. 27.

### 🐾 Try this in the classroom

**Ruth and Jo**

*Ruth makes this pattern using multilink cubes.*

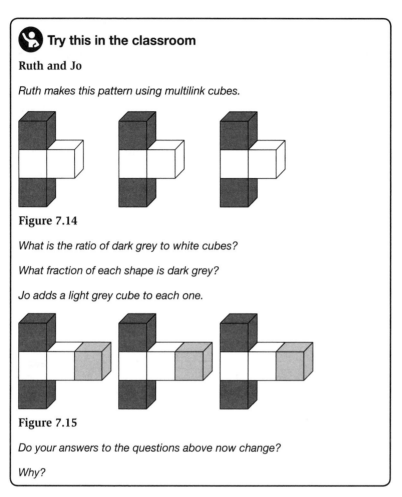

**Figure 7.14**

*What is the ratio of dark grey to white cubes?*

*What fraction of each shape is dark grey?*

*Jo adds a light grey cube to each one.*

**Figure 7.15**

*Do your answers to the questions above now change?*

*Why?*

When should students use cubes, and when should they use a number line? How can teachers help students to make connections between a word problem, a diagram, a 'traditional' calculation and a mental method?

Students manipulate objects and work with pictures and diagrams to give abstract mathematical concepts meaning and relevance.

Several studies have found that the long-term use of manipulatives (enactive learning) has a positive effect on student achievement, as the use of concrete objects allows students to visualise, model and internalise abstract mathematical concepts.[51]

---

[51] **E. Sowell**, *op. cit.*
**R. Ruzic and K. O'Connell**, *op. cit.*
**J. Heddens**, *op. cit.*

### Long-term use of manipulatives has a positive effect on student achievement

 **Evidence**

**R. Ruzic and K. O'Connell** 2001.[52]

**The study:** Through reviewing the literature, researchers found that long-term use of manipulatives has a positive effect on student achievement. Through using concrete objects, students observe, model and internalise abstract concepts.

**What it tells us:** From their review of the literature, four general principles emerged: a) use a manipulative consistently, over a long period of time; b) begin with highly transparent concrete representations and move to more abstract representations over time; c) avoid manipulatives that resemble everyday objects or have distracting irrelevant features; and d) explicitly explain the relation between the manipulatives and the mathematics concept.

Of course, it's one thing to demonstrate that certain principles have a positive effect on achievement, and quite another to fully incorporate these principles into daily classroom practice.

### Raising the profile of concrete manipulatives

 **Case study**

**The school context:** To facilitate students using a manipulative consistently, over a long period of time, all classrooms at Academy 360, Sunderland, UK, are equipped with packs containing cubes, beads and geoboards and other manipulatives. These packs are out on tables during all mathematics lessons. By making manipulatives available in this way, teachers are more easily able to avoid using manipulatives that resemble everyday objects or have distracting irrelevant features. It also encourages students to use them as a learning aid without prompting.

Teachers understand the importance of making explicit the relationship between the manipulative and the mathematical concept it represents. They use questioning to probe student responses and strategies.

**Their impact:** Students are overwhelmingly positive about their learning in mathematics. On a learning walk, several students stated it was their favourite subject. Students are asking an increasing number of questions and are improving in confidence.

---

[52] **R. Ruzic and K. O'Connell**, *op. cit.*

**Try this in the classroom**

**Always, sometimes or never true?**

| | |
|---|---|
| $n + 4 = 7$ | $u + 2 = u + 14$ |
| $2n + 3 = 3 + 2n$ | $2r - 4 = 4 - 2r$ |
| $4y + 3 = 7y$ | $m + 6 < 20$ |
| $x^2 = 5x$ | $4t > 8 + t$ |

**Figure 7.16**

 **Preparing to teach – do the mathematics!**

In preparing to teach 'Always, sometimes or never true?', you might consider the following points:

- When talking about each equation or inequality, when do you use the term 'variable' and when 'unknown'? Does your use of these terms pre-suppose the statement being 'sometimes' or 'always' true? What term would you expect students to use to refer to these letters?

- Ask students to explain and justify their answers using manipulatives.

Howard Gardner advanced the theory that different people are intelligent in different ways.[53] Unfortunately, some schools interpreted Howard Gardner's theory of multiple intelligences as a reason to label students as particular types of learner who were then taught in different ways. But students who are not yet confident visual thinkers or kinaesthetic learners arguably need to work with pictorial and concrete representations more than anyone.

# Mixing up the order – multiple representations

Concrete manipulatives need not always be seen as the first and easiest step on a journey to understanding. Naturally, there will be learning sequences where it is appropriate to begin with concrete manipulatives, and progress through to the abstract. However, on some occasions students' understanding will be deepened through beginning work with symbols, and asking them to represent the ideas using diagrams or objects.

---

[53] **H. Gardner**, *Frames of Mind: The Theory of Multiple Intelligences* (New York, NY: Basic Books, 2008, 2011).

The phrase 'concrete – pictorial – abstract' has become established in Singapore and teachers tend to introduce these representations in this order. However, observers report that Japanese lessons often focus on one or two problems, with a variety of ways of modelling and solving them being explored in a single lesson, and concrete representations being explored alongside and in parallel to more abstract representations. This parallel use of concrete representations is different from an approach that starts with the concrete, with the expectation of this providing a foundation for the abstract, and follows on with the concrete gradually being withdrawn.[54]

Representations do not always need to be progressed through in a certain order – beginning with concrete objects, moving on to diagrams or pictures, and ending up with abstract symbols. On the contrary, moving from working with abstract algebraic symbols to representing the same ideas using diagrams or objects is an effective way to challenge students to deepen their understanding.

Effective teachers have been found to work with a connected range of representations in parallel.[55] The school inspectorate in England, Ofsted, has cautioned that the introduction and use of interactive whiteboards has reduced the use of practical resources.[56] However, many areas of mathematics focus on relationships. For topics such as functions, a dynamic graph may be the closest thing to a concrete representation.

Students can use algebra area tiles representing one, $x$, and $x^2$ to represent, think about and manipulate quadratic expressions.

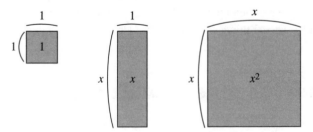

Figure 7.17

---

[54] **M. Askew et al.,** *Values and Variables: Mathematics Education in High-Performing Countries* (London: Nuffield Foundation, 2010), pp. 34–35.

[55] **M. Askew et al.**, *op. cit.*

[56] **Ofsted**, *Mathematics: Understanding the Score* (London: Ofsted, 2008). On page 28 this report notes that 'Teachers generally underused practical resources ... to develop pupils' understanding of mathematical ideas and help them to make connections between different topics.'

**Try this in the classroom**

Give students, individually or in pairs, an $x^2$ square, five rectangles representing $x$, and six 'ones' (little squares). These can be made from cardboard – coloured and laminated if you're feeling extra generous.[57]

The expression $x^2 + 5x + 6$ can be represented as a rectangle. It is a linear expression multiplied by another linear expression. Any expression of the form $(x \pm a)(x \pm b)$ can be represented as a rectangle with sides of length $x \pm a$ and $x \pm b$.

Challenge students to arrange the big square (representing $x^2$), five strips (representing $x$), and six little squares (each representing one) to make one big rectangle.

Once they have arranged the pieces, ask students to discuss how the rectangle they have made connects with this equation:

$(x + ?)(x + ?) = x^2 + 5x + 6$

Factorise: $x^2 + 5x + 6$
So the total area is made up of 1 piece of $x^2$, 5 pieces of $x$ and 6 pieces of 1.

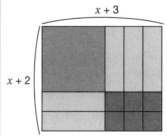

*x + 3*

*x + 2*

The total area is:
$$x^2 + 5x + 6$$
The area of the rectangle is also given by:
$$(x + 3)(x + 2)$$
So we know that;
$$x^2 + 5x + 6 \equiv (x + 3)(x + 2)$$
$x^2 + 5x + 6$ is the product of $(x + 3)(x + 2)$
$(x + 2)$ and $(x + 3)$ are factors of $x^2 + 5x + 6$

**Figure 7.18**

 **Consider**

What role did the concrete manipulatives – in this case the algebra area tiles – play in deepening students' understanding?

---

[57] Algebra area tiles are also available to buy from educational suppliers.

The value of students becoming comfortable working symbolically is arguably as strong with the topic of quadratic expressions as with any other. Algebraic manipulation is a central skill here, and no teacher would be pleased to find their students dependent on algebra tiles to factorise a quadratic.

Experience of a range of representations, including manipulatives, can ensure that students have a deep understanding of algebra.

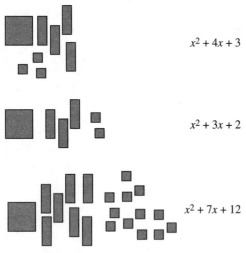

$$x^2 + 4x + 3$$

$$x^2 + 3x + 2$$

$$x^2 + 7x + 12$$

**Figure 7.19**

---

### Winning people round to manipulatives 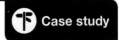 Case study

**The school context:** At Ark Bolingbroke Academy, London, the mathematics team have significantly increased their use of concrete manipulatives. While some teachers, students and parents were initially sceptical, particularly where higher-attaining students were concerned, they are now confirmed converts.

**Their impact:** A teacher from the mathematics team describes how using manipulatives has been a vital step in demonstrating that mathematics can be fun and accessible:

*At the same time, it enhances students' deeper conceptual understanding of different topics. Now they request to use them at the start of lessons. They are genuinely excited about mathematics!*

---

The value of using manipulative materials to investigate a concept, of course, depends not only on whether manipulatives are used, but also how they are used. The resources do not, in themselves, bring an understanding of mathematics.[58] It is through interaction between student and teacher that the apparatus comes to represent a mathematical idea.[59]

Used well, manipulatives can enable students to enquire themselves – becoming independent learners and thinkers. They can also provide a common language with which to communicate cognitive models for abstract ideas.

 **Try this in the classroom**

Begin by asking students to take six cubes. These could be unifix or multilink cubes. Inform them that the six cubes represent one whole. Ask students to show you one-half of the whole, followed by one-third of the whole. Now ask them to add one-half to one-third.

- Why did we choose six cubes for this question?

- If the question was changed to $\frac{1}{5} + \frac{1}{2}$, what is the smallest number of cubes needed to represent this?

Research into use of concrete and visual resources in mathematics learning internationally[60] has tended to conclude that a relatively small, carefully considered range of manipulatives supports student learning most effectively. These should be versatile, so they can be used to model a wealth of mathematical concepts and processes.

This is an encouraging research finding, because it makes the shift to using manipulatives more frequently in the secondary mathematics classroom that bit more realistic. Rather than requiring the purchase and storage of a vast variety of different tools, a department might focus on investing in a large class set of Cuisenaire rods, or of Dienes blocks, that are used to represent and to connect a range of concepts.

[58] **D.L. Ball**, 'Magical Hopes: Manipulatives and the Reform of Mathematics Education', *American Educator* 16(2) (1992): pp. 46–47.

[59] **K. Delaney**, 'Teaching Mathematics Resourcefully', in *Issues in Mathematics Teaching*, edited by P. Gates (London: Routledge Falmer, 2001), p. 124.

[60] For example, **Rousham** (2003), comparing England and the Netherlands, and **Wittman** (1995), discussing the Dortmund Mathe 2000 project.

**L. Rousham**, 'The Empty Number Line: A Model in Search of a Learning Trajectory', in *Enhancing Primary Mathematics Teaching*, edited by I. Thompson (Buckingham: Open University Press, 2003), pp. 29–39.

**E.Ch. Wittmann**, 'Mathematics Education as a "Design Science"', *Educational Studies in Mathematics* 29 (1995): pp. 355–374.

**Weekly hands-on learning increases attainment**

**H. Wenglinsky** 2000.[61]

**The study:** Harold Wenglinsky examined data about classroom activity.

**What it tells us:** Use of manipulatives is most effective when it is a frequent element of classroom practice. By examining data about classroom activity, this analysis suggests that 'when students are exposed to hands-on learning on a weekly rather than a monthly basis, they prove to be 72% of a grade level ahead in mathematics'.

# Differentiation using manipulatives

Are you used to seeing cubes and counters used to support students when they're finding a concept tricky? That was certainly my experience. One classic way to differentiate is to give objects to some students and not to others.

You will rarely see this in an effective lesson taught in schools that have adopted the *Mathematics Mastery* programme, because the teachers will have asked themselves: 'Why am I taking the manipulatives away from the students who've made sense of this more quickly? Will the removal of manipulatives deepen students' understanding?' In many learning situations, working with manipulatives or images alongside the abstract will be more powerful for deepening conceptual understanding than working with the abstract in isolation.

There can be a temptation to view concrete manipulatives as a tool most suitable for students who seem to be struggling. However, studies have shown that flexible use of representations is a useful advanced skill in working with mathematics.[62] The highest-performing students need to develop real fluency with multiple representations.

---

[61] **H. Wenglinsky**, *How Teaching Matters: Bringing the Classroom Back into Discussions of Teacher Quality* (Princeton, NJ: Educational Testing Service, 2000), p. 27.

[62] **T. Dreyfus**, 'Advanced Mathematical Thinking Processes', in *Advanced Mathematical Thinking*, edited by D. Tall (Dordrecht: Kluwer, 1991).

Students must have regular opportunities to work with manipulatives, diagrams and mental images – this is a key component of mathematics learning.

Concrete representations certainly can be used to support students who are still struggling to make sense of a concept, but they are equally effective for offering stretch and challenge to those who appear to have quickly grasped a new concept or skill.

Manipulatives don't always make mathematics easier – if demonstrated and modelled correctly by the teacher, and used correctly by the students, they often make students think more deeply.

Manipulatives can be used to increase, rather than reduce, challenge. They can promote deeper thinking about a concept, and provide a way for every student to access more complex ideas.

In working with students to develop their mathematical understanding, we can offer them concrete manipulatives, pictures and diagrams and symbolic representations. These can be used for both demonstrations by the teacher and hands-on student engagement, and it is important that demonstration does not replace engagement.

It is rare in an effective mastery lesson to see the teacher modelling with symbols without objects or diagrams, as a good practitioner would consider this a missed opportunity for depth.

Instead, you may see:

- the same manipulatives being used in different instances: for example, students finding a concept tricky may be representing examples that have already been modelled as a whole class, while those who are more confident with the concept are working out how to represent new examples

- the same examples being used with different manipulatives: for example, some students may be representing examples using the same manipulative that was used as a whole class, while students ready for additional challenge work out how to use a new manipulative

- the same manipulatives and examples being used, but the task presented in a different way: for example, students finding the concept more challenging might be given expressions and their representations using manipulatives, and asked to match them, while those who seem to be grasping the concept more quickly are given only the expressions and asked to represent them with manipulatives, or vice versa.

**Discuss**

Choose one of the lesson purposes above. Can you think of an alternative way to differentiate the task for depth?

Think of a different task involving manipulatives for a different lesson purpose. How could you differentiate your task for depth? What did you keep constant for every student – the type of manipulative, the examples worked with, or both?

 **Try this in the classroom**

Each pair of students takes two white cubes and six black cubes, and arranges them in two piles – a pile of white cubes and a pile of black cubes.

There are three times as many black cubes as white cubes.

Will there still be three times as many black cubes as white cubes if you ....

- add two cubes to each pile?
- double the number of cubes in each pile?
- add four to each pile?
- take two cubes from each pile?
- halve the number of cubes in each pile?

What else can you do to the pile of cubes so that the ratio of white to black remains as 1:3?

### Use of Cuisenaire rods

If the length of the brown rod is equal to one whole, define the lengths of the pink, red and white rods.

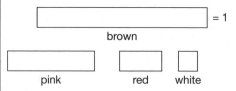

**Figure 7.20**

If you had an unlimited number of each colour of rod, how many different ways could you arrange the rods so that the total lengths equal one whole?

| 1 | | | | |
|---|---|---|---|---|

| brown | | | | | brown |
|-------|---|---|---|---|-------|
| pink | | | | | pink |
| pink | | | | | red |
| red | | | | | red |
| red | | | | | white |
| red | | | | | white |

**Figure 7.21**

$$\frac{1}{4} + \frac{1}{4} + \frac{1}{4} = \frac{3}{4}$$

What other calculations can you write?

Find sets of fractions that sum to $\frac{5}{8}$

How many sums can you find?

---

 **Preparing to teach – do the mathematics!**

In preparing to teach the task above, you might consider the following points:

- Try this task using Cuisenaire rods. Narrate your thinking once using the colours of the rods, and then again using the fraction names. What are the affordances and constraints of each of these two labelling methods?

- How might you adapt this task to make a new task? You could alter the requirement from using addition to using subtraction. How many expressions can you find that use subtraction and are equal to $\frac{5}{8}$? What happens if you use both addition and subtraction?

- How many calculations can you find with the answer $\frac{13}{16}$? Can you find a general rule for which fractions it is and is not possible to make by adding and subtracting the fractions $\frac{1}{2}$, $\frac{1}{4}$ and $\frac{13}{16}$?

There are more ideas on the use of Cuisenaire rods to enhance conceptual understanding in the Association of Teachers of Mathematics' recent publication.[63]

 **Discuss**

Is there more you could do to help students to understand the deep structure of key concepts and skills? Could you make more use of diagrams or hands-on manipulatives?

[63] **M. Ollerton, H. Williams and S. Gregg,** *Cuisenaire – from Early Years to Adult* (Derby: Association of Teachers of Mathematics, 2017).

# Summary

Successful reasoning and problem solving require deep conceptual understanding. To teach for mastery is to teach with the highest expectations for every learner, so that their understanding is deepened, with the aim that they will be able to solve non-standard problems in unfamiliar contexts.

Why is conceptual understanding important?

- Understanding is motivational in itself.

- Understanding of key concepts provides the foundation for future learning.

- Mathematics makes sense.

- Understanding structure and making connections improves achievement.

An important component of a deep understanding in mathematics is being able to represent ideas in many different ways.

Abstract mathematical concepts can be represented using objects, diagrams, words and symbols. The representation is not a tool to achieving an answer or solving a problem. The representation is there to help students understand the structure of the concept.

*Visual representations:* visual aids can be used to illustrate key concepts. They can also facilitate reasoning, problem solving and proof.

*Bar models:* in working with these representations, students deepen their understanding of conceptual relationships. Bar models are useful for representing arithmetic and proportional reasoning problems, as well as algebraic problems.

*Digital technology:* students' understanding of graphs, variables, functions and the modelling process can be aided by digitally supported multiple representations.

*Manipulatives:* offer students direct experience with concrete objects every week – put them in the students' hands.

Representations do not always need to be progressed through in a certain order – beginning with concrete objects, moving on to diagrams or pictures, and ending up with abstract symbols.

# Chapter 8

## Can you help your students to think like mathematicians?

**A**s one aim of the mastery approach is to develop a much greater number of high-achieving mathematicians, it is essential that students not only have deep conceptual understanding (as we saw in Chapter 7), and the ability to explain and prove mathematical ideas (which we will explore in Chapter 9), but also that they can generalise, specialise and seek out patterns.

A 'key discriminator between good and weaker provision', according to England's school inspectorate, Ofsted, is 'the degree of emphasis on problem solving and conceptual understanding'. It points out that, too often, 'many pupils spend too long working on straightforward questions, with problem solving located at the ends of exercises or set as extension tasks so that not all tackle them'.[1]

Deep understanding of core concepts and procedures is vital for achievement in mathematics. Students who benefit from significant exposure to core content are more successful. By learning about content such as equations and formulas, students increase their chances of mathematical success. Common sense and cognitive science unite on this point – students are ill-equipped to tackle problems for which they have limited knowledge.

When we think, when we solve problems, we depend on working memory and long-term memory. Because working memory is so restricted – it can hold just four to seven items of information at any one time[2] – the more we have committed to long-term memory, and the more connections we have made between those items, the more we are able to engage with and think about the task in hand.

---

[1] **Ofsted**, *Better Mathematics Conference Keynote Spring 2015*, paper presented at the Better Mathematics Conference, Norwich, Norfolk (2015).

[2] **K.A. Ericsson and W. Kintsch**, 'Long-term Working Memory', *Psychological Review* 102 (2) (1995): pp. 211–245.

As we have established, when it comes to tackling familiar or relatively straightforward questions that can be solved by applying taught procedures, understanding core concepts is the key to success.

However, increased exposure to core content is not sufficient for student success with more complex problems. Students need to learn to think and reason mathematically, as the OECD's PISA study has demonstrated: 'Exposure to mathematics concepts and procedures matters for performance, but is not sufficient for higher-order thinking skills'.[3] As well as teaching students mathematical content, we need to teach them mathematical thinking.

There is a distinction here, perhaps, between what teachers do to impart core concepts and what they do to inculcate mathematical habits of mind. There's a tendency in the research literature to come down strongly on the side of the importance of knowledge, or of habits of mind. By implication or explicitly, the other is seen as less important (or not at all important). This is unhelpful.

Furthermore, as we saw in Chapter 6, studies suggest that memory is the product of thought: the more thought happening, the better the memory.

Students need not, indeed cannot, discover all the mathematics they are entitled to for themselves. Mathematics teachers need to impart knowledge, and to do all they can to help students both to remember and to understand this core knowledge. How teachers might achieve this was our focus in Chapters 6 and 7. But we are doing students a disservice if we do not also introduce them to mathematics as an academic discipline.

If teachers focus on conceptual understanding at the expense of developing mathematical thinking, they are reducing, not increasing, their students' chances of achieving mastery of mathematics.

In this chapter, we will consider what we mean by mathematical thinking and look at how teachers might go about developing it.

---

[3] **OECD**, *Equations and Inequalities: Making Mathematics Accessible to All* (Paris: OECD Publishing, 2016), p. 14.

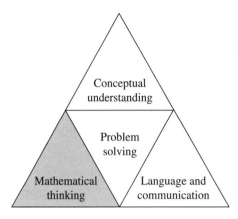

**Figure 8.1:** The three dimensions of depth: mathematical thinking

# Does mathematical thinking mean thinking like a mathematician?

I often hear teachers and teacher trainers lament how far the mathematics taught in school seems to be removed from the activity of *real* mathematicians. Most mathematics curricula emphasise facts and techniques. Very few mathematics lessons encourage students to think as mathematicians do – that is, to invent their own theorems and proofs. Teachers sometimes ask me what they can do to get their students to think like mathematicians.

The answer – and by now this might feel like a familiar answer in relation to teaching for mastery – is that learning to think like a mathematician is a long-term endeavour.

As we saw in Chapter 3, one responsibility of mathematics teachers is to train the next generation of mathematicians. But learning to be a mathematician takes many years. A growing number of researchers are endorsing the finding that it takes ten years to become an expert in any given field.[4]

Real mathematicians are experts. They have worked hard at mathematics day in day out for years. Those years of practice mean that mathematicians don't just think more about mathematics, they think about it differently.

Experts have a lot of background knowledge about their fields. Mathematicians know a lot of mathematics. But they can also access the most relevant information from memory with speed and accuracy.

---

[4] **H. Simon and W. Chase**, 'Skill in Chess', *American Scientist* 61 (1973): pp. 394–403.

Working memory is a 'bottleneck' to effective thinking, as Daniel Willingham describes: 'Working memory is the workspace in which thought occurs, but the space is limited, and if it gets crowded, we lose track of what we're doing and thinking fails.'[5]

It's not just that there is a wealth of knowledge in a mathematician's long-term memory. The information in an expert's memory is organised differently from the way the information in a novice's long-term memory is organised.

Ultimately, we want students to be able to solve novel problems in unfamiliar contexts. New problems differ in surface structure, but experts recognise the deep, abstract structure. Students tend to focus on surface features. They are less effective at seeing the abstract, functional relationships between problems.

Mathematicians have abstract representations of problems and situations in their long-term memories. This means they can think functionally, ignoring unimportant details and focusing on useful information. They save room in working memory through acquiring extensive deep structural knowledge, and by making mental procedures automatic.

As we saw in Chapter 6, students need to practise procedures so they become automatic. Mathematical thinking is practically no use in isolation. The conceptual understanding we've been thinking about in the previous chapter is absolutely vital.

Expert mathematicians do not just understand their field, they also add new knowledge to it. Mathematicians create. They create proofs and descriptions of complex patterns. A student may not be able to develop their own proof of Pythagoras' theorem, but they can understand an existing proof. A teacher might ask students to explain why or prove a theorem, although not with the expectation that, through this, they will learn to think like mathematicians.

Mathematicians discover new knowledge. It does not follow that students should learn through discovery, because there are significant differences between how experts and novices think.

Of course, exploring a new area of mathematics can be motivating. Students may be motivated by sometimes being asked to create new knowledge. But because they are still novices, success with such tasks is almost inevitably beyond their reach.

---

[5] **D. Willingham**, *Why Don't Students Like School?* (San Francisco, CA: Jossey-Bass, 2009), p. 132.

# Mathematical thinking in Japan

A mathematics lesson in Japan is often based around one key problem. Students work on this problem individually or in small groups for 20 minutes or so. Students are then encouraged to present and discuss alternative solution methods. The students are sometimes encouraged to create their own variations on the original problem.

It seems that Chinese and Japanese students may be more highly involved in mathematics tasks posed by the teacher than American students.[6] A comparison of Japanese and American lesson videotapes found that Japanese teachers appeared to place a greater emphasis on mathematical thinking.

## Emphasis on thinking in Japanese teaching 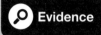 Evidence

**J.W. Stigler, C. Fernandez and M. Yoshida** 1996.[7]

**The study:** The researchers compared 20 Japanese and 20 American videotapes of classes of 10–11-year-old students. The lessons focused on the topic of how to find the area of a triangle.

**What it tells us:** The lessons differed in their approach to establishing the formula. The Japanese lessons were structured around children manipulating images to find informal methods for calculating the areas of triangles and with the teacher subsequently drawing these together into the accepted formula at the end of the lesson. The American teachers introduced the formula early in the lesson: the students then applied this to several problems.

*Typical US lesson*

- Teacher reviews concept of perimeter (1 minute).

- Teacher explains area of rectangle, then students do practice examples (8 minutes).

- Teacher explains area of triangles, then students do practice examples (25 minutes).

---

[6] **S.Y. Lee**, 'Mathematics Learning and Teaching in the School Context: Reflections from Cross-Cultural Comparisons', in *Global Prospects for Education: Development, Culture, and Schooling*, edited by S.G. Garis and H.M. Wellman (Washington, DC: American Psychological Association, 1998), pp. 45–77.

[7] **J.W. Stigler, C. Fernandez and M. Yoshida**, 'Tradition of School Mathematics in Japanese and American Elementary Classrooms,' in *Theories of Mathematical Learning*, edited by L.P. Stefte and P. Nesher (Mahwah, NJ: Lawrence Erlbaum Associates, 1996), pp. 149–175.

- Students work individually on an exercise (11 minutes).

*Typical Japanese lesson*

- Teacher presents a complex problem (4 minutes).

- Students attempt to solve the problem on their own or in groups (15 minutes).

- Students' presentations and class discussion of student solutions to the problem, combined with teacher explanations, leading to general solution (21 minutes).

- Students work on practice problems (5 minutes).

  The researchers found three significant differences between Japanese and American lessons:

  1. Japanese teachers' *lesson plans emphasised students' thinking.* The lesson plans were always structured to facilitate students' coherent representation. The Japanese teachers also wrote down before the lesson how they anticipated students would respond.

  2. Japanese teachers used a number of techniques to *give students opportunities to think* during instruction. These techniques included providing time for students to solve problems during the lesson; not hurrying students for solutions; providing opportunities for public discourse about mathematics; asking students the kinds of question that would elicit lengthy and thoughtful responses; using students' errors as opportunities for reflection and discussion, and using manipulations as tools for representing mathematical ideas.

  3. When conveying a view of mathematics, Japanese teachers tended to *put the authority, not in the teachers, but in the methods* themselves. There are multiple ways to solve a single problem, and the methods of solving problems must be evaluated by mathematical discourse and argument.

The Japanese lesson structure expects all students to engage with complex mathematical situations. Students are asked to make decisions about what to do when tackling an unfamiliar problem – a problem that they have not previously been shown how to solve.

The emphasis on thinking observed in this study is also evident in schools' reporting systems. In lower secondary schools in Japan, termly report cards to parents describe both how students are doing compared with their peers (norm-referenced evaluation) and how they are doing at gaining the expected knowledge and skills (criterion-referenced evaluation). In mathematics, teachers use the following four aspects of criterion-referenced evaluation:

**1** interest, eagerness, and attitude towards mathematics or natural phenomena

**2** mathematical or scientific thinking

**3** expression and processing

**4** knowledge and understanding.

Japanese teachers place a high value on developing students' mathematical thinking. The TIMSS Videotape Classroom Study, carried out by a group of researchers also led by J.W. Stigler, found that almost three-quarters of Japanese teachers wanted to teach students to think in a new way.

## Mathematics as a set of relationships

**J.W. Stigler et al. 1999.[8]**

**The study:** A nationally representative sample of 100 German, 50 Japanese and 81 American classrooms were videotaped and analysed. The researchers found an astonishing amount of similarity between teaching within each country, and an equally surprising amount of difference between the different countries.

**What it tells us:** The researchers said: 'Japanese lessons appear to be generated by different beliefs about the subject. Teachers act as if mathematics is a set of relationships between concepts, facts and procedures.'[9]

In a teacher questionnaire, asked what the main thing was that they wanted students to learn, 73 per cent of the Japanese teachers reported that the main thing they wanted was for their students to think in a new way and see the relationships between mathematical ideas. This contrasts with teachers in Germany and the United States, of whom 55 per cent and 61 per cent respectively wanted students to learn skills.

---

[8] **J.W. Stigler et al.**, *The TIMSS Videotape Classroom Study: Methods and Findings from an Exploratory Research Project on Eighth-Grade Mathematics Instruction in Germany, Japan, and the United States* (NCES 10999-074) (Washington, DC: National Center for Education Statistics, 1999).

[9] **J.W. Stigler and J. Hiebert**, *The Teaching Gap* (2nd ed.) (New York, NY: The Free Press, 1999), p. 89.

It seems that a much greater proportion of time in Japan is spent on exploration and application than in other countries. What is perhaps surprising is that there is still a commitment to clarification and practice.

This is because a task focused on application of one topic can begin to explore others. A task with the main purpose of exploring a new topic can provide opportunities to clarify and practise previous topics.

For example, in applying finding fractions of an amount, students can begin to explore pie charts. A task with the main purpose of exploring surface area can motivate students to clarify the names of three-dimensional shapes and to practise calculating with decimals.

It is important to spend a significant chunk of time in learning each concept or skill the first time; it's equally important to ensure that the skill or concept does not become neglected and forgotten. Whatever topic is the central focus of teaching, it's important to plan in and to allow for exploration, clarification, practice and application of other topics.

Exploration will tend to focus on those topics that have not yet been explicitly taught; clarification and practice will usually focus on topics that have very recently been taught, or will be taught in forthcoming weeks (at least they are likely to be topics on the curriculum for that year group). Opportunities can be planned and spontaneously seized to apply topics studied earlier in the year or key stage to new problems and contexts.

# Mathematicians solve problems – should students?

Let's take a look at the different advantages that teaching through problem solving can bring.

### Problem solving can be enjoyable and motivational

Puzzles have been shown to inspire students to engage with mathematics. They support students' mathematical development. Award-winning mathematician Sarah Flannery reported that her mathematical success and enthusiasm resulted from the puzzles she was given to solve.[10]

Presenting a problem and developing the mathematical skills needed to solve that problem can be more motivational than teaching the skills in

---

[10] **S. Flannery**, *In Code: A Mathematical Journey* (Chapel Hill, NC: Algonquin Books, 2002), p. 38.

isolation. Such motivation gives problem solving special value as a vehicle for learning new concepts and skills or the reinforcement of skills already acquired.[11] This is the 'joy of banging your head against a mathematical wall, and then discovering that there might be ways of either going around or over that wall'.[12]

Problems can also offer motivational contexts for practising mathematics that has already been learned. Practice can take place in the context of a problem, for example, in carrying out a number of calculations to reach a solution, as it does in the problem below.

## Problematic palindromes

Choose a two-digit number (for example, 73), reverse the number and add (73 + 37 = 110). If the answer is not a palindrome, repeat as before (110 + 11 = 121). The answer is now palindromic. It took two addition calculations for 73 to generate a palindromic answer.

The problem is … what happens with other two-digit numbers?

 **Preparing to teach – do the mathematics!**

In preparing to teach the task above, you might consider the following points:

- How would you define the term 'palindromic'?

- How might use of Dienes apparatus help explain why this process produces palindromic numbers?

- How might you support students who are finding it difficult to get started?

- What if you use three-digit or four-digit numbers?

This problem can provide a motivational context for mental or written addition of two-digit numbers.

---

[11] **G. Stanic and J. Kilpatrick**, 'Historical Perspectives on Problem Solving in the Mathematics Curriculum', in *The Teaching and Assessing of Mathematical Problem Solving*, edited by R.I. Charles and E.A. Silver (USA: National Council of Teachers of Mathematics, 1989), pp. 1–22.

[12] **I. Olkin and A. Schoenfeld**, 'A Discussion of Bruce Reznick's chapter', in *Mathematical Thinking and Problem Solving*, edited by A. Schoenfeld (Hillsdale, NJ: Lawrence Erlbaum Associates, 1994), pp. 39–51.

## Problem solving can prepare students for the workplace

A problem-solving approach contributes to the practical use of mathematics by helping people to develop the facility to be adaptable. Lauren Resnick argued that, when students leave education and enter the workplace, those who learned mathematics through solving problems would be more adaptable and cope better with challenge.[13] Resnick expressed the belief that 'school should focus its efforts on preparing people to be good adaptive learners, so that they can perform effectively when situations are unpredictable and task demands change'.[14]

## Problem solving can promote student autonomy

Problem solving can provide a vehicle for students to construct their own ideas about mathematics and to take responsibility for their own learning. One of the aims of teaching through problem solving is to encourage students to refine and build on to their own processes over a period of time as their experiences allow them to discard some ideas and become aware of further possibilities.[15]

As well as developing knowledge, students are also developing an understanding of when it is appropriate to use particular strategies. Through using this approach, the emphasis is on making the students more responsible for their own learning rather than letting them feel that the algorithms they use are the inventions of some external and unknown 'expert'.

## Problem solving can help students apply mathematics in unfamiliar situations

A learner is more likely to persevere in seeking solutions if they have experience of struggling initially with problems and then subsequently succeeding. This observation might lead a teacher to maximise students' engagement with problems, perhaps through the kind of group-based problem solving described in Jo Boaler's work. However, a learner is also more likely to persevere in seeking solutions if they have a well-connected understanding of a wealth of mathematical concepts and techniques to draw on.

---

[13] **L.B. Resnick**, 'Learning in School and out', *Educational Researcher* 16 (1987): pp. 13–20.

[14] *Ibid.*, p.18.

[15] **T.P. Carpenter**, 'Teaching as Problem Solving', in *The Teaching and Assessing of Mathematical Problem Solving*, edited by R.I. Charles and E.A. Silver (USA: National Council of Teachers of Mathematics, 1989), pp. 187–202.

It seems that students who are used to tackling non-routine problems are better able to apply the mathematics they know in new and challenging situations.

## Teaching through problem solving

 **Evidence**

**J. Boaler** 1997.[16]

**The study:** Jo Boaler led a research project in England comparing the GCSE (16+) results of matched samples of students from two similar schools. In one school, students were taught through complex mathematical activity, solving problems and enquiring into mathematics. In the other, they were taught more procedurally and from a textbook.

**What it tells us:** The examination scripts showed that the students taught through complex mathematical activity were more willing to tackle unfamiliar mathematics questions as problems to be solved, where the latter group tended to not attempt anything they had not been taught explicitly. It seemed that what the first group of students 'transferred' from one task to another was not knowledge of facts and methods but a general approach to mathematics.

It seems that students who have spent time on complex mathematical activity, such as modelling and problem solving, are not disadvantaged when they are tested on procedural questions against students who have had more preparation for these. Other research supports these results.[17] Students who spend most of their time on complex problems can also work out how to solve 'ordinary' mathematics questions.

It is, however, worth noting that the students who experienced the more complex, problem-solving approach remained constrained by their limited mathematical knowledge. Although their attainment on high-stakes tests exceeded that of their peers in schools with similar socio-economic intake,

---

[16] **J. Boaler**, *Experiencing School Mathematics: Teaching Styles, Sex and Setting* (Buckingham: Open University Press, 1997).

[17] **R. Hembree**, 'Experiments and Relational Studies in Problem Solving: A Metaanalysis', *Journal for Research in Mathematics Education* 23(3) (1992): pp. 242–273.

**A. Watson and E. De Geest**, 'Principled Teaching for Deep Progress: Improving Mathematical Learning Beyond Methods and Materials', *Educational Studies in Mathematics* 58(2) (2005): pp. 209–234.

they achieved substantially less than those in schools with more advantaged student bodies.

## Teaching through problem solving

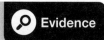

**S.L. Senk and D.R. Thompson** 2003.[18]

**The study:** Researchers at the University of Chicago analysed results from eight mathematics teaching projects in the United States looking at students' fraction computation skills and algebraic competence, alongside their problem-solving capabilities.

This followed on from an earlier study[19] in which students who were given a curriculum based on problems and a variety of exploratory activities did better on open-ended and complex, multi-stage tasks, than comparable groups taught in more conventional ways. They also did just as well on traditional questions.

**What it tells us:** Students taught through problem solving were better at applying their knowledge in complex problem-solving situations, and did as well or better than comparative students on tests of their fraction and algebraic competence.

In the search for mathematical success for all, researchers often ask whether students learn mathematics best by being taught routines efficiently (such as with computerised and other learning packages designed to minimise cognitive load) or through problem solving in complex situations (such as through Realistic Mathematics Education).

Unfortunately, these studies tend to adopt an either/or approach where the achievement of students immersed in problem solving, discovery and enquiry is compared with the achievement of students rarely exposed to problems.

In studies comparing approaches in this way, the achievement of students learning through problem solving tends to be strong in aspects that require and yield to situationally specific problem solving. While this undoubtedly offers an advantage in some ways, students taught only through problems

---

[18] **S.L. Senk and D.R. Thompson**, *Standards-Based School Mathematics Curricula: What Are They? What do Students Learn?* (Mahwah, NJ: Lawrence Erlbaum, 2003).

[19] **D. Thompson and S. Senk**, 'The Effects of Curriculum on Achievement in Second-Year Algebra: The Example of the University of Chicago School Mathematics Project', *Journal for Research in Mathematics Education* 32(1) (2001): pp. 58–84.

are denied access to the generality and abstraction that lead to technical competence and lay the foundation for higher mathematical study.

Analysis of this research shows that the significant difference is not about the speed and retention of learning but what is being learned. Whatever the approach, the main question for progression is whether the students learn new concepts well enough to apply them to non-routine problems.

Focus too much on efficient transfer of knowledge and skills and the risk is that students are ill-equipped to independently apply what they know. Rely entirely on learning through enquiry, and students may be deprived of the knowledge and skills they need to solve problems.

Both approaches – the efficient and routine focused, and the complex and realistic – have an inherent weakness when it comes to students being able to independently apply the mathematics they have learned to a totally new problem in an unfamiliar situation. In other words, both have weaknesses when it comes to students mastering mathematics.

Many teachers are reluctant to teach entirely through problem solving, with good reason: exploration of non-routine problems can be frustrating and inefficient. To increase the efficiency of teaching mathematics – to teach mathematics better – surely it's possible to use problems *enough*, so that all their advantages can be harnessed, and their disadvantages minimised?

In *Mathematics Mastery* teaching programmes, problem solving sometimes provides a medium through which mathematical concepts and skills can be learned – as a starting point for learning mathematics – and at other times there's evidence to suggest that it's best to learn the concepts and skills first, and apply them to problems later. The most important thing is that students have the required depth of understanding.

Teachers and department heads beginning to consider a shift to teaching for mastery frequently voice this concern. They explain, often in a confessional tone, that while they have always understood the importance of problem solving, in the classroom 'problems' often manifest themselves as word problems and questions requiring lengthy written working.

The nature of the schemes of work they are using, often lead students through core skills and knowledge and then expose them to problems that require connections between the individual key ideas and that also introduce 'real-life' or 'functional' contexts. The issue with this structure is that the jump from practising skills to solving problems can prove to be challenging for many students. Some students may rarely attempt such questions, if at all.

These teachers often express a desire to include problem solving as an integral aspect of every lesson and not something that is taught or considered separately.

 **Discuss**

George Halmos argues that:

> *The major part of very meaningful life is the solution of problems; ... It is the duty of all teachers, and of teachers of mathematics in particular, to expose their students to problems much more than to facts.*[20]

- Do you agree?
- How important are 'facts' in teaching mathematics?
- What proportion of teaching time do you spend on problem solving?
- Would you like your students to spend more, or less time solving problems than they currently do?

Simply exposing students to lots of facts is not an effective way to teach. But there is a body of essential facts that must be learned. Rather than *exposing* students to these, we need to actively ensure that they commit them to memory.

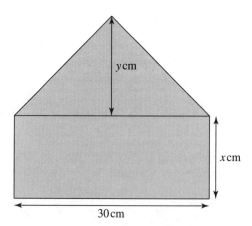

Given that the ratio of the area of the rectangle to the triangle is 5:4, find some possible values for $x$ and $y$.

**Figure 8.2**

---

[20] **P. Halmos**, 'The Heart of Mathematics', *American Mathematical Monthly* 87 (7) (1980): p. 523.

This problem offers application of:

- calculating the area of a rectangle and a triangle
- given the ratio between two parts, and the value of the first part, finding the value of the second part.

The problem could be used to generate practice questions, as students could select (or randomly generate) values of $x$, and calculate the value of $y$. A practice exercise generated in this way would provide an opportunity to meaningfully consider questions such as:

- What's the same and what's different?
- What is the largest and smallest possible value (of $x$, and of $y$)?
- What effect does changing the value of $x$ have on the value of $y$?

# What is mathematical thinking?

Higher-order thinking is difficult to define exactly, but we can recognise it when it occurs, as Lauren Resnick described in the late 1980s:

*Consider the following:*

- *Higher order thinking is non-algorithmic. That is, the path of action is not fully specified in advance.*

- *Higher order thinking tends to be complex. The total path is not 'visible' (mentally speaking) from any single vantage point.*

- *Higher order thinking often yields multiple solutions, each with costs and benefits, rather than unique solutions.*

- *Higher order thinking involves nuanced judgment and interpretation.*

- *Higher order thinking involves the application of multiple criteria, which sometimes conflict with one another.*

- *Higher order thinking often involves uncertainty. Not everything that bears on the task at hand is known.*

- *Higher order thinking involves self-regulation of the thinking process. We do not recognize higher order thinking in an individual when someone else 'calls the plays' at every step.*

- *Higher order thinking involves imposing meaning, finding structure in apparent disorder.*

- *Higher order thinking is effortful. There is considerable mental work involved in the kinds of elaborations and judgments required.*[21]

---

[21] **L.B. Resnick**, *Education and Learning to Think* (Washington, DC: National Academies Press, 1987), pp. 2–3.

**Discuss**

Have a go at the question below. Do you use any higher-order thinking?

How many different ways can you find to make this statement true?

☐ × ☐.☐☐ = 1

**Figure 8.3**

✎ **Preparing to teach – do the mathematics!**

In preparing to teach the task above, you might consider the following points:

- Is what is missing in each of the four empty boxes a 'number' or a 'digit'? Or could it be called either? Does it matter?

- What term do you use to describe the second number – the three-digit number with a decimal point? Do you refer to it as 'the decimal number', for example? Might your chosen term have the potential to cause confusion?

- Why is it incorrect to describe either of the numbers being multiplied together as 'factors' of 1?

- Could you represent the problem using a diagram? Perhaps you could draw a square of area 1, and divide the square into equal parts, considering whether the area of the parts can be written as a number with two decimal places.

- You may have adopted a systematic approach, first considering whether the first missing digit could be 2, then 3, then 4, etc. Can you think of any alternative ways of working systematically?

- How could you extend the problem? Perhaps you might change the '1' to a '2', a '3', or other values. You might investigate which values have the most or the fewest different ways of completion.

Higher-order thinking in the domain of mathematics is often described as 'mathematical thinking'. As you tackled the problem above, you will have been thinking mathematically. For instance, you had to make sense of the problem and decide how to get started. You may have needed to persevere when you got stuck.

These practices have been termed 'mathematical habits of mind' by educationalists, including Al Cuoco and colleagues.[22] They identify habits, including reasoning by continuity, looking at extreme cases, performing thought experiments and using abstraction. Their work has informed the United States' Common Core State Standards for Mathematical Practice, which are summarised in the table below.

**Table 8.1**: Common Core State Standards for Mathematical Practice

| Standard 1 | Standard 2 | Standard 3 | Standard 4 | Standard 5 | Standard 6 | Standard 7 | Standard 8 |
|---|---|---|---|---|---|---|---|
| Make sense of problems and persevere in solving them. | Reason abstractly and quantitatively. | Construct viable arguments and critique the reasoning of others. | Model with mathematics. | Use appropriate tools strategically. | Attend to precision. | Look for and make use of structure. | Look for and express regularity in repeated reasoning. |
| <ul><li>MPs 1 and 6 – overarching habits of a productive mathematical thinking</li><li>MPs 2 and 3 – reasoning and explaining</li><li>MPs 4 and 5 – modeling and using tools</li><li>MPs 7 and 8 – seeing structure and generalizing</li></ul> | | | | | | | |

In working with students on developing mathematical thinking, it can be helpful to have a shared language for describing them. Teacher-researcher Leone Burton described mathematical behaviours to students in her class as follows:

*Mathematicians:*

- *Have imaginative ideas*

- *Ask questions*

- *Make mistakes and use them to learn new things*

- *Are organised and systematic*

- *Describe, explain and discuss their work*

- *Look for patterns and connections*

- *Keep going when it is difficult*

*Together we can learn to be mathematicians.*[23]

---

[22] **A. Cuoco, E. Goldenburg and J. Mark**, 'Habits of Mind: An Organising Principle for Mathematics Curricula', *Journal of Mathematical Behaviour* 15 (1996): pp. 375–402.

[23] **L. Burton**, 'Mathematicians as Enquirers: Learning about Learning Mathematics' (Springer, 26 May 2004). Cited in A. Watson, 'School Mathematics as a Special Kind of Mathematics', *For the Learning of Mathematics* 28(3) 3–7 (2008): p. 3.

Her definition combines some quite mathematics-specific traits, such as looking for patterns and connections, with behaviours that might be considered effective for learning any subject, such as viewing mistakes as opportunities to learn and being resilient. You might find a list like this helpful to use with students.

Another useful mathematics-specific taxonomy is that of the eight 'mathematical powers' identified by John Mason. Students whose teachers foster and develop these powers are able to reason about mathematics and solve problems. The powers, which come in pairs, are as follows:

- conjecture and convince

- organise and classify

- imagine and express

- specialise and generalise.[24]

---

 **Consider**

Have a go at the following task. As you tackle it, and once you have completed it, reflect on:

- which habits of mind you employed

- which mathematical behaviours you displayed

- which mathematical powers you used.

Decide if the following descriptions are possible.

Use sketches to justify your answers.

> A rectangle with perimeter numerically five times the area

> A triangle with an area of 12 cm² and perimeter greater than 16 cm

**Figure 8.4**

---

[24] **J. Mason and S. Johnston-Wilder**, 'Learners' Powers', in *Fundamental Constructs in Education* (London: Routledge Falmer, 2004), pp. 115–142.

**Preparing to teach – do the mathematics!**

In preparing to teach the task above, you might consider the following points:

- How would you define perimeter and area?

- Was it more helpful to draw lots of different sketches, or to draw one sketch and annotate it with different length values?

- If you used algebraic notation, at what stage did you start to use it?

- The descriptions are designed to address some of the difficult points around the concepts of area and perimeter. Can you design another question that is similar to these two?

Combine two different rectangles in as many ways as you can.

What happens to the perimeter?

 **Consider**

Which mathematical powers might students use in tackling this problem?

For example:

- Students might *conjecture* (incorrectly) that the perimeter will remain the same, however they arrange the shapes.

- Students might *organise* the shapes they can make into groups or categories, such as those where the two rectangles connect with two squares joining, and those where they connect with three squares joining.

- Students might *generalise*, and find that whatever way they arrange the two rectangles, the perimeter always equals 2 × (the longest length + the longest width).

What other opportunities are there to conjecture, organise and generalise? What about the other mathematical powers?

**Discuss**

What does it mean to be good at mathematics? Beyond the general classroom norms, and social and communication skills that make for a good learner in any subject, what intellectual and mental activity is demonstrated by those students who are successful with mathematics?

## The skills shared by gifted mathematics learners

 **Evidence**

**The study:** Krutetskii studied gifted mathematics learners.[25]

**What it tells us:** He concluded that good mathematicians were those who could:

- grasp formal structure
- think logically in terms of spatial, numerical and symbolic relationships
- generalise rapidly and broadly
- curtail mental processes
- be flexible with mental processes
- appreciate clarity and rationality
- switch from direct to reverse trains of thought
- memorise mathematical objects.

 **Consider**

- To what extent do the activities you listed in the discussion task above match with the faculties described by Krutetskii?
- Compare the frameworks developed by Leone Burton, Al Cuoco and John Mason described above.
- What's the same and what's different? How do these relate to the faculties identified by Krutetskii?

How do we make sure the students we teach are thinking mathematically? How to take this from theory to practice?

---

[25] **V.A. Krutetskii**, *The Psychology of Mathematical Abilities in School Children* (Chicago: University of Chicago Press, 1976).

For students to have greater opportunities for developing mathematical habits of mind, we must immerse them in classroom experiences that let them engage in learning mathematical concepts through problem solving, and making and applying generalisations.

A framework for developing such thinking in 'ordinary' lessons can be found in Anne Watson and John Mason's book *Questions and Prompts for Mathematical Thinking.*[26] Great questions prompt children to:

- think of another example

- give a general rule

- explain how to do a process

- explain why a process works

- say what is the same and what's different

- say whether something is sometimes, always or never true

- change one aspect such that....

In early secondary school, students are expected to select and use appropriate calculation strategies to solve increasingly complex problems. For some students, this might not seem too challenging. But have they really mastered it?

Let's look at a word problem, and think about using it as a starting point for teaching 11–12-year-olds. To do this, we will incorporate multiple representations, scaffold and challenge with language, and draw on *Questions and Prompts for Mathematical Thinking*[27] for inspiration.

### Fin buys some fish

Smoked haddock costs £26.80 per kg. Salmon is £3.25 per 100g. Fin spends £16.45 on fish. He buys some salmon and 250g of smoked haddock. How much salmon does he buy?

- Explain how you would solve this problem.

- Represent the problem using a bar model. Can you think of more than one way?

---

[26] **A. Watson and J. Mason**, *Questions and Prompts for Mathematical Thinking* (Derby: Association of Teachers of Mathematics, 1998).

[27] *Ibid.*

- What calculations did you do to find the answer? Could you have used different calculations to arrive at the same answer?

- Demonstrate using base ten blocks.

- Can you demonstrate how you would solve this using a bead string? Using a number line?

- What is different about your explanation when you use different manipulatives?

- What stays the same about your explanation whichever manipulative you use?

- Make up another word problem that uses the same numbers and has the same answer, but in a new context. And another. And another.

- Make up a word problem that uses the same numbers and has the same answer, that is in a context that no one else will have thought of.

- Look at this second word problem. What has changed and what has stayed the same?

Smoked haddock costs £26.80 per kg. Salmon is £3.25 per 100 g. Fin spends £17.99 on fish. He buys some salmon and 550 g of smoked haddock. How much salmon does he buy?

- Solve the second problem. Is it easier or harder? Why?

- Explain how you would solve the second problem (which includes multiplying decimals). Demonstrate using base ten blocks or number counters.

- What is the same and what's different about these two calculations?

  $26.80 \times 0.55$

  $0.0268 \times 550$

- What do they mean in the context of the word problem?

- Make up and solve five word problems that are the same as this problem, but with different numbers.

- Alex says, 'Whatever the numbers, Fin always buys more smoked haddock than salmon.' Is this true? Is it sometimes true (or always true, or never true)?

- Can you find a rule for the numbers so that Fin has bought more smoked haddock than salmon?

**Preparing to teach – do the mathematics!**

In preparing to teach the task above, you might consider the following points:

- Talk yourself through the process of carrying out the calculations with the decimals. What language do you use?

- Did you represent the problem using a bar model? What were the affordances and constraints of this?

- How do the questions asked above relate to each of the mathematical powers? For example, which questions prompt students to specialise? Which questions prompt students to classify or to convince?

 **Discuss**

Choose a question from an exercise or textbook for a year group you teach. Use the question as a starting point to create at least three different tasks designed to deepen students' understanding. Try to include multiple representations, scaffolding and challenge through language, and prompts for mathematical thinking.

# It's not just the task …

Task design and task selection is certainly an important route to developing students' mathematical thinking. But it is not the task itself that promotes such thinking, rather the way in which teacher and students interact with it.

As Rongjin Huang observed in his doctoral thesis:

> *Good teaching seems to take place in larger Chinese classrooms because the teachers emphasize exploratory activities, justification, and variation exercises, as well as paying attention to helping students engage in the learning process.*[28]

---

[28] **R. Huang**, 'Mathematics Teaching in Hong Kong and Shanghai: A Classroom Analysis from the Perspective of Variation', unpublished doctoral dissertation (The University of Hong Kong: Hong Kong, 2002).

Anne Watson offers three challenges for teachers to apply even when working in simple mathematical situations:

- Structure work so that higher-order thinking is encouraged and noticed.

- Trust all students, including previously lower-attaining students, to think in mathematically sophisticated ways.

- Recognise higher-order approaches when they are being used, then value them by making them explicit for others.[29]

The good news is that highly effective teachers are not all busy asking a succession of complex, pre-planned questions! Teachers bring about great classroom discussion with a look, a nod, a smile or a pause.

These 'dynamics of questioning' are offered by Watson:

- *varying wait-time, before and after answers;*

- *using a mixture of open and closed questions;*

- *not commenting on answers but asking for more;*

- *bringing in other people;*

- *collecting a range of responses on the board;*

- *seeking agreement, alternatives or dissent;*

- *using, or not using, 'hands-up';*

- *using names to get particular people to answer;*

- *remaining silent until something else is said.*[30]

You may want to refer to this list occasionally to see whether there are any strategies you would like to be using more frequently.

There can be temptation to promote participation and accuracy through praising students who give the correct answer. In developing students' thinking and reasoning skills, the 'answer' is just the beginning of a discussion and not the ultimate goal. To help students to develop deep-thinking skills and resilience, it's important to praise the thinking behind

---

[29] **A. Watson**, 'Low attainers exhibiting higher-order mathematical thinking', *Support for Learning* 16(4) Nov (2001): pp. 179–183.

[30] **A. Watson**, 'Working with Students on Questioning to Promote Mathematical Thinking', *Mathematics Education Review* 15 (2002): pp. 31–41. The second bullet is updated from the 2002 publication at Anne's request in personal correspondence.

their answer as much as – or more than – the answer itself. The answer is just the beginning.

There is also a balance to be considered between asking students to engage in overt and covert mathematical thinking. At times when you want to hold students accountable to think and participate, you might ask them to discuss with a partner, indicate (for example, with thumbs up) whether they agree, or write down their answer on a mini-whiteboard.

At other times, to increase students' sense of safety and success, you might ask them to close their eyes and visualise or imagine something, think to themselves, or rehearse a solution in their own mind.

Teaching students to reason and think mathematically is far from straightforward, as PISA 2012 confirmed:

> Introducing problem-solving strategies – such as teaching students how to question, make connections and predictions, conceptualise and model complex problems – requires time and is more challenging in disadvantaged schools.[31]

But emphasising the importance of mathematical thinking – shifting mathematics lessons from merely carrying out given techniques and routines – is often the key to success in working with previously disengaged and underperforming students.

# But aren't there some students who struggle to think mathematically?

It can be assumed that 'mathematical thinking' is the preserve of the lucky few – that it is somehow innate and unusual. On the contrary, such thinking is actually a very natural human behaviour. Andy Noyes argues that 'many children are trained to do mathematical calculations rather than being educated to think mathematically'.[32] This may well be down to the low expectations we sometimes have of some students.

---

[31] **OECD**, *op. cit.*

[32] **A. Noyes**, *Rethinking School Mathematics* (London: Paul Chapman Publishing, 2007), p.11.

[33] **S. Norton, C. McRobbie and T. Cooper,** 'Teachers' Responses to an Investigative Mathematics Syllabus: Their Goals and Practices', *Mathematics Education Research Journal* 14(1) (2002): pp. 37–59.

## Teachers expect less mathematical thinking from lower-attaining students

**S. Norton, C. McRobbie and T. Cooper** 2002.[33]

**The study:** The researchers explored how secondary mathematics teachers in Queensland, Australia, were responding to a syllabus that encouraged investigative teaching and learning. Through survey responses and lesson observations, they sought to investigate nine teachers' beliefs and practices.

**What it tells us:** Most of the teachers had calculation-based goals for students with lower prior attainment and conceptual goals for students with higher prior attainment. Several teachers used investigative methods with 'able' students and 'show and tell' methods with 'less able' students.

Anne Watson found that low-achieving students in the early years of secondary school could display the thinking skills, generalisations and abstractions which characterise high performance in mathematics learning.[34]

Through studying the early language acquisition of children, Caleb Gattegno analysed four common 'powers of the mind' possessed by everyone who is able to master their first language.[35] These are:

- the power of extraction – finding 'what is common among so large a range of variations'

- the power to make transformations – for example, my Dad ~ my Mum's partner ~ my sister's Dad ~ my uncle's brother

- handling abstractions – for example, any noun is a label for a general set of objects

- stressing and ignoring – for example, focusing on one aspect of perception to the exclusion of others.

By speaking their first language, children demonstrate that they already have all of these 'powers', which are so essential to mathematical thought. Simply through learning their first language, the students we teach have

---

[34] **A. Watson and E. De Geest**, 'Principled Teaching for Deep Progress: Improving Mathematical Learning Beyond Methods and Materials', *Educational Studies in Mathematics* 58, 2 (2005): pp. 209–234.

[35] **C. Gattegno**, *What We Owe Children: The Subordination of Teaching to Learning* (London: Routledge Kegan Paul, 1971). The 'powers' are discussed on page 9.

demonstrated extremely sophisticated thinking skills. It is the role of mathematics education to develop and hone these thinking skills within every student. We can support every student to think mathematically.

Perhaps because of frequent, relatively high-stakes testing, we sometimes feel pressure for teaching mathematics to involve simplification of the mathematics until it becomes a sequence of small, smooth steps which can be easily traversed. Unfortunately, this approach is unlikely to result in deep or sustained learning, as the students are insufficiently engaged with the mathematics to retain it in the long term.

Afzal Ahmed worked with teachers teaching low-attaining students.[36] His study showed that nearly all students were able to use sophisticated thinking skills in learning mathematics. The teachers in the study found that students learned better if they were given time to make choices, to discuss and to explore mathematics.

Over the past few decades, we seem to have been presented with a false dichotomy between teaching standard curriculum topics and developing students' mathematical thinking.

What if we could do both at the same time?

## Low-attaining students think mathematically

 **Evidence**

**A. Watson** 2002.[37]

**The study:** Anne Watson set out to see if some low-achieving students in the early years of secondary school could display the thinking skills, generalisations and abstractions that characterise both pure esoteric mathematics and the artificial word 'problems' arising in textbooks and tests.

**What it tells us:** The tasks we use should be accessible and extendable, encourage decision making, promote discussion, encourage creativity, and encourage 'what if' and 'what if not?' questions.

---

[36] **A. Ahmed**, *Low Attainers in Mathematics Project*. Better Mathematics (London: HMSO, 1987).

[37] **A. Watson**, 'Instances of Mathematical Thinking among Low Attaining Students in an Ordinary Secondary Classroom', *Journal of Mathematical Behavior* 20 (2002): pp. 461–475.

Reinforcing the findings of Anne Watson,[38] a study by Els De Geest and colleagues demonstrated that students with low prior attainment are capable of thinking mathematically, providing their teachers have high expectations of them and put the necessary conditions in place.[39]

Other studies have similarly found that previously low-attaining students are capable of making shifts in their thinking and of improving their mathematics attainment when challenged with higher-order thinking tasks.[40]

Recent research on the brain suggests that we all have a natural inborn propensity towards mathematical thinking and conceptual understanding.[41] The natural brain function that enables us to recognise and compare small numbers can be adapted to become the foundation of mathematical thinking.[42]

As we saw in Chapter 5, a focus on exam preparation is not necessarily the best preparation for exams. Of the three dimensions of depth – conceptual understanding, mathematical thinking and language and communication – it is often mathematical thinking that is most at threat from teachers' behaviours under the pressure of high-stakes student testing.

The English school inspectorate, Ofsted, raised concerns about this over-emphasis on examinations and the implications for the development of mathematical thinking. It observed that schools were 'focusing heavily on examination questions', and that this 'enabled students to pass examinations, but did not necessarily enable them to apply their knowledge independently in different contexts'.[43]

Ofsted inspectors have reported that they have often found that teaching 'presented mathematics as a collection of arbitrary rules and provided a

---

[38] **A. Watson** 2001, *op. cit.*

[39] **E. De Geest, A. Watson and S. Prestage**, 'Thinking in Ordinary Lessons: What Happened When Nine Teachers Believed Their Failing Students Could Think Mathematically', in *27th Conference of the International Group for the Psychology in Mathematics Education Conference*, Vol. 2 (2003): pp. 300–308.

[40] **A. Zohar and Y.J. Dori**, 'Higher Order Thinking Skills and Low-Achieving Students: Are They Mutually Exclusive', *Journal of the Learning Sciences* 12(2) (2003): pp. 145–181.

**M. Cardelle-Elawar**, 'Effects of Metacognitive Instructions on Low Achievers in Mathematics Problems', *Teaching & Teacher Education* 11(1) (1995): pp. 81–95.

[41] For example: **B. Butterworth**, *The Mathematical Brain* (London: Macmillan, 1999); **S. Dehaene**, *The Number Sense: How the Mind Creates Mathematics* (London: Allen Lane, 1997).

[42] **G. Lakoff and R.E. Nunez**, *Where Mathematics Comes From* (New York, NY: Basic Books, 2000).

[43] **Ofsted**, *Evaluating Mathematics Provision for 14–19-year-olds* (Crown Copyright. Ref Number: HMI 2611, 2006).

narrow range of learning activities [that] did not motivate students and limited their achievement'.[44]

# How to develop mathematical thinking

As I hope this chapter has already made clear, there is a wealth of ways in which to think mathematically. I have found it helpful to put these into five groups, as follows:

- Exemplify

- Generalise

- Modify

- Explain

- Compare

Over the next few pages, we'll take a closer look at the first three of these, and consider some ideas for tasks, or task adaptations, that promote exemplification, generalisation and modification as central to the learning and doing of mathematics.[45]

## Mathematicians exemplify

The creation of examples can involve transforming and reorganising knowledge. In 'Mathematics as a constructive activity',[46] Anne Watson and John Mason explain and demonstrate the teaching strategy of asking students to construct their own examples of mathematical objects. They argue that learner-generated examples or example variations, as explicit stimuli, could prompt access to the essential aspects of concepts.

An effective way to prompt exemplification is to give students a statement and ask them to give you examples that meet the statement, and then ask for another example, and another … .

---

[44] **Department for Education**, *Making Mathematics Count: the Report of Sir Adrian Smith's Inquiry into Post-14 Mathematics Education* (937764) (London: The Stationery Office, 2004).

[45] For further examples of ways to promote these, and other, habits of mind, a practical source of inspiration is: **M. Swan**, *Improving Learning in Mathematics: Challenges and Strategies* (Department for Education and Skills Standards Unit, 2005).

[46] **A. Watson and J. Mason**, 'Mathematics as a Constructive Activity: Learners Generating Examples', *Studies in Mathematical Thinking and Learning* (Mahwah, NJ: Lawrence Erlbaum Associates, 2005).

### Another, another and another

*Can you give me a fraction between $\frac{2}{7}$ and $\frac{3}{7}$? And another, another, another …
Can you think of a fraction that's closer to $\frac{2}{7}$? One that's exactly half-way?*

Another type of task that prompts exemplification is to ask students to give you an example of a 'hard' and 'easy' answer to a question, explaining why one is 'hard' and the other 'easy'.

### Hard and easy

*Give me a hard and easy example of a missing angle problem.*

Example creation is often carried out by textbook authors and teachers. If some of the responsibility for making examples is transferred to students, their knowledge structures can be developed and extended.

Since exemplification requires a sense of structure, domain, or generality, the teacher can help learners shift to more complex cognitive levels by asking for examples.[47]

It is worth emphasising that learner-generated examples are intended to supplement, not replace, the use of carefully crafted practice exercises. Such question sets, designed by teachers, curriculum writers or textbook authors, offer considered variation to deepen conceptual understanding and promote mathematical thinking.

## Mathematicians generalise

To encourage generalisation, teachers can give students a statement and ask whether it is always, sometimes or never true. One useful source of prompts for these tasks is the Inquiry Maths website run by Andrew Blair.[48]

### Always, sometimes, never

*Is it always, sometimes or never true that the product of two even numbers is even?*

### What is the question?

A useful prompt for shifting the focus onto structures rather than answers is to ask, *'If this is an answer, what might the question be?'* Give students an

---

[47] **P. Sadovsky**, 'Arithmetic and Algebraic Practices: Possible Bridge Between Them', in *Proceedings of the 23rd Conference of the International Group for the Psychology of Mathematics Education*, Vol. 4, edited by O. Zaslavsky (1999): pp. 145–152.

[48] www.inquirymaths.com accessed 17 August 2017.

answer and ask them to come up with as many questions as possible that could have that answer.

*The answer is 36, what could the possible questions be?*

## Mathematicians modify

An effective way to engage students in thinking about the mathematics they are learning is to ask them to identify and correct errors. One *Mathematics Mastery* student workbook includes this exercise:

8. True or false?

a) $3 - 8 = 5$

b) $6 = -4 - 2$

c) $-99 - -99 = 0$

d) $-1.3 - -2.6 - -1.1 = 2.4$

e) $8 - -5 = 3$

f) $4 = 1 - -3$

g) $-0.2 - -1.5 = 1.7$

h) $-\frac{3}{8} - -\frac{1}{4} - -\frac{1}{12} = \frac{1}{3}$

**Figure 8.5**

With a similar focus on addressing common misconceptions, this task asks students to identify the error in the process of adding fractions.

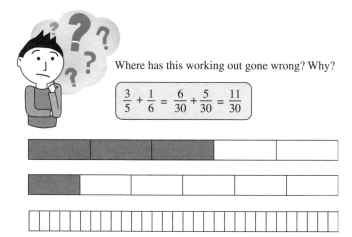

Where has this working out gone wrong? Why?

$$\frac{3}{5} + \frac{1}{6} = \frac{6}{30} + \frac{5}{30} = \frac{11}{30}$$

**Figure 8.6**

# Summary

Learning to think like a mathematician is a long-term endeavour.

Why teach problem solving? Problem solving can:

- be enjoyable and motivational
- prepare students for the workplace
- promote student autonomy
- help students to apply mathematics in unfamiliar situations.

There are a number of frameworks for mathematical thinking.

It is not the task itself that promotes mathematical thinking, rather the way in which teacher and students interact with it.

Mathematical thinking is not just the preserve of the lucky few.

How to develop mathematical thinking:

- Ideas for encouraging students to exemplify include 'another, and another, and another'.
- To promote generalisation, teachers can ask students whether a claim is 'sometimes, always or never true'.
- To raise the profile of *modification* in learning to think mathematically, students can be asked to identify and correct errors.

# Chapter 9

## What gets students talking about mathematics?

**A**s mathematics teachers, we quite rightly tend to see ourselves as just that – teachers of mathematics. But it is becoming increasingly clear that secondary students need our support in making sense of the literacy demands of the subject.[1]

Mathematics educators, and others, often state that 'mathematics is a language'. This can lead to the view that the development of spoken and written natural language is less important to the study of mathematics than it is to subjects such as geography or history.

Students' natural language proficiency might be seen as not mattering. The idea that 'mathematics is a language' is a useful metaphor. But even one of its key advocates, David Pimm, warns that the metaphor should not be allowed to obscure the complex role of language in learning mathematics.[2]

Talking, reading and writing about mathematics can be really difficult. It's traditionally an abstract subject, with its own special vocabulary (a *product* isn't something to make or to buy; *sum* is more specific than it seems; even *differentiation* has its own meaning!).

In this chapter, we first consider why communication in mathematics is so important. We then take a look at what teachers can do to develop communication in the mathematics classroom.

---

[1] **R.J. Draper** *et al.*, 'What's More Important – Literacy or Content? Confronting the Literacy-Content Dualism', A*ction in Teacher Education* 27(2) (2005): pp. 12–21.

[2] **D. Pimm**, *Speaking Mathematically: Language in Mathematics Classrooms* (London: Routledge, 1987).

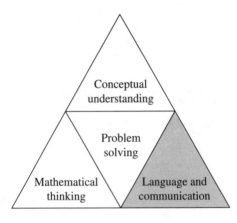

**Figure 9.1:** The three dimensions of depth: language and communication

# Why is mathematical communication so important?

Mathematics is an abstract subject. It can be experienced and learned only through language, symbols, diagrams, models or applications. Language and reasoning are an integral part of mathematics.

Communication – including reading, writing and discussion – is vital to learning mathematics. Students find it difficult to explain their mathematical thinking and understanding of concepts.

Students with more advanced communication skills achieve more in mathematics.

In this section, we take a look at each of these three assertions in turn. We draw on our own experiences of mathematics and communication, as teacher and as learner. We also consider what the research literature can tell us about each statement.

## Language is integral to mathematics

Language is vital to mathematics. Mathematical modelling (consideration of a 'real-life' situation, and using mathematics to solve it) is a crucial part of the subject, and understanding and 'mathematising' spoken and written English is vital for success with this. Academic mathematicians communicate mathematical ideas precisely and efficiently using accepted terminology.

In Hong Kong, they go so far as to include communication in their definition of mathematics: 'Mathematics is a mode of thinking, a powerful *means of communication*, a tool for studying other disciplines and an intellectual endeavour'[3] [author's emphasis].

In Singapore, the first of three mathematical processes identified in the national curriculum is 'Reasoning, Communication and Connections', which includes 'Use appropriate representations, mathematical language (including notations, symbols and conventions) and technology to present and communicate mathematical ideas.'[4]

Improving students' ability to articulate mathematical ideas, concepts and reasoning has a profound effect on the way that students see themselves, as Clare Lee describes.[5] The better a student can communicate using the mathematics 'register', the more they feel themselves to be a mathematician.

Inspired by the work of Wittgenstein and Vygotsky, many educationalists argue that human thinking is a form of communication. This results from the observation that all human activities are either purely communicational or imbued with and shaped by discourse. One such academic, Anna Sfard, argues that 'learning mathematics may now be defined as an initiation to mathematical discourse'.[6]

At college level, students' troubles are customarily ascribed to the lack of specific content in their high-school curricula. Pier Ferrari claims that students' competence in ordinary language and in the specific languages used in mathematics are other sources of trouble.[7]

He demonstrates that mathematical language shares a number of properties with written literate registers of ordinary language. This means that being

---

[3] **Curriculum Development Council, HKSAR,** *Learning to Learn: The Way Forward in Curriculum Development* (Hong Kong: Government Printer, 2001).

[4] The same mathematical processes are referenced in all Singapore's mathematics syllabuses. See, for example, www.moe.gov.sg/docs/default-source/document/education/syllabuses/sciences/files/mathematics-syllabus-sec-1-to-4-expressn(a)-course.pdf.

[5] **C. Lee,** *Discussion in a Mathematics Classroom: Developing a Teacher's Awareness of the Issues and Characteristics* (Oxford: Centre for Research into Mathematics Education, 1998).
**C. Lee,** *Language for Learning Mathematics – Assessment for Learning in Practice* (Buckingham: Open University Press, 2006).

[6] **A. Sfard,** 'There is More to Discourse than Meets the Ears: Looking at Thinking as Communicating to Learn More about Mathematical Learning', *Educational Studies in Mathematics* 46 (2001): pp. 13–57. Quote is from page 28.

[7] **P.I. Ferrari,** 'Mathematical Language and Advanced Mathematics Learning', in *Proceedings of the 28th Conference of PME*, edited by M. Johnsen Hoines and A. Berit Fuglestad (Bergen, Norway: Bergen University College, 2004), pp. 383–390. www.emis.de/proceedings/PME28/RR/RR177_Ferrari.pdf accessed 18 August 2017.

familiar with literate registers and their use is a good starting point, if not a prerequisite, to learning to use mathematical language.

As an abstract subject, mathematics can only be communicated through language, symbols, diagrams, models or applications.

Learning mathematics involves:

- working mathematically for yourself
- translating what you know into communicable terms
- interpreting others' attempts at communication.

Language is one important way in which we represent mathematical ideas.

 **Try this in the classroom**

**Three squares**

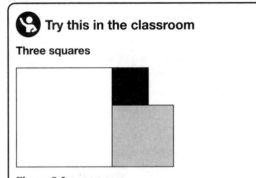

Figure 9.2

The area of the grey square is 49 cm$^2$.

The perimeter of the black square is 12 cm.

What are the area and perimeter of the white square?

**Preparing to teach – do the mathematics!**

In preparing to teach 'Three squares', you could consider the following points:

- How do you define area and perimeter? To yourself? To your students? How would your students define these terms?

- When you think about the phrase 'the perimeter of the black square is 12 cm', what representation supports this? By what process do you conclude that the length of the side of the black square is 3 cm? How could you explain this process using concrete manipulatives or dynamic visual representations? What language would you use to accompany these representations?

Ask students to tackle the 'Three squares' problem. Once they have the answer (individually, or through discussion in pairs) set them these three challenges:

- Explain your full method to a partner in silence, using annotation and jottings only.

- Explain your full method to a partner in full spoken sentences, using correct mathematical vocabulary.

- Write down your full method using full sentences and correct mathematical vocabulary.

Ask students to reflect on:

- which of the three challenges was easiest, and hardest, and why

- which of the three explanations was the most convincing, and why.

## Communication is vital to learning mathematics

Reading, writing and discussion are important routes for students to understand mathematics.

By solving problems collaboratively through talk, students clarify their own ideas as well as supporting their peers to clarify theirs.[8] Through talk, students improve their understanding and gain new insights into the problem. Studies show that encouraging students to verbalise problems before giving a written response increases the rate of correct answers.[9]

Many recommendations for classroom practice are founded on a socio-cultural model of education, in which talking to learn is central. These are often based on the work of Vygotsky, who argued that students learn through their interactions with more capable peers and adults.[10]

The Cockcroft Report (introduced in Chapter 6) stated that:

*The ability to 'say what you mean and mean what you say' should be one of the outcomes of good mathematics teaching. This ability develops as a result of opportunities to talk about mathematics. Pupils*

[8] **P.W. Thompson**, 'Experience, Problem Solving, and Learning Mathematics: Considerations in Developing Mathematics Curricula', in *Teaching and Learning Mathematical Problem Solving: Multiple Research Perspectives*, edited by E.A. Silver (Hillsdale, NJ: Lawrence Erlbaum Associates, 1985), pp. 189–236.

[9] **T. Lovitt and K. Curtis**, 'Effects of Manipulating Antecedent Event on Mathematics Response Rate', *Journal of Applied Behaviour Analysis* 1 (1968): pp. 329–333.

[10] **L.S. Vygotsky**, *Thought and Language* (Cambridge, MA: MIT Press, 1986).

*need the explicit help, which can only be given by extended discussion, to establish these relationships, even pupils whose mathematical attainment is high do not easily do this for themselves.* [11]

The importance of high-quality discussion in learning mathematics is widely acknowledged.[12] Celia Hoyles suggests three aspects to discussion between students that lead them to examine their own reasoning:

- Articulating ideas brings about reflection on those ideas.

- Discussion involves framing ideas in a way that will be accepted by others.

- Listening to others modifies your own thoughts.[13]

The Expert Panel for the National Curriculum in England found that:

*There is a compelling body of evidence that highlights a connection between oral development, cognitive development and educational attainment. We are strongly of the view that the development of oral language should be a particular feature of the new National Curriculum.* [14]

The National Curriculum in England does, indeed, include a statement about spoken English, which emphasises the importance of language to mathematics:

*The quality and variety of language that pupils hear and speak are key factors in developing their mathematical vocabulary and presenting a mathematical justification, argument or proof. They must be assisted in making their thinking clear to themselves as well as others, and teachers should ensure that pupils build secure foundations by using discussion to probe and remedy their misconceptions.* [15]

---

[11] **Department of Education and Science**, *Mathematics Counts: Report of the Committee of Inquiry into the Teaching of Mathematics in Schools* (Cockcroft Report) (London: HMSO, 1982). p. 72.

[12] **M. Walshaw and G. Anthony**, 'The Teacher's Role in Classroom Discourse: A Review of Recent Research into Mathematics Classrooms', *Review of Educational Research* 78(3) (2008): pp. 516–551.

[13] **C. Hoyles**, 'What is the Point of Group Discussion in Mathematics?', *Educational Studies in Mathematics* 16(2) (1985): pp. 205–214.

[14] **Department for Education**, *The Framework for the National Curriculum. A report by the Expert Panel for the National Curriculum Review* (London: Department for Education, 2011), pp. 9–10.

[15] **Department for Education**, *Mathematics Programmes of Study: Key Stage 3 National Curriculum in England* (London: Department for Education, 2013).

## Teachers access students' thought through their talk and writing

Teachers find the discussion between students and the writing they produce to be useful tools for gaining insight into their understanding of mathematics. But it is not clear how teachers make this assessment. There is a risk that we assume that what a student says or writes conveys their intentions without distortion or alteration. Candia Morgan describes this as a problematic 'myth of transparency' which assumes that through students' talk and text, teachers can access their thoughts.[16]

### Students find it difficult to explain their mathematical thinking

**C. Lawson and C. Lee** 1995.[17]

**The study:** Clare Lee and Christine Lawson, as Mathematics and English teachers respectively, explored how students use language in order to think through concepts, express and communicate their learning. They studied the language used by Year 10 students working through a mathematical problem.

**What it tells us:** The students were confident in tackling the problem, and were 'competent users of spoken and written language'. They were asked to be sure that everyone understood their ideas and ways of working. However, despite this, the students:

*... speak in short phrases, mainly just numbers ... The conversation is made up of half-finished sentences, often containing mathematical operations but never related specifically to the problem ... They seem unable to use specific terminology to express their mathematical conclusions.*

---

[16] **C. Morgan**, *Writing Mathematically: The Discourse of Investigation, Studies in Mathematics Education* (London: Falmer Press, 1998), p. 197.

[17] **C. Lawson and C. Lee,** *Numeracy through Literacy. Proceedings of the Joint Conference of the British Society for Research into Learning Mathematics and the Association of Mathematics Education Tutors* (Loughborough: BSRLM/AMET, 1995), pp. 43–46. www.bsrlm.org.uk/wp-content/uploads/2016/02/BSRLM-IP-15-2-8.pdf accessed 18 August 2017.

## Better communication improves mathematics achievement

It seems that improving students' communication skills may improve their mathematics achievement. In fact, communication skills may predict mathematics achievement.

Reading skills are a powerful predictor for mathematical performance. A study in Finland found that the reading factor explained 52 per cent of the variance in mathematics performance.[18] To me, this is a powerful argument for using mathematics learning time to improve students' mathematical communication.

Improved language processing appears to be linked to mathematical performance, according to Chinese psychologists.

**Improved language processing accounts for gender differences in arithmetic**

**W. Wei** *et al.* 2012.[19]

**The study:** Psychologists in Beijing set 1556 eight- to eleven-year-old students ten cognitive tasks. Aware that, on average, female children consistently outperform male children in arithmetic, the researchers set out to analyse students' arithmetic and language processing skill.

**What it tells us:** Results showed that girls outperformed boys in arithmetic tasks (including simple subtraction and complex multiplication). Girls also performed better than boys in numerosity-comparison, number-comparison, number-series-completion, and word-rhyming tasks. Controlling for scores on the word-rhyming task eliminated gender differences in arithmetic. These results suggest that girls' advantage in arithmetic is likely to be due to their advantage in language processing.

This Beijing study indicates that supporting students to improve their language processing may well contribute to improved fluency with arithmetic.

Another reason that improved language and communication skills lead to higher mathematics achievement is the high literacy demands of high-stakes mathematics exams.

---

[18] **J. Korhonen, K. Linnanmäki and P. Aunio**, 'Language and Mathematical Performance: A Comparison of Lower Secondary School Students with Different Level of Mathematical Skills', *Scandinavian Journal of Educational Research* 56(3) (2012): pp. 333–344.

[19] **W. Wei** *et al.*, 'Gender Differences in Children's Arithmetic Performance are Accounted for by Gender Differences in Language Abilities', *Psychological Science* Vol 23, Issue 3 (2012): pp. 320–330.

# How to develop mathematical communication

When I began teaching in the early 2000s, the English government's education department published a guide and resources for teaching students who began their secondary schooling below national expectations.

The publication offered me this useful advice:

> You should make sure pupils have a good grasp of mathematical vocabulary and notation. Pupils should understand key mathematical words and symbols and use them correctly in oral and written work.[20]

The only trouble was, the students I was teaching didn't yet have a good grasp of mathematical vocabulary and notation, and they weren't using key mathematical words and symbols correctly in oral and written work. What was I supposed to do about it?

Since then, I have looked to the research literature, effective practitioners across the UK, and ideas from overseas, to find out how best to develop students' language and communication skills.

I hope that the three approaches described in this section will give you some useful ideas as to how you might develop your students' mathematical communication.

As with the recommendations for all three dimensions of depth, these techniques are as relevant for high-attaining students as they are for students who have previously underperformed.

# Get students talking

In order to deepen students' mathematical understanding through language, I advocate including a task involving student talk, in pairs or small groups, in every single mathematics lesson. Whatever their background or prior attainment, students benefit from scaffolding of language to further deepen their mathematical communication.

Relatively low-attaining students might struggle to discuss their mathematical ideas because they lack either the vocabulary or the ability to use it in

---

[20] **Department for Education and Skills**, *Springboard 7: A Mathematics Catch-up Programme for Pupils Entering Year 7* (London: DfES, 2001), p. 512.

sentences. Some comparatively high-attaining students might feel that they can get 'the answer' on their own, and that talk is peripheral to the business of doing mathematics. Students across the full range of attainment therefore benefit from explicit modelling of mathematical talk, both to teach them its words and structures, and to demonstrate its importance.

---

### A talk task in every lesson

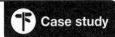 **Case study**

**The school context:** The mathematics team at London Academy in the UK include 'talk tasks' in every mathematics lesson. When learning about decimals, for example, students are asked to find and share different ways of sorting decimals, or to find different ways of describing a decimal number (describing 2.6 in tenths or in ones and tenths, for example).

With nine new teachers in the mathematics team in one year, the team find that including talk tasks in all lessons across the department is helpful in increasing students' experience of consistent and coherent teaching, and offers a structure for developing staff skills and sharing effective practice.

Teachers use questioning to draw out key ideas and concepts. They encourage students to justify their answers and give reasons by asking, 'Explain what you mean …', 'Can you find another way?', or 'How can you check that your answer is correct?'

**Their impact:** By demonstrably raising the profile of talk in learning mathematics, mathematics teachers at London Academy have given students ownership of subject-specific vocabulary and developed their understanding of important concepts.

At the start of their second year of teaching for mastery, a learning walk through Year 8 classrooms found students confidently and correctly using vocabulary learned in the previous year. For example, in an introductory discussion about their new topic of fractions, students introduced the terms vinculum, numerator and denominator, and engaged in informed discussion about their meaning. Students explained each part of the vulgar fraction, stating, for example, that 'the denominator represents the number of equal parts in the whole'.

---

Some teachers are initially concerned that all this emphasis on talk will put off shy students from learning mathematics. I am often asked about those children who prefer not to talk, but 'just to get on with it'. While I can see why this might be a concern, a greater concern for me is that by letting them 'just get on with it', teachers may be limiting their mathematical achievement.

 **Try this in the classroom**

In working on the task below, students practise structuring sentences in the form 'If ..., then ...'. These are valuable foundations for mathematical reasoning.

**What will happen?**

$a \div b = c$

What will happen to the value of $c$ if we ...

- double the value of $a$

- multiply $b$ by 10

- multiply $a$ by 100

- halve the value of $b$

- multiply both $a$ and $b$ by 10

- multiply $a$ by 10 and $b$ by 100?

Substitute numbers for $a$, $b$ and $c$ to see if you are correct.

 **Preparing to teach – do the mathematics!**

In preparing to teach the task above, you might consider the following points:

- What language might you expect to hear for a clear mathematical explanation?

- What questions might help to support development of multiplicative understanding?

- What would you expect to happen if $a$ increases? Why?

- What would you expect to happen if $b$ increases? Why?

- What happens if $b$ is very small/large?

- What could have happened to $a$ and $b$ if $c$ was 20 times greater?

- How many different possibilities can you think of?

- What other 'What if ... ?' questions could you ask?

# Structure mathematical talk

One conception of talk is 'our use of language for thinking together, for collectively making sense of experience and solving problems'.[21] However, such 'interthinking' is only possible when every student is confident in their use of language in the mathematics classroom.

Mathematical language and verbal reasoning must also be explicitly introduced and practised. Researchers have identified the use of repetition and recitation as a significant factor in the success of East Asian countries, even allowing for the impact of their cultural orientation towards achievement and examination performance.[22] By repeating key words and phrases, students' attention is focused on the ideas that lead to better understanding.

It is important that all students talk about mathematics in complete sentences, using correct mathematical vocabulary. This includes teachers asking students to listen to and build on what their peers have said. For example, they might ask, 'Can you say what he just said?' or 'Can you build on what he just said?'

Teachers teaching for mastery do not let children who are 'good at mathematics' but who struggle with English (which is inevitably the dominant language in the classroom) remain in the symbolic, avoiding use of words and sentences (unless it's beneficial to their learning in a particular situation), because to do so would not be fair to them. Building the foundations needed to study mathematics at A-level and beyond involves a facility to justify and prove.

One key way that teachers in the *Mathematics Mastery* partnership emphasise language and communication is through an insistence on complete sentences. This is in order to give students the maximum amount of practice in constructing complete sentences.

This pedagogic technique was noticed to be effective by Doug Lemov, who watched thousands of classes and videos of classes taught by teachers in

---

[21] **N. Mercer**, *Words and Minds: How We Use Language to Think Together* (London: Routledge, 2000). On page 1 Neil Mercer describes this as 'interthinking'.

[22] **F.K.S. Leung**, 'The Traditional Chinese Views of Mathematics and Education: Implications for Mathematics Education in the New Millennium', in *Mathematics Education in the 21st Century*, edited by C. Hoyles, C. Morgan and G. Woodhouse (London: Falmer Press Ltd, 1999), pp. 240–247.

**J. Biggs**, 'What are Effective Schools? Lessons from East and West' (The Radford Memorial Lecture), *Australian Educational Researcher* 21 (1994): pp. 19–39.

the United States whose students were particularly successful.[23] As well as supporting students to construct grammatically correct sentences, this gives students plenty of opportunity to use mathematical terminology themselves.

In the absence of this expectation, students might mostly experience a word such as 'equivalent' when they hear the teacher say it, or read it as part of a written mathematics question. By requesting that they speak in full sentences, students get the opportunity to use the words themselves and hear them used by their peers.

- Ask students to reword their peers' sentences to ensure relevant terminology is used.

- Plan tasks and exercise sets so that purposeful discussion can take place using key vocabulary.

An exchange between teacher and student might go as follows:

Teacher: 'What is the sum of the angles in a triangle?'

Student: 'One-hundred and eighty.'

Teacher: 'The sum of ...'

Student: 'The sum of the angles in a triangle is equal to one-hundred and eighty degrees.'

Other ways the teacher might remind the student to give a full-sentence answer include the prompt 'full sentence' or a non-verbal hand signal.

As students' mathematical vocabulary grows, they can be encouraged to give full-sentence answers that vary the word choice from the question. For example:

Teacher: 'What is the sum of the angles in a triangle?'

Student: 'If you add together the internal angles of a triangle they always total one-hundred and eighty degrees.'

In this way, students' understanding of mathematical concepts – in this case 'sum', 'addition' and 'total' – is deepened.

---

[23] **D. Lemov**, *Teach Like a Champion: 49 Techniques that Put Students on the Path to College* (San Francisco, CA: Jossey-Bass, 2010). Expecting pupils to answer in complete sentences is part of Technique 4: Format Matters, which is introduced on page 47.

**Try this in the classroom**

For one whole-class question-and-answer or discussion-based task, insist that everyone (you included!) speaks only in complete sentences. What becomes harder? What becomes easier? What might the impact of this approach be in the long term?

A number of *Mathematics Mastery* partner schools have found that it is not just students' mathematics that is improving – their students' literacy improves too. The expectation that students will speak in full sentences gives students a level of confidence that is born through being able to fully understand and make up their own sentences. Their deep understanding of constructing sentences soon begins to show through in all subjects, not just mathematics.

The best way to prepare students to speak in full sentences is to speak in full sentences yourself when working on mathematics with colleagues.

In the *Mathematics Mastery* team, we engage in some mathematics together every week. We try to speak in full sentences ourselves, partly to support our own continued learning of mathematics, and partly so we can reflect on the affordances and constraints of this classroom expectation.

Analysis of work by the Mathematics Quality Analysis Group within the TIMSS Video Study found that, although Hong Kong classrooms were dominated by teacher talk, the quality of learning and instruction was nevertheless high.[24] It seems that teacher talk in Hong Kong is highly mathematically structured.

It seems somewhat paradoxical that, even though teacher talk is not the best way for students to learn, countries with very high student attainment seem to have high levels of teacher talk. An interesting explanation for this is that preparing to model and explain content, and doing so in the majority of lessons, acts as a form of professional development for teachers.

Remember Liping Ma's study comparing the depth of conceptual understanding of US and Chinese teachers from Chapter 7? Ma noted that though the US teachers and Chinese teachers both spoke at similar length, the US teachers' answers were, generally speaking, 'less mathematically relevant and mathematically organized'.[25]

---

[24] **F.K.S. Leung**, 'Some Characteristics of East Asian Mathematics Classrooms Based on Data from the TIMSS 1999 Video Study', *Educational Studies in Mathematics* 60 (2005): pp. 199–215.

[25] **L. Ma**, *Knowing and Teaching Elementary Mathematics: Teachers' Understanding of Fundamental Mathematics in China and the United States* (Mahwah, NJ: Lawrence Erlbaum Associates, 1999), p. 104.

She proposes that the Chinese teachers' proficiency in communicating mathematics may be a result of their teaching style, which involves a significant component of lecture presentation. In preparing to teach a lesson, Chinese teachers therefore spend time preparing a presentation on the topic, thereby practising and training their mathematical communication skills.

There is no argument here for a shift towards lecture-style teaching. But it is worth thinking about the possibility that teachers taking time to organise and gather their ideas before teaching a topic is of benefit. The research does indicate that teachers in East Asia have acquired well-developed communication skills in mathematics.

# Grow students' vocabulary

One challenge in mathematical problem solving is the large number of new or unfamiliar words that may inhibit connections to students' existing knowledge and create barriers to comprehension.[26]

A very helpful distinction between two types of mathematics curriculum content has been made by Dave Hewitt. He distinguishes between those things that cannot be known by a student without that student being informed (he refers to these as 'arbitrary') and those things that can be figured out and known to be correct by a student for him or herself (which he calls 'necessary').

For example, the fact that all three angles of a triangle add up to the same number (180 degrees) is necessary, but the fact that we call the shape a 'triangle', the corners 'angles', and measure them in 'degrees' is entirely arbitrary (and based only on a choice made a long time ago).

> What is arbitrary is arbitrary for everyone, in that no one can know the arbitrary without being informed by others. The arbitrary concerns names and conventions which have been established within a culture and which need to be adopted by students if they are to participate and communicate successfully within this culture. The arbitrary is in the realm of memory as students cannot work out these things through their own awareness. So the students' role is to memorise the arbitrary.[27]

---

[26] **M.J. Kieffer and N.K. Lesaux**, 'Morphing into Adolescents: Active Word Learning for English Language Learners and Their Classmates in Middle School', *Journal of Adolescent & Adult Literacy* 54(1) (2010): pp. 47–56.

[27] **D. Hewitt**, 'Arbitrary and Necessary. Part 2: Assisting Memory', *For the Learning of Mathematics: an international journal of mathematics* 21(1) (2001): pp. 44–51.

Hewitt makes the powerful case that 'mathematics' consists of the necessary (to be made aware of) rather than the arbitrary (to be memorised). But we cannot afford to let this lead us to conclude that mathematics teachers can abdicate responsibility for helping students with the arbitrary.

Just as it is an important part of the student's role to memorise the arbitrary, so it is a vital part of the teacher's role to make this process as efficient as possible.

I recommend a structured approach to language for mathematics, which involves cumulative mastery of vocabulary. Key words are not just listed for lessons as a one off, some never to be seen again.

Many teachers in the *Mathematics Mastery* partnership make it clear to students which key words they want to hear the students using during that lesson. Some even go so far as to offer rewards if they hear the words in use.

Mathematics vocabulary is unique in that many words have both general and specific meanings, while at the same time key terms must be defined in a precise manner – for example, a student must know that prime refers to a *positive integer with exactly two distinct positive factors*. Prime also means perfect, chief, or of the highest grade, but none of these non-mathematical meanings really aids understanding of the mathematical meaning.[28]

Thinking carefully not just about what mathematics you want students to talk about, but also about exactly what sentences and vocabulary you expect them to use to talk about it, significantly increases the chance that every child will be successful.[29] As Robert Marzano and Debra Pickering observe:

> *Teaching specific terms in a specific way is the strongest action a teacher can take to ensure that students have the academic background knowledge they need to understand the content they will encounter in school.*[30]

Timing is important here. Rather than introducing vocabulary and notation 'just in time', students can start using the correct mathematical terminology

---

[28] **T. Shanahan and C. Shanahan**, 'Teaching Disciplinary Literacy to Adolescents: Rethinking Content Area Literacy', *Harvard Educational Review* 78(1) (2008): pp. 40–59.

[29] **P.J. Fisher and C.L.Z. Blachowicz**, 'Vocabulary Instruction in a Remedial Setting', *Reading & Writing Quarterly* 21 (2005): pp. 281–300.

[30] **R.J. Marzano and D.J. Pickering**, *Building Academic Vocabulary: Teacher's Manual* (Alexandria, VA: ASCD, 2005).

as soon as it is relevant. For example, students can use the terms expression and equation when working with numbers, even before they use them algebraically.

We need to choose vocabulary that will help students to both understand new concepts and make connections between real-world experiences and existing background knowledge. These kinds of connection help students build conceptual models and deepen their understanding of mathematics.[31]

It takes time to learn mathematical vocabulary – students must be provided with multiple exposures in meaningful contexts, direct instruction focused on individual words, and opportunities to explore the conceptual relations between words.[32] Teachers need to support students in learning what Isabel Beck, Margaret McKeown and Linda Kucan describe as tier 2 words (high-utility words found in written text but less common in everyday conversation) and tier 3 words (words specific to mathematics).[33]

The need to explicitly teach tier 3 words such as reciprocal, proportion, expression, equation and variable is well understood. What might be less obvious is that tier 2 words such as manipulate, combine, introduce, arrange or organise may benefit from focused teaching in mathematics lessons.

The most difference can be made by selecting a relatively small number of words and focusing on building a deep understanding of them.[34]

---

[31] **M.W. Conley**, 'Cognitive Strategy Instruction for Adolescents: What We Need to Know about the Promise, What We Don't Know about the Potential', *Harvard Educational Review* 78 (2008): pp. 84–106.

[32] See, for example: **M.F. Graves**, *The Vocabulary Book: Learning & instruction* (New York, NY: Teachers College Press, 2006).

**S.A. Stahl and W.E. Nagy**, *Teaching Word Meanings* (Mahwah, NJ: Lawrence Erlbaum, 2006).

**R.T. Vacca and J.A. Vacca**, *Content Area Reading: Literacy and Learning Across the Curriculum* (6th ed.) (Menlo Park, CA: Longman, 1999).

[33] **I.L. Beck *et al.***, *Bringing Words to Life: Robust Vocabulary Instruction* (New York, NY: Guilford Press, 2002).

[34] **C.L.Z. Blachowicz *et al.***, 'Vocabulary Questions from the Classroom', *Reading Research Quarterly* 41 (2006): pp. 524–539.

# Summary

Mathematical communication is important because:

- *language is integral to mathematics* itself – mathematics is abstract and can only be communicated through language, symbols, diagrams, models or applications

- *communication is central to teaching and learning mathematics* – reading, writing and discussion are key to learning mathematics, and teachers access students' thoughts through their talk and writing; students find it difficult to explain their mathematical thinking and understanding of concepts

- *better communication improves mathematics achievement* – communication skills predict mathematics achievement; high–stakes mathematics examinations have high literacy demands.

How to develop students' mathematical communication skills:

- *Get students talking:* build opportunities for student talk into every lesson. Insist that students use mathematical vocabulary and sentence structures.

- Structure mathematical talk: expect students to speak in full sentences. Model grammatically correct sentences.

- *Grow students' vocabulary:* ensure students have the vocabulary they need to communicate mathematically.

# Chapter 10

## How can you make this happen in your school?

One teacher can make a significant difference, but real transformation comes when teachers work together in collaboration across the school's mathematics department. In this chapter, we take a look at the transformation that is possible across a mathematics department, and the leadership required to make this happen.

Congratulations! If you're reading this chapter, it's highly likely that you are seriously considering driving forward a really significant change in the way mathematics is taught – not only in your own classroom, but across your school's mathematics department. It's a brave step, and a very exciting one. In this chapter, I offer some advice and resources in the hope of making this very difficult but worthwhile challenge a bit easier.

By adopting a shared approach across your department you can make a real difference for every student. It has been demonstrated that the school a student attends has a greater influence on their progress than their background characteristics such as age, gender or socio-economic disadvantage.[1] You can make sure that the mathematics education provided by your school really transforms students' life chances – that every student succeeds and a significant proportion excels.

## Expert teachers for every class

Successful teaching and learning can be achieved when expert teachers deliver lessons that have been designed together, reviewed and improved over time.

---

[1] **J. MacBeath and P. Mortimore**, eds, *Improving School Effectiveness* (Buckingham: Open University Press, 2001), p. 72.

Wherever possible, classes should be taught by expert teachers. Teaching by non-experts, particularly in the lower years of secondary, can result in poor foundations being laid for later learning.

Where teacher subject knowledge is weaker, students can experience mathematics as a set of disparate and disjointed procedures and techniques. A two-year study into learners' needs found that 'Lack of specialist knowledge can also make it harder for teachers to understand the connections and relationships between key mathematical ideas.'[2]

Mary Kennedy suggests that:

> *Teachers need not only to understand the content deeply, but also to know something about how that content is taught and learned. If they learn a series of specific teaching techniques without understanding their rationale and without help in adapting them to particular students and classrooms, they will be unable to make lasting changes in their practice.*[3]

On a study visit to Shanghai, a group from the National College for School Leadership were impressed that all secondary school teachers are qualified to degree level to teach their specialist subject.[4] This may or may not be the case in your own school.

In the *Mathematics Mastery* partnership, we work with departments fully staffed with mathematics graduates, and teams almost entirely made up of non-specialists. I've noticed that, though many of the highly mathematically-qualified teams we work with certainly do an excellent job, there isn't the correlation between level of mathematics qualification and quality of teaching you might expect. So it was interesting to read that a study in the United States found no significant difference between the key concept understanding of teachers who graduated in the subject they taught, and teachers who did not.

---

[2] **ACME**, *Mathematical Needs: The Mathematical Needs of Learners* (Advisory Committee on Mathematics Education, 2011). www.acme-uk.org/media/7627/acme_theme_b_final.pdf accessed 21 August 2017.

[3] **M.M. Kennedy**, 'Some Surprising Findings on How Teachers Learn to Teach', *Educational Leadership* 49(3) (1991): pp. 14–17. www.ascd.com/ASCD/pdf/journals/ed_lead/el_199111_kennedy.pdf accessed 21 August 2017.

[4] **National College for School Leadership**, *Report on Research into Maths and Science Teaching in the Shanghai Region*, research by National Leaders of Education and Subject Specialists in Shanghai and Ningbo, China, 11–18 January 2013.

> ## A surprising finding about teacher qualifications
>
>  **Evidence**
>
> **M.M. Kennedy** 1991.[5]
>
> **The study:** Mary Kennedy reported on findings from the Teacher Education and Learning to Teach (TELT study) in the United States. This large-scale study from the National Center for Research of Student Learning included more than 700 trainee teachers on pre-service and in-service programs as well as induction programs and alternative routes.
>
> **What it tells us:** Majoring in an academic subject in college did not guarantee that teachers would have the kind of subject knowledge they need for teaching. When the study contrasted teachers who majored in a discipline with others who did not, it was found that the majors were often no more able than other teachers to explain fundamental concepts in their subject.

If you feel subject expertise may be lacking in your team, the findings of the TELT study might be reassuring. You may not be as far 'behind' as you think, so it really is well worth tackling teacher subject knowledge. For teams who find themselves in the fortunate position of being relatively well qualified in mathematics, this finding may act as a reminder that there is still much work to be done.

To teach, we need an explicit and deep understanding of the subject we teach, as the TELT study emphasised:

> *Teaching requires a variety of kinds of knowledge and requires that these bodies of knowledge be integrated in a unique way. Teachers need an understanding of subject matter that is more explicit and deeper than the subject knowledge needed by other practitioners.*[6]

In supporting teachers to make changes in their teaching, to teach for mastery, the challenge is, as Mary Kennedy puts it, 'to find a way to help teachers in all aspects of teaching, not just the subject matter, not just the pedagogy, but both. And not separately, but in relationship to one another.'[7]

---

[5] **M.M. Kennedy**, 'Some Surprising Findings on How Teachers Learn to Teach', *Educational Leadership* 49(3) (1991): pp. 14–17. www.ascd.com/ASCD/pdf/journals/ed_lead/el_199111_kennedy.pdf accessed 21 August 2017.

[6] *Ibid.*

[7] *Ibid.*

For several decades, researchers have been exploring the idea that 'there is content knowledge unique to teaching – a kind of subject matter specific professional knowledge'.[8] The idea was proposed by Lee Shulman in the 1980s.[9]

Shulman distinguished this category of teacher knowledge from six other categories: knowledge of general pedagogical strategies, of learners, of educational contexts, of educational philosophies, of subject content, and of the curriculum. He used the term 'pedagogical content knowledge' to refer to this seventh category of teacher knowledge – 'that special amalgam of content and pedagogy that is uniquely the province of teachers, their own special form of professional understanding'.[10] This specialised body of professional knowledge, pedagogical content knowledge, is deemed necessary for teachers to develop effective teaching.[11]

What is required is development of teachers' understanding of the *teaching of mathematics* – their mathematical 'pedagogical content knowledge'. This is a big ask, especially given the many demands already fighting for teachers' time and attention.

A secondary school mathematics department can be a difficult place to admit to gaps in your own mathematics knowledge.

A spirit of collaborative experimentation creates a culture in which it's OK to say:

- I never thought of that!

- I didn't know 68 per cent of 50 was equal to 50 per cent of 68!

- I've always wondered if there was a better way to explain that!

---

[8] **D.L. Ball et al.**, 'Content Knowledge for Teaching: What Makes it Special?', *Journal of Teacher Education* 59(5) (2008): pp. 389–407.

[9] **L.S. Shulman**, 'Those Who Understand: Knowledge Growth in Teaching', *Educational Researcher* 15(2) (1986): pp. 4–14.

[10] **L.S. Shulman**, 'Knowledge and Teaching: Foundations of the New Reform', *Harvard Educational Review* 57 (1987): pp. 1–22.

[11] **L. Darling-Hammond**, 'Teacher Learning that Supports Student Learning', *Educational Leadership* 55(5) (1998): pp. 6–11.

**M.M. Kennedy,** *op. cit.*

**Teacher professional activities in learning in East Asia and America**

**S.Y. Lee** 1998.[12]

**The study:** Shin-Ying Lee examined differences in pre-service and in-service professional activities of teachers.

**What it tells us:** She found that East Asian teachers had more opportunities to work together, prepare lessons, grade student work, and meet students individually than American teachers.

For a successful department-wide approach to the teaching of mathematics, serious consideration must be given to teacher development that goes beyond training about general pedagogy, such as behaviour management, or about specific learner needs, or curriculum changes, or any of the many other important areas that are relevant across the curriculum. Not only that, but this training must do more than simply develop teachers' mathematics subject knowledge.

A review of the research literature carried out by the Nuffield Foundation aimed 'to identify the issues that are fundamental to understanding children's mathematics learning'.[13] From these, they offer implications for classroom practice.

For example, from their research into learners' understanding of fractions, the team concluded that:

*Teaching should make it possible for students to:*

- *use their understanding of quantities in division situations to understand equivalence and order of fractions*

- *make links between different types of reasoning in division and measurement situations*

- *make links between understanding fractional quantities and procedures*

- *learn to use fractions to represent relations between quantities, as well as quantities.*[14]

---

[12] **S.Y. Lee**, 'Mathematics Learning and Teaching in the School Context: Reflections from Cross-Cultural Comparisons', in *Global Prospects for Education: Development, Culture, and Schooling*, edited by S.G. Garis and H.M. Wellman (Washington, DC: American Psychological Association, 1998), pp. 45–77.

[13] **T. Nuñes, P. Bryant and A. Watson**, *Key Understandings in Mathematics Learning* (London: Nuffield Foundation, 2009), p. 3.

[14] *Ibid.*, p.11.

The research synthesis made similar recommendations for the topics of whole numbers, relations, space, algebra and modelling. These provide a useful starting point for departmental work on developing subject and pedagogic content knowledge.

 **Try this in the classroom**

Choose a topic that you have recently taught or will be teaching in the near future. Ask your colleagues to read the relevant papers from *Key Understanding in Mathematics Learning*. Where does it give evidence for a practice that's already established? Did the recommendations challenge any of your existing classroom practice?

However rich your discussions in putting together your scheme of work, most written schemes will record mathematical content such as 'compare and order fractions, decimals and mixed numbers', but find it harder to convey what students will learn about what mathematics is, or about what it is to be mathematical. It's very difficult to list these kinds of awareness and skills. Instead, they emerge as a result of discussion and collaboration with colleagues.

In planning professional development opportunities, you can go some way to supporting colleagues with considering these less tangible skills through activities such as doing mathematics together, discussing student learning, co-planning, trialling and reflecting on lessons.

 **Discuss**

Paul Halmos argues that: 'A teacher who is not always thinking about solving problems – ones he does not know the answer to – is psychologically simply not prepared to teach problem solving to his students.'[15]

Do you agree?

Teachers' own mathematics knowledge can affect student success. For example, it has been suggested that mathematics teachers in high-performing China may have a more profound understanding of mathematics than those in the United States.[16]

---

[15] **P. Halmos,** *I want to be a Mathematician: An Automathography* (New York, NY: Springer-Verlag, 1985), p. 322.

[16] **L. Ma,** *Knowing and Teaching Elementary Mathematics: Teachers' Understanding of Fundamental Mathematics in China and the United States* (Mahwah, NJ: Lawrence Erlbaum Associates, 1999).

Every year, term, week and lesson, teachers' knowledge of mathematics content and pedagogy should be increasing. The best professional development is focused on teachers' knowledge of subject content and how students learn it.

Mathematics teachers sometimes give themselves a hard time about this. There are plenty of successful English teachers who are not amateur poets and essayists, and I know numerous highly effective modern foreign language teachers who developed a good level of fluency with a second language at university and have seen no need to take things further since.

This is not to say that these practitioners' practice would not be improved still further through continued study of the subject they teach, only that mathematics teachers should not feel guilty if they choose not to spend every spare minute on recreational mathematics.

It might be constructive to move away from consideration of extremes – teachers engaging in no mathematics at all versus teachers passionate about puzzles and on a perpetual quest to learn mathematics – and think about what can be achieved in the small amount of time teachers have in the working week.

If the mathematics team is to spend a little time each week or fortnight working individually or collectively on mathematics, what mathematics might they most profitably engage with?

 **Discuss**

- Should teachers tackle the tasks they will set their students, or more challenging problems to which they do not yet know the solution?

- Should teachers focus on their own mathematical thinking when doing mathematics, or think about the different approaches their students are likely to take?

- Should discussion focus on the experience of learning the mathematics, or consider ideas for teaching it?

There is no single right answer to each of these questions. They merit consideration and discussion as a department.

Throughout this book, each mathematical task has been accompanied by a 'Preparing to teach – do the mathematics!' box. In the box below, you can find some guidance as to the questions it's generally useful to ask yourself when preparing to use a mathematical task with learners.

**Preparing to teach – do the mathematics!**

In preparing to teach a mathematical task, you might consider the following points:

- What key vocabulary does this task require? What language structures might deepen student understanding? How can the ideas discussed in Chapter 9 be applied here?

- What are the affordances and constraints of the representations (whether concrete, pictorial, or abstract) offered by the task? Is there scope to introduce additional representations that would deepen students' conceptual understanding? How can the principles of deepening conceptual understanding, related in Chapter 7, be put into practice?

- In what ways does this task already scaffold students' learning? Might some students need additional support? What form might that take? What is already challenging about this task? How could the level of challenge be increased to deepen students' understanding of this content?

- How does this task foster mathematical thinking? What opportunities are there to use the techniques for deepening mathematical thinking described in Chapter 8?

The teacher-led whole-class teaching model used in Japanese and Chinese classrooms has meant that teachers give considerable thought, preparation and reflection to their exposition and modelling, which enhances their subject knowledge.[17]

# Change is possible

School leadership has the second-largest impact on student outcomes after teacher quality.[18] In every school I've worked with where a high proportion of students have excelled with mathematics, the key to success has been down to leadership. This includes the leadership of the school's headteacher, of the senior team, of the head of mathematics and, in many cases, of another

---

[17] **H.W. Stevenson and S.Y. Lee**, 'The East Asian Version of Whole-class Teaching', *Education Policy* 9 (1995): pp. 152–168.

[18] **K. Leithwood *et al.***, *Review of Research: How Leadership Influences Student Learning* (Center for Applied Research and Educational Improvement, University of Minnesota, 2004). http://hdl.handle.net/11299/2035 accessed 21 August 2017.

key individual who is championing transformative teaching and learning in mathematics.

In every case of a school transforming achievement through mastery, the mathematics department exhibits strengths across these three areas:

- *Buy-in:* their commitment to transforming achievement and belief in the potential of every learner.

- *Clarity:* their alignment around a shared vision for teaching and learning.

- *Training:* the high-quality professional development and learning they engage in.

In some cases, these three areas are strengths across the school. High expectations are prevalent, with a culture of discussing and experimenting with teaching approaches. The school leadership prioritises the necessary time, money and leadership to provide high-quality training. These strengths have been shown to result in schools becoming highly effective.[19]

You may be in the lucky position of leading the mathematics department of a school that enjoys a universal emphasis on scholarship and a shared commitment for teachers to support one another to develop. I very much hope that you are, as they can be such exciting places to work, with students truly benefiting from really effective teaching.

But please don't despair if you feel you aren't in such a privileged position – such a culture can be developed within the mathematics team.[20] It is generally accepted that it is the subject department that most closely affects what is taught and how it is taught,[21] so you have a real opportunity to make a difference.

---

[19] **B. Mulford, H. Silins and K. Leithwood,** *Educational Leadership for Organisational Learning and Improved Student Outcomes* (Dordrecht: The Netherlands: Kluwer, 2004). B. Mulford and H. Silins, 'Revised Models and Conceptualisation of Successful School Principalship that Improves Student Outcomes', *International Journal of Educational Management* 25(1) (2011): pp. 61–82.

[20] **A. Watson and E. De Geest,** 'Secondary Departments Making Autonomous Change', *Proceedings of BCME* (2010), pp. 130 ff. www.bsrlm.org.uk/wp-content/uploads/2016/02/BSRLM-IP-30-1-30.pdf accessed 21 August 2017.

[21] **L.S. Siskin,** *Realms of Knowledge: Academic Departments in Secondary Schools* (London: Falmer, 1994).

## A mathematics department can make a difference

 Evidence

**A. Watson and E. De Geest** 2010.[22]

**The study:** Three mathematics departments were studied by Anne Watson and Els De Geest as they went through autonomous change.

Before the three departments began their work to transform achievement, most lessons took the form of a starter, main and plenary with defined, small-scale learning targets, although some more varied teaching approaches were used from time to time. The majority of lessons included demonstrations of techniques or concepts, followed by individual or pair work on questions.

All departments included core members who overtly learned together. Several members of each team were well informed, read professional literature and sought research-based approaches to teaching.

**What it tells us:** The departments made a number of changes. They focused on key ideas in mathematics and/or mathematical thinking (albeit defined in different ways by different teachers). They had a culture of frequent, informal discussions about teaching mathematics. They all provided protected timetabled time for co-planning where possible.

Over the two years of the self-initiated change, the study found that 'departments shifted from talking about tasks and activities as if they would somehow "deliver" learning to developing focused teaching approaches'. Planning centred around discussion of parallel groups and also vertical planning, so that students' experience would be coherent year-on-year.

At the end of three years (during which the national proportion of students achieving at least level 5 rose by just one percentage point from 71 to 72 per cent) two of the schools saw significant improvements in attainment, and in the third school, results were steady against a whole-school background of a fall in results.

The impact on attainment of the three departments in this study demonstrates how, regardless of the wider school context, it is possible for mathematics teams to make a difference to student achievement.[22]

Success with the mastery approach comes down to the extent to which the entire mathematics department develops buy-in, clarity and high-quality training.

---

[22] **A. Watson and E. De Geest**, *op. cit.*

In your leadership of the mathematics department, you can take significant control of these three important levers – you can establish shared goals and expectations, agree on effective teaching practices and lead teacher learning and development.

To maximise the impact of any courses, conferences, articles and networks you and your team engage with, you need to think carefully about how they will cohere with and contribute to these three levers. To bring about real change, you need to form a coherent plan for developing the culture, alignment and practice of your team over time.

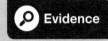

## Three key levers: commitment to goal, shared theory of teaching and teacher development

**V. Robinson** 2011.[23]

**The study:** Viviane Robinson identified five leadership practices associated with increased learning and well-being of students, in a meta-analysis of school leadership.

**What it tells us:** While there are no hard-and-fast rules about how to interpret effect sizes in educational research, an effect of 0.2 is usually considered small, 0.4 a moderate effect and 0.6 and above a large effect.

The three practices with the largest effect size were found to be:

- establishing goals and expectations (effect size 0.42)

- having a defensible and shared theory of effective teaching that forms the basis of a coherent teaching programme with collective teacher responsibility for student learning (effect size 0.42)

- leading teacher learning and development (effect size 0.84).

The two lower-impact practices identified were 'resourcing strategically' and 'ensuring an orderly and safe environment', which are perhaps more appropriately tackled at a whole-school than a departmental level.

The three levers that emerged from the meta-analysis mesh with the three we identified on page 231 – buy-in, clarity and training. Establishing goals and expectations is about buy-in. The shared theory of effective teaching

---

[23] **V. Robinson**, *Student-Centered Leadership* (San Francisco, CA: Jossey-Bass, 2011).

**J. Hattie**, *Visible Learning: A Synthesis of Over 800 Meta-analyses Relating to Achievement* (London: Routledge, 2009).

**233**

translates to clarity. Leading teacher learning and development is what our third lever – training – is all about.

These three levers frame our discussion in this chapter. We begin with buy-in. How can you build a team-wide commitment to achievement for every single student, no matter what their background or prior attainment?

We then look at the importance of getting all mathematics teachers, and all members of the senior team, on the same page regarding what they want teaching to look like.

The chapter culminates in consideration of how to develop mathematics teachers' subject knowledge and further improve their teaching. No matter where in the world you're working, professional development is the key to transforming achievement (emphasised by the OECD[24]).

# Buy-in: share a commitment to enjoyment and achievement

It has repeatedly been shown that high expectations of learning are a critical factor in successful professional development projects.[25] Teaching for mastery requires a commitment to achievement for every single student, no matter what their background or prior attainment.

A whole-school focus on achievement has been shown to be vital in highly effective schools. Success doesn't just come from the belief that every child can achieve, it's about being determined that this belief will become a reality.

Robust monitoring of the performance of individual students[26] and evaluation of school performance[27] have been shown to be important features of

---

[24] **A. Schleicher**, *Building a High-Quality Teaching Profession: Lessons from Around the World* (Paris: OECD Publishing, 2011).

[25] **H.S. Timperley**, 'Instructional Leadership Challenges: The Case of Using Student Achievement Information for Instructional Improvement', *Leadership and Policy in Schools* 4(1) (2005): pp. 3–22.

**S. Nickerson and G. Moriarty**, 'Professional Communities in the Context of Teachers' Professional Lives: A Case of Mathematics Specialists', *Journal of Mathematics Teacher Education* 8 (2005): pp. 113–140.

**A. Watson and E. De Geest**, 'Principled Teaching for Deep Progress: Improving Mathematical Learning Beyond Methods and Materials', *Educational Studies in Mathematics* 58 (2005): pp. 209–234.

[26] **P. Mortimore *et al.*,** *School Matters: The Junior Years* (Salisbury: Open Books, 1988).

[27] **D.H. Hargreaves and D. Hopkins**, *The Empowered School: The Management and Practice of Development Planning* (London: Cassell, 1991).

effective schools. Such monitoring and evaluation are beneficial only where expectations remain high, and the focus is on how teaching can be altered to ensure all succeed, rather than on labelling certain students as destined for failure.

## Successful professional communities share a belief that every student can learn

 **Evidence**

**S. Nickerson and G. Moriarty** 2005.[28]

**The study:** Susan Nickerson and Gail Moriarty led a professional development project with urban schools in the United States. The project goal was to increase teachers' mathematics content knowledge and to help them improve in practice.

They studied the characteristics of those communities which lasted beyond the project. Using two contrasting school sites as examples, they describe five aspects of the teachers' individual and collective professional lives that influenced the emergence of teachers' professional communities.

**What it tells us:** The professional communities who sustained their effort over time were influenced by:

- leadership
- relations within the institution
- respect for each other's knowledge
- expectations that every child can learn.

High expectations – shared across the team – are vital to significantly improve teachers' practice and students' learning.

## Team not keen?

There's no need to rush. If several members of your department are reluctant to adopt a mastery approach wholesale, try starting with small but visible changes that make a positive difference, such as using a bar model representation when teaching learners to calculate a fraction of an amount, or trying out the same 'think, pair, share' task with all groups in a given year group. As these small 'wins' accumulate, your colleagues will become more open to trying out new things.

---

[28] **S. Nickerson and G. Moriarty**, *op. cit.*

If you try something and it doesn't work or has unintended consequences, don't hide it. Failure is a learning experience for teachers, just as it is for students. Dealing effectively with setbacks is critical if change is going to be an accepted part of your team's culture.

Jumping in with both feet – trying to impose significant change on a team before its members are comfortable with new ideas and processes – may doom your adventures in mastery before they've even started.

Of the three dimensions of depth, multiple representations perhaps lends itself best to this kind of small-scale change. This may be because the change is (literally!) more visible than adopting strategies to improve language and communication, or mathematical thinking.

## Developing teaching for mastery 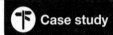 Case study

**The school context:** The team at Cramlington Learning Village, Northumberland, UK, thought carefully about when and how to introduce a mastery approach. They identified mathematics as a key area on their School Improvement Plan. Although Key Stage 3 had always been a strong focus for the school, GCSE (i.e., 16+) outcomes often took priority. The decision to teach mathematics for mastery saw the start of a clear emphasis on developing pedagogical approaches in Year 7. This is expected to quickly have an impact on teaching and learning across all years, and improve outcomes in the long term.

Central to the school's long-term emphasis on effective teaching is the timetabling of a weekly one-hour session every Wednesday after school. This is kept separate from the weekly department meeting for administrative matters. Teachers look together at key tasks for the following week's Year 7 lessons, 'doing the mathematics' and discussing possible questions and scope for additional challenge and scaffolding.

The Year 7 teaching team includes newly qualified teachers, non-specialists from other departments and experienced mathematics teachers. The school and department leadership have viewed this as an opportunity. The head of mathematics finds that the mix of experience has led to a positive environment for professional development sessions, with some teachers using them as a platform to develop their existing practice, and others as a starting point for teaching mathematics.

**Their impact:** Within the first term of this work, the senior leadership team member noticed positive feedback from staff and students. In particular, several experienced members of the mathematics team have embraced the opportunity to reflect on their mindset and try new classroom approaches.

A learning walk through Year 7 lessons found students in all classes to be highly engaged with learning, and enjoying opportunities to use manipulatives, explain their reasoning and engage in problem solving. The mathematics team are finding that the mastery approach is supporting students who are not secondary-ready when joining the school, particularly boys, in accessing and engaging in mathematics. A student voice survey of over 240 respondents found that students have positive attitudes towards mathematics, and believe they have the opportunity to engage in problem solving.

## Why change? Where's the evidence?

The teaching approach described in this book is evidence-based by design. It begins with an ambition that every student will succeed in mathematics and a significant proportion will excel. It draws on worldwide effective practice, and on established research findings, to develop a coherent approach that will achieve this ambition.

Evidence of impact, then, can be seen as falling into three main types:

**1** evidence of high achievement in the countries which inspired this approach

**2** evidence for specific recommendations in the approach, such as use of concrete manipulatives, or student feedback

**3** evidence of impact of the *Mathematics Mastery* programme in UK schools.

An introduction to the evidence base for all three of these has been integrated throughout this book.

International comparisons have been drawn on, as relevant, in the preceding chapters. Case studies from schools implementing this programme have been included throughout the book.

In this section, I summarise key international high achievement. This section also includes early evidence of impact of the *Mathematics Mastery* programme. The intention here is to offer some indication that combining the specific, research-informed recommendations described in this book has the potential to transform student achievement.

In addition to the usual challenges of measuring the impact of any educational initiative,[29] a significant obstacle to evidencing the impact of a mastery approach stems largely from the very many ways that the term has been adopted and interpreted.

Although some attempts have been made to analyse the impact of 'mastery' approaches more broadly, it would be easy to overstate their relevance to the approach we're looking at here. The term 'mastery' as described in this book and elsewhere[30] shares some key ideas with previous uses of the word in education research, but there are also key differences.

'Mastery' approaches tend to emphasise the potential of every student, and spending longer on understanding key concepts. However, the term *mastery learning*, predominantly used in the United States, refers to programmes in which learners continue a cycle of studying and testing until the mastery criteria are met. Using the *mastery learning* method, all students must achieve a pre-specified level of mastery on one topic before they can progress to the next.

It is easy to confuse the mastery approach to teaching mathematics and the concept of *mastery learning* as used in the education literature. The toolkit from the UK Education Endowment Foundation (EEF) evaluates the evidence for the effectiveness of 'mastery'.[31] Although it acknowledges that there is a wide range of definitions of 'mastery', an overall definition of mastery is arrived at that is more aligned with 'mastery learning' than with the mastery approach as defined here. This developed from ideas in American schools in the 1920s, and was revived in the form of programmed instruction in the late 1950s.

The EEF looks at approaches that break subject matter and learning content into units with clearly specified objectives that are pursued until they are achieved. Students work through each block of content in a series of sequential steps. They must demonstrate a high level of success on tests, typically at about the 80 per cent level. The Education Endowment Foundation review of the available meta-analyses of mastery learning is therefore of limited relevance to the mastery approach as defined here.

---

[29] For a clear summary of the threats to the conclusions commonly based on test scores, see **D. Koretz**, *Measuring Up: What Educational Testing Really Tells Us* (Cambridge, MA: Harvard University Press, 2008), pp. 316–317.

[30] For example, by the National Centre for Excellence in the Teaching of Mathematics in its short paper: www.ncetm.org.uk/public/files/19990433/Developing_mastery_in_mathematics_october_2014.pdf accessed 21 August 2017.

[31] https://educationendowmentfoundation.org.uk/evidence/teaching-learningtoolkit/mastery-learning accessed 21 August 2017.

## Evidence of international high achievement

International studies TIMSS and PISA offer us a broad-brush picture of mathematics education.

### Success in East and South-east Asian countries

**OECD** 2016.[32]

**The study:** The Programme for International Student Assessment (PISA) is a triennial international survey that aims to evaluate education systems worldwide by testing the skills and knowledge of 15-year-old students.

In 2015, over half a million students, representing 28 million 15-year-olds in 72 countries and economies, took the international PISA test. Students were assessed in science, mathematics, reading, collaborative problem solving and financial literacy.

**What it tells us:** According to the study, students from East and South-east Asian countries such as Singapore, Japan, South Korea and China are, on average, up to three years ahead in mathematics compared with 15-year-olds in England.

Of course, international comparisons are not without their shortcomings.[33] There are differences between jurisdictions in the extent to which the curriculum content matches that of the test. There are differences in the extent to which schools and students feel the tests are important. The sampling methods used differ from jurisdiction to jurisdiction, although the TIMSS and PISA surveys address sampling error by emphasising that we should only be interested in differences among the means which are large enough to be statistically significant.[34] The problematic aspects of these studies mean that they should be interpreted with caution.[35]

[32] **OECD**, *PISA 2015 Results (Volume I): Excellence and Equity in Education* (Paris: OECD Publishing, 2016). DOI: *http://dx.doi.org/10.1787/9789264266490-en* accessed 21 August 2017.

[33] **M. Brown**, 'The Tyranny of the International Horse Race', in *School Effectiveness for Whom? Challenges to the School Effectiveness and School Improvement Movements*, edited by R. Slee, G. Weiner and S. Tomlinson (London: Falmer Press, 1998), pp. 33–47.

[34] **D. Koretz**, *op. cit.*

[35] **H. Goldstein**, 'International Comparisons of Student Attainment: Some Issues Arising from the PISA Study', *Assessment in Education: Principles, Policy and Practice* 11(3) (2004): pp. 319–330.

Findings from TIMSS suggest that, while teaching has a significant effect on mathematical learning, international differences are explained primarily by differences in the match between curriculum and test items.

*All we can safely say (we hope) is that students do experience different types of instructional arrangements cross-nationally and the influence of these arrangements generically appears weak relative to such matters as prior learning and the contents of learning opportunities during the course of study.*[36]

With data from several sources, including several iterations of both PISA and TIMSS, we can see that some East Asian countries consistently score far above the rest.

### Early evidence for the *Mathematics Mastery* partnership programme

Evaluating any initiative in education is fraught with difficulties. It is almost impossible to control for school context and differences in quality of teaching, and there are threats to internal validity such as novelty, halo and Hawthorne effects.[37]

An additional challenge for the *Mathematics Mastery* secondary programme is its relative youth – the programme only began to work with teachers of Year 7 (11- and 12-year-old) students in 25 schools in 2012. These students have not yet taken their GCSE (16+) exams, let alone made decisions about studying mathematics post-16, or had the opportunity to demonstrate any long-term impact of the mastery approach on the depth of their understanding.

The *Mathematics Mastery* programme began as a project funded by the Education Endowment Foundation, so evaluation of the approach was built in from the start. Although it is evaluation over the long term – including, but absolutely not restricted to, GCSE results – that will give the most insight into the approach's effectiveness, the EEF also commissioned an independent evaluation to look at the effects of adopting a mastery approach in the first year.

---

[36] **L. Burstein**, ed., *The IEA Study of Mathematics III: Student Growth and Classroom Processes* (Oxford: Pergamon Press, 1992), p. 278.

[37] **D. Ary et al.**, *Introduction to Research in Education* (Belmont, CA: Cengage Learning, 2014).

### *Mathematics Mastery* programme impact in the first year

**J. Jerrim and A. Vignoles** 2015.[38]

**The study:** An independent, randomised controlled trial funded by the Education Endowment Foundation (EEF) found that the *Mathematics Mastery* programme had a positive effect on student attainment after its first year.

In their working paper series, independent evaluators John Jerrim of the University of London's Institute of Education and Anna Vignoles of the University of Cambridge report on this EEF study of *Mathematics Mastery*.

The study involved 10,114 students, from 127 schools. The schools were randomly assigned to receive the treatment and implement the *Mathematics Mastery* programme, or to join the control group. Sixty-two schools received the treatment, and 65 were allocated to the control.

**What it tells us:** The study found evidence of a positive impact. On average, students in classes where the approach was used made one additional month's progress in the school year compared with similar classes without the programme.

At secondary, the study used a test where 40 per cent of the items were likely to have been covered in 'control' schools, but were not taught to students in the 'treatment' schools. *Mathematics Mastery* students matched the control group on areas not yet covered within the *Mathematics Mastery* programme curriculum. On topics included on the curriculum, 'treatment' students outscored the control group on 90 per cent of topics. This suggests that aspects of the approach – such as more time on key topics, use of representations, higher expectations or an emphasis on problem solving – may improve student learning.

The schools involved reported that students felt more confident about applying their mathematics and more successful.

As well as improving learning outcomes for covered content, the EEF study suggests that students' capacity to tackle unknown mathematics may be improved by the programme. This will be an interesting area to explore in future research.

---

[38] **J. Jerrim and A. Vignoles**, 'The Causal Effect of East Asian "Mastery" Teaching Methods on English Children's Mathematics Skills', Department of Quantitative Social Science working paper series (2015).

The EEF also funded a trial of the *Mathematics Mastery* programme at primary level. The findings from the primary and secondary trials were combined. The meta-analysis was of one trial with Year 1 students, using an arithmetic test, and another trial with Year 7 students, using a different test with wider curriculum coverage. When the two studies' results are combined, the results are statistically significant. However, the number of students and the effect size at secondary are not great enough for the secondary study to be statistically significant on its own.

The high performance of overseas jurisdictions that expect success in mathematics for all mainstream students, teach for deep understanding, and hold solving problems to be the ultimate aim of teaching and learning mathematics, is inspiring. The early, tentative findings of the impact of the *Mathematics Mastery* partnership programme are encouraging. However, the most important evidence of impact is the evidence for an individual school, class or student. Planning to evaluate impact is therefore a key part of leading any departmental change in practice.

## Evaluating impact

### How will you know your mastery approach is working?

What are your priorities right now? If they're getting your team excited about mastery, thinking through what to change when, and getting started, you're not unusual. Once you've decided a mastery approach is right for your school, you understandably want to get cracking!

But in six weeks, a term, a year, or five years, how will you be sure that your hard work is paying off? How will you know that your mastery approach is working? The mastery approach is a long-term approach to transforming achievement in mathematics, and it's important not to chase short-term goals. That said, if you select the right outcome measure, it's possible to check for positive impact without introducing adverse short-term targets. Impact on student learning is what adopting a mastery approach is all about, so it's important to design and evaluate your professional development programme in terms of impact on students.

It is always difficult to attribute one specific organisational initiative to an improvement in attainment, but without an evaluation plan it will be even harder. Adding in evaluation methods after the mastery approach has been running for a time is almost impossible, so it's important to design a systematic evaluation from the start.

Earlier in this chapter, we looked at evaluations of mastery approaches that have taken place across large groups of schools and been led by full-time researchers, mostly as randomised controlled trials. Such evaluations can be useful – they provide a robust estimate of an approach's average effectiveness.

However, the average effect of teaching for mastery will not always match its impact in a given school. An approach may be more effective in some contexts than in others.

In order to determine whether or not the changes you're making are having the impact that you hoped for in your setting, you will need to carry out your own school-based evaluation.

Before making changes in your department, make a plan. You'll find useful support with this on the Education Endowment Foundation website. Here's a quick guide to getting started, based on its guidance.[39]

**1** *Frame your research question*

Identify the question you are going to investigate as clearly as possible. For example:

- What impact does spending more time on fewer topics in Year 7 have on students' mathematics attainment?

- What impact does using bar models have on Year 9 students' attainment in proportional reasoning?

- What impact does including a talk task in every Year 8 lesson have on students' attitudes to learning mathematics?

You need to state three things – what is being changed (the 'choice'), what 'outcome' will be measured, and the 'context' – which students will be involved.[40] If you are particularly interested in impact on a specific group – for example, students who were previously lower-attaining-you may want to focus on them.

**2** *Decide on an outcome measure*

Your outcome measure may involve student attitudes, take-up of mathematics post-16, or depth of understanding of a particular topic. However, with a focus on student achievement, it is likely that one, if not all, of your outcome measures will be academic.

---

[39] **R. Coe and S. Kime**, *DIY Evaluation Guide* (Endowment Education Foundation, 2013).

[40] **M.Q. Patton**, *Utilization-Focused Evaluation: The New Century Text* (3rd ed.) (Thousand Oaks, CA: Sage, 1997).

There are three main possibilities for outcome measures:

- national assessments

- standardised tests from reputable suppliers

- design your own.

A discussion of the advantages and disadvantages of each of these is beyond the scope of this book; the EEF site[41] offers a useful summary.

**3** *Construct your comparison group*

There are three broad categories for establishing a comparison group:

- random allocation

- matching

- simple comparison.

*Random allocation* involves half the students receiving the new approach, and half not, at random. This is the most robust option but is often not very practical. *Simple comparison*, where the attainment of the study group is compared with the attainment of students in a previous cohort or another school, is much more practical, but considerably less robust.

*Matching* offers a compromise. Creating a matched comparison group involves matching similar students to the students in your intervention group who do not receive the intervention. The matched students may be taken from a different school or from a different cohort of students. It is important to match students on important characteristics that might affect their progress such as prior attainment, gender or special educational needs and disabilities. One important tool in creating a matched comparison group is the 'pre-test'.

**4** *Make the changes!*

It's important to record in advance what you plan to change and to record, as you go, what actually happens.

**5** *Carry out a post-test and analyse the results*

Use the test you planned, and analyse the results. The EEF website offers support with this stage.[42]

---

[41] https://educationendowmentfoundation.org.uk/tools/diy-guide/your-measure accessed 21 August 2017.

[42] https://educationendowmentfoundation.org.uk/tools/diy-guide/analysis accessed 21 August 2017.

# Clarity: agree a shared understanding of effective teaching and learning

Before we look at the principles underpinning effective professional development, which are in the section on training, let's take some time to consider what your team is aiming towards.

 **Consider**

When you hear a colleague talking about a lesson, or you pop into their classroom, what do you consider 'successful' or 'effective' teaching and learning?

We saw at the start of the chapter how it was vital to have 'a defensible and shared theory of effective teaching that forms the basis of a coherent teaching programme'.[43]

You may want to use the lesson observation guidelines at the end of this book as a starting point for developing your department's shared understanding of effective teaching and learning.

 **Consider**

In your school, are there clear, shared expectations around what *teaching for mastery* looks like, which are consistently adhered to when teaching is being *observed*?

- Do senior leaders and mathematics leads regularly teach mathematics with a mastery approach?

- Is there a schedule of observations and clear guidelines for observation and feedback?

- Can all senior leaders explain expectations of mathematics teaching to external observers?

As you lead the adoption of a mastery approach in your department, your work will be framed by your school's approach to student grouping, assessment and intervention, and by the extent to which your department is obliged to work within them.

---

[43] **V. Robinson**, *op. cit.*

**Consider**

What room for manoeuvre do you have with regard to schemes of work, assessment, setting and intervention?

The context in which you are leading your department – wider school culture and policies, anticipated inspections, local authority or multi-academy trust guidance – may in effect seem to be imposing: setting; objective-led lessons; target-setting; regular testing; a 'coverage' approach to the curriculum; and a lesson format of three parts: starter, main teaching, and plenary evaluation against the objective.

Arguably, a 'pure' mastery approach involves:

- all students in each year group following the same scheme of work

- students with mixed prior attainment being taught together

- ongoing formative assessment to assess the depth of students' understanding, with formal written assessments once or at most twice a year

- same-day intervention to ensure all students keep up.

Depending on your own school context, you may decide to:

- adopt a mastery curriculum gradually, over time

- continue with existing setting policies and, if introducing mixed-attainment grouping, do so in Year 7 initially and work up over the years

- continue with current assessment policies

- continue with existing intervention systems.

In this section, we look at schemes of work, setting, assessment and intervention in turn, to inform your decision making about what to change and what to keep constant as you move towards a mastery approach with your team.

## Selecting or designing schemes of work

Schemes of work aligned to a mastery approach are available with published resources, are available free of charge online,[44] and can, of course, be created

---

[44] For example, www.mathematicsmastery.org, whiterosemathshub.co.uk and www. glowmathshub.com provide schemes of work designed for teaching for mastery.

from scratch. Each of these options is equally valid, and all can result in a highly effective curriculum for mastery.

A curriculum for mastery is one where every student is entitled to access key concepts and skills, where there are explicit connections between areas of mathematics, and where learning builds over time. The design principles of a mastery curriculum were explored in greater detail in Chapter 2. If you decide to use an existing scheme, acquaint yourself with Chapter 2 before making your selection. Make sure you are happy with the way your chosen scheme addresses each of the key features of a curriculum for mastery, and that you and your team understand this well enough to explain, justify and implement the scheme with integrity.

You may decide to develop your own scheme of work, either individually or with your team. In creating your own scheme, you miss out on the potential collaboration advantages of preparing to teach, on teaching, and on reviewing topics at the same time as teachers in other schools, and of course, it is a time-consuming process. That said, there is really no better way to really get your head around the rationale of a curriculum than to write it yourself.

> **◯ Discuss**
>
> In what ways does our current scheme of work promote mastery? Does it have any features that are a barrier to mastery?

If you do decide to go for it and plan your own, here are some pointers to get you started:

**1** *Start with the end.* For each of the three aims of teaching mathematics – as an academic discipline, as preparation for the workplace, and for life skills – make a list of the topics (the concepts and skills) students need to have learned by age 16. Group together any concepts or skills you are sure you would teach at the same time (for example, percentage increase with percentage decrease, addition of fractions with subtraction of fractions), but if in doubt, keep topics separate – though 'factors and multiples' and 'area and perimeter' have become common bedfellows, you may decide there are more advantages to working on them separately, at least initially, before making connections later.

**2** *Reality check.* For success in both academia and the workplace, students will need the qualifications as well as the understanding. Look at the requirements for A-level mathematics and check you've laid the groundwork. Look at the requirements for GCSE (i.e., 16+) mathematics and ensure you have the content covered.

**3** *Get things in order.* You may want to put each concept or skill on an index card for this part. Start by identifying any cards that you didn't need for the three aims, but which are on the exam syllabus or national curriculum. Put these towards the end of Year 11. Then look for those extremely connected topics, such as place value, which are linked to the vast majority of other topics. Put these towards the start of Year 7, so they can be practised and applied across the five years.

**4** *Think timings.* All topics do not deserve equal time. By investing time in the fundamentals – place value, additive relationships, multiplicative relationships, proportional reasoning – students will get their heads round later concepts and skills much more quickly and easily. Invest time in the big ideas at Key Stage 3 so your students have strong foundations for success at 16+ and beyond.

## All set for success?

The vast majority of secondary schools group students in attainment-based sets for learning mathematics.[45] Of these, some set only at the end of Year 7, say, or only for Key Stage 4. Of course, some mathematics teams choose to teach in mixed attainment groups right up to 16+.

 **Discuss**

What is the impact of our current departmental setting policy? Are we clear about the purpose of any setting or grouping by prior attainment? Are we realising the intended advantages?

Different teaching and learning approaches are experienced by different sets within the same year group.[46]

Reduced use of grouping by prior attainment can reduce the influence of socio-economic status on students' opportunities to learn.

---

[45] **D. Wiliam and H. Bartholomew**, 'It's Not Which School but Which Set You're In that Matters: The Influences of Ability Grouping Practices on Student Progress in Mathematics', *British Educational Research Journal* vol. 30 (2004): pp. 279–293.

[46] **P. Kutnick et al.**, *Pupil Grouping Strategies and Practices at Key Stage 2 and 3: Case Studies of 24 Schools in England, Report RR796* (London: Department for Education and Skills, 2006).

Setting has been shown time and time again to have negative effects on the mathematical learning of students with difficulties.[47] Setting students can lead to them achieving below their potential, as it can result in us:

- teaching students a limited number of concepts and skills

- lowering our expectations of students in lower sets

- giving students less choice and opportunity to work at their own pace.[48]

This is a social justice issue, as lower streams and sets tend to include disproportionate numbers of students of low socio-economic status, from particular ethnic minority groups, boys, and those born in the summer.[49] The justification for setting is based on the view that attainment is mainly determined by some innate ability, and that it is stable over time. Is this view realistic or is it defeatist?

## Lower set, less progress

**D. Wiliam and H. Bartholomew** 2004.[50]

**The study:** Dylan Wiliam and Hannah Bartholomew studied the impact of placement in sets on student outcomes. Between 1996 and 2000 they followed a cohort of 955 students, in six secondary schools in the

Greater London area, as they moved from Year 8 in 1996–97 to Year 11 in 1999–2000. All the students in the six schools were taught mathematics in mixed-ability groups in Year 7, but by Year 11, all the students were being taught in subject-specific ability groups or 'sets'.

**What it tells us:** Comparing students with the same Key Stage 3 scores, the study found that students placed in top sets averaged nearly half a GCSE grade higher than those in the other upper sets, who in turn averaged a third of a grade higher than those in lower sets, who in turn averaged around a third of a grade higher than those students placed in bottom sets.

---

[47] **J. Ireson and S. Hallam**, 'Raising Standards: Is Ability Grouping the Answer?', *Oxford Review of Education* 25(3) (1999): pp. 341–358.

**J. Boaler**, *Experiencing School Mathematics: Teaching Styles, Sex and Setting* (Buckingham: Open University Press, 1997).

[48] **J. Boaler, D. Wiliam and M. Brown**, 'Students' Experiences of Ability Grouping – Disaffection, Polarisation and the Construction of Failure', *British Educational Research Journal* 26(5) (2000): pp. 631–648.

[49] **S. Hallam and I. Toutounji**, *What Do We Know about the Grouping of Pupils by Ability?* (London: Institute of Education, 1996).

[50] **D. Wiliam and H. Bartholomew**, *op. cit.*

Many high-performing jurisdictions, Singapore for example, teach students in sets according to prior attainment, but seem to have few of the negative consequences. Perhaps it is not the structure of setting that is inherently damaging, but rather the mindset and behaviours this seems to encourage.

For example, it is possible that teachers of mixed-attainment groups feel more ownership over and responsibility for all the students in the class. If teachers feel they can make a case that an under-performing student is simply in the 'wrong set', they may feel less responsible for ensuring success for all.

 **Consider**

If your department currently teaches students in sets according to prior attainment, and a shift to mixed-attainment grouping is not on the cards, think about what you can do to:

- give all students access to the full curriculum
- give teachers 'ownership' of the groups they teach
- promote high expectations for every student
- encourage teaching methods that support success.

Consider other experiences students might have where they are grouped according to their prior performance. Perhaps there are A and B teams for football and other sports? Students allocated to the B team often find themselves motivated to try harder, improve their performance, and get promoted to the A team. Is there anything the mathematics department could learn from this?

### One curriculum

When teaching lower sets, there can be a strong temptation to repeat material from earlier years, and focus on areas of knowledge in which the students have previously failed.

International studies have shown that the two factors most strongly associated with growth in student achievement in mathematics are the proportion of students who have been taught the material contained in the tests, and the extent to which all students have access to the same curriculum.[51]

---

[51] **E. Kifer and L. Bursten**, 'Concluding Thoughts: What We Know, What it Means', in *The IEA Study of Mathematics III: Student Growth and Classroom Processes*, edited by L. Bursten (Oxford, UK: Pergamon, 1992), pp. 329–341.

If some students seem to be ahead of others at the start of Year 7, it is important to deepen the understanding of these students, and to give others of their age the chance to 'catch up'. By teaching all students in the same year group the same mathematics, right from the start, we can ensure that every student is able to keep up, with no one left behind.

### Aim high

Whether the students who have previously been lower-attaining are taught in a 'bottom set' or in a group with a mix of previous attainment, we must give consideration to what we really believe they are capable of.

Simply being told that they are teaching a set rather than a mixed-attainment group can affect how teachers teach.

## Variety of teaching approach can reduce with setting

**J. Boaler and J. Greeno** 2000.[52]

**The study:** Jo Boaler and James Greeno analysed interviews with 48 high school students from six schools. The teachers of the six classes were experienced and well respected in their departments. The students had elected to take an advanced mathematics class and could all be regarded as successful students of mathematics.

The students were asked to describe mathematics lessons; they were asked about lessons they particularly liked and disliked, the extent of discussion in mathematics, and the nature of mathematical confidence.

**What it tells us:** The researchers found that teachers of sets employed a more restricted range of teaching approaches than they did when teaching groups of students with mixed prior attainment. This had a strong negative effect on students.

### Keep it complex

Breaking content down into increasingly less challenging, step-by-step, simplified, procedural activities has become an established approach for working with lower-attaining students. However, the TIMSS seven-nation comparative study shows that high-achieving countries adopt approaches

---

[52] **J. Boaler and J. Greeno**, 'Identity, Agency and Knowing in Mathematics Worlds', in *Multiple Perspectives on Mathematics Teaching and Learning,* edited by J. Boaler (Westport, CT: Ablex, 2000).

which *preserve* the complexity of concepts and methods for all students, rather than simplifying them.[53]

## Assessment

High-stakes national examinations place considerable pressures on schools, departments, teachers and students. We saw in Chapter 5 how a performance culture can develop in which over-frequent summative assessment distorts teaching and learning.

A particular challenge when introducing a new approach such as teaching for mastery is the tension between assessing in a way that is aligned with a curriculum for mastery, and assessing in a way that makes student attainment comparable with that of previous cohorts.

Many of the schools I have worked with have navigated this by using mastery curriculum-aligned assessments for any weekly or half-termly formative checks and standardised or national tests (or tests written in the style of national tests) termly or biannually. This has enabled staff to be confident that students are making greater progress with the mastery approach than previous cohorts have done prior to its implementation.

 **Discuss**

Does our assessment system support a mastery approach? How will we monitor student progress and achievement?

## Intervention

Secondary schools in England cannot continue to rely on on-to-one and small group interventions in the way they are at present. In recent years, a wealth of time and money has been committed to intervention programmes designed to help students 'get the grade'.

If we can redirect that energy and expense into radically improving the quality and consistency of teaching and learning in mathematics lessons, our dependence on intervention will reduce. The most successful mathematics improvement programmes are those that focus on changing daily teaching practices.[54] Heads of department and school leaders who work with teachers

---

[53] **J. Hiebert et al.**, *Teaching Mathematics in Seven Countries: Results from the TIMSS 1999 Video Study* (Washington, DC: US Department of Education National Center for Education Statistics, 2003).

[54] **R.E. Slavin, C. Lake and C. Groff**, 'Effective Programs in Middle and High School Mathematics: A Best Evidence Synthesis', *Review of Educational Research* 79(2) (2009): pp. 839–911.

to equip and empower them to teach for mastery can radically reduce their need to 'intervene'.

The evidence base on intervention in mathematics is patchy and less developed than the evidence base on literacy interventions, particularly in terms of comparing progress between different mathematics intervention schemes. Interventions work best when they are targeted on an individual student's weaknesses;[55] the most efficient way of doing this is to directly tackle such 'weaknesses' as and when they crop up in the classroom. From my experience of schools in the UK and abroad, the most effective interventions seem to be those that take place on the same day as the lesson.

 **Discuss**

Do our approaches to intervention support a growth mindset? Might targeted and focused sessions for students identified using formative assessment be more effective than fixed long-term intervention classes?

In Shanghai, for example, mathematics is taught at the start of the day, so that work can be marked and intervention given the same day to students who need it. We may not have the luxury of daily non-contact time to review students' work, but you may be able to find a way to organise same-day interventions. This means finding innovative ways to guarantee time for each mathematics teacher to work with a small number of students on mathematics *every day*. For example, you might be able to take a creative approach to the use of afternoon registration, break or lunch times, or after-school clubs. Perhaps additional adults, such as learning support assistants, could take on some pastoral responsibilities, freeing qualified mathematics teachers to work with the students who most need it?

Alternatively, if this option is impractical in your current school context, you might want to think differently about how you use the lesson time allocated to mathematics. Twenty minutes, once or twice a week, might be carved out of lesson time. While the rest of the class engage in deliberate practice, the teacher can work with a small group of students who would benefit from additional input.

In this section, we have established the importance of a shared understanding of effective teaching and learning, and clarified the parameters of curriculum, student grouping, assessment and intervention. We conclude with a section on professional development.

---

[55] **A.D. Dowker**, *What Works for Children with Mathematical Difficulties?* (London: DfES, 2004).

# Training: high quality, coherent opportunities for teachers to learn

To transform achievement in mathematics in your school, you need to provide your colleagues with high-quality, coherent opportunities to learn. Teaching quality is one of the main determinants of learning, with at least three times the effect on student achievement as any other factor.[56]

Several significant reviews are available on the evidence of the impact of teacher professional development on students' learning. These literature reviews consistently lament the lack of research into the impact of teachers' professional development on students' learning outcomes. What research there is shows that the right kinds of professional development can produce great benefits for students. Unfortunately, the studies also conclude that most of the professional development that teachers undertake is not of this kind.[57]

The suggestions and approach offered in this chapter are supported by the Department for Education for England and Wales's guidelines on effective professional development, which recommend that professional development should:

- have a clear focus on improving and evaluating student outcomes

- be underpinned by robust evidence and expertise

- include collaboration and expert challenge

---

[56] **J. Hattie**, *Teachers Make a Difference: What is the Research Evidence?* (Australian Council for Educational Research, October 2003).

**S.G. Rivkin, E.A. Hanushek and J.F. Kain**, 'Teachers, Schools, and Academic Achievement', *Econometrica* 73(2) (2005): pp. 417–458.

**T.J. Kane** et al., 'Have We Identified Effective Teachers? Validating Measures of Effective Teaching Using Random Assignment', research paper, MET Project (Bill & Melinda Gates Foundation, 2013). www.metproject.org/downloads/MET_Validating_Using_Random_Assignment_Research_Paper.pdf accessed 21 August 2017.

[57] **K.S. Yoon** *et al.*, *Reviewing the Evidence on How Teacher Professional Development Affects Student Achievement (Issues & Answers Report, REL 2007–No. 033)* (Washington, DC: US Department of Education, Institute of Education Sciences, National Center for Education Evaluation and Regional Assistance, Regional Educational Laboratory Southwest, 2007). Retrieved from http://ies.ed.gov/ncee/edlabs/regions/southwest/pdf/rel_2007033.pdf accessed 21 August 2017.

**R.C. Wei** *et al.*, *Professional Learning in the Learning Profession: A Status Report on Teacher Development in the United States and Abroad* (Dallas, TX: National Staff Development Council, 2009).

**P. Cordingley and M. Bell**, *Understanding What Enables High Quality Professional Learning: A Report on the Research Evidence* (Centre for the Use of Research Evidence in Education (CUREE); Pearson School Improvement, 2012).

- be sustained over time

- be prioritised by school leadership.[58]

The positive impact of working in a whole-school environment that supports collaborative experimentation is becoming increasingly well documented.

The importance of establishing a school-wide community of professional learners has been recognised in England by the Department for Education's Standard for Teachers' Professional Development:

> *Effective professional development for teachers is a core part of securing effective teaching. It cannot exist in isolation, rather it requires a pervasive culture of scholarship with a shared commitment for teachers to support one another to develop so that pupils benefit from the highest quality teaching. The thousands of professional decisions that must be made every day need to be informed by the best evidence, knowledge and professional wisdom.*[59]

The professional development that makes the most difference to teachers is:

(a) *active* and classroom-based, with opportunities to try things out and discuss them with peers

(b) *supported* by effective school leadership with external feedback and networks to improve and sustain

(c) *sustained* over at least two terms, with at least 15 contact hours, preferably 50.

Let's take a look at the evidence base and rationale behind each of these three features.

## Active: the power of collaborative experimentation

Learning through practice should be a key feature of professional development. There is evidence that East Asian countries have recognised this need more effectively than their Western counterparts.

Japanese teachers have a relatively high involvement in developing their national curriculum. They are also typically involved in researching how

---

[58] **Department for Education**, *Standard for Teachers' Professional Development: Implementation Guidance for School Leaders, Teachers, and Organisations that Offer Professional Development for Teachers* (Department for Education, 2016). www.gov.uk/government/uploads/system/uploads/attachment_data/file/537031/160712_-_PD_Expert_Group_Guidance.pdf accessed 21 August 2017.

[59] *Ibid.*

to teach.[60] Their approach to classroom-based action research has often been referred to as lesson study.[61] In this approach, teachers work with their colleagues to develop, revise, demonstrate and share their teaching ideas.[62]

Teachers in China also tend to spend comparatively large amounts of time thinking about how to improve their teaching. Class contact time in Shanghai is dramatically lower than in the UK, at between 25 and 30 per cent, although classes are larger, with 40 or more students.[63] The Grattan Institute estimated that Shanghai teachers spend an average of 10–12 hours teaching per week.[64]

Much of the resulting non-contact time is used to work with students in various ways. Teachers run extension classes and give students individual support. But there is also time for considered planning and preparation. Because teacher planning and preparation do not have to be fitted into evenings and weekends, teachers can plan collaboratively.[65]

Discussion time is built into the day, especially the collaborative planning of lessons. The focus is on ensuring student progression and the development of knowledge through the careful organisation of the topic to be taught. Teachers engage in group planning. Because they have only two or three classes to teach, their preparation and focus on these teaching groups is intense.

---

[60] **H.W. Stevenson and J.W. Stigler**, *The Learning Gap: Why our Schools are Failing and What We Can Learn from Japanese and Chinese Education* (New York, NY: Summit Books, 1992).

[61] **C. Fernandez and M. Yoshida**, *Lesson Study: A Japanese Approach to Improving Mathematics Teaching and Learning* (Studies in Mathematical Thinking and Learning) (Hillsdale, NJ: Lawrence Erlbaum Publishers, 2004).

[62] **H. Stevenson, S. Lee and R. Nerison-Low**, *The Educational System in Japan: Case Study Findings* (National Institute on Student Achievement, Curriculum, and Assessment, Washington, DC: US Department of Education, Office of Educational Research and Improvement, 1998).

[63] **National College for School Leadership**, *Report on Research into Maths and Science Teaching in the Shanghai Region*, research by National Leaders of Education and Subject Specialists in Shanghai and Ningbo, China 11–18 January 2013. https://www.gov.uk/government/uploads/system/uploads/attachment_data/file/340021/report-on-research-into-maths-and-science-teaching-in-the-shanghairegion.pdf accessed 21 August 2017.

[64] **B. Jensen et al.**, *Catching Up: Learning from the Best School Systems in East Asia* (Grattan Institute, 2012). https://grattan.edu.au/wp-content/uploads/2014/04/129_report_learning_from_the_best_main.pdf accessed 21 August 2017. This estimate was obtained via an interview with the Shanghai Municipal Education Commission in 2011.

[65] *Ibid.*

Classrooms in China seem to be often open for observation, study and discussion. To develop their teaching skills, teachers are expected to observe each other regularly. Non-judgemental observation, in which the observer takes on the role of learner, is widespread. These often involve collaborative planning, and group observation, with a focus on what all teachers involved can do to improve student learning in future.[66]

Although, as teachers, we often limit the definition of 'professional development' to attendance at courses, conferences and in-service training days, there is increasing evidence pointing to the importance of 'on the job' learning. [67]

It may be more helpful to consider professional development as encompassing all behaviours that are intended to effect change in the classroom. We might therefore adopt a definition of professional development such as that of Christopher Day:

*Professional development consists of all natural learning experiences and those conscious and planned activities which are intended to be of direct or indirect benefit to the individual, group or school, which contribute, through these, to the quality of education in the classroom.*

*It is the process by which, alone and with others, teachers review, renew and extend their commitment as change agents to the moral purpose of teaching; and by which they acquire and develop critically the knowledge, skills and emotional intelligence essential to good professional thinking, planning and practice with children, young people and colleagues throughout each phase of their teaching lives.*[68]

---

[66] **National College for School Leadership**, op. cit.

[67] See: **S. Edmonds and B. Lee**, 'Teacher Feelings about Continuing Professional Development', *Education Journal* 61 (2002): pp. 28–29; **D. Hustler *et al.***, *Teachers' Perspectives of Continuing Professional Development*, Department for Education and Skills Research Report No. 429 (London: Department for Education and Skills, 2003).

**C. Robinson and J. Sebba**, *A Review of Research and Evaluation to Inform the Development of the New Postgraduate Professional Development Programme* (TTA/University of Sussex, 2004).

[68] **C. Day**, *Developing Teachers: The Challenges of Lifelong Learning* (London: Falmer Press, 1999), p. 4.

[69] **B.R. Joyce and B. Showers**, *Student Achievement through Staff Development* (3rd ed.) (Alexandria, VA: Association for Supervision & Curriculum Development, 2002).

## The importance of experimentation

**B.R. Joyce and B. Showers** 2002.[69]

**The study:** Bruce R. Joyce and Beverly Showers review the research evidence to identify which forms of staff development produce the most substantial gains.

**What it tells us:** Their research shows that only one broad approach works: collaborative action research. They find that change in classroom practice requires teachers to experiment with new methods, and to discuss resulting difficulties with colleagues, along with other improvement issues. Otherwise, most teachers try ideas suggested in training only once or twice at best, and then revert to their usual practice.

The result is a continuous improvement model based on collaborative action research, with the teacher as researcher.

The researchers identify four important stages to this process:

1. Identify an agreed training need – one common goal to change curriculum, teaching methodology or student culture so as to improve student outcomes.

2. Design staff training to meet agreed outcomes for knowledge, attitudes, skills, and transfer to the classroom.

3. Deliver training, including studying the theory, demonstration or modelling, simulated practice and setting up peer coaching.

4. Peer coaching.

All learning requires time, practice and support, and the time for change to classroom practice is often underestimated. The research found that teachers must practise with a new method 20–25 times to learn to use it as effectively as their usual methods. The first few attempts with a new method may fail, and the teacher may then be tempted to abandon further experiments – this is where the support provided by peer coaching is so vital.

Over time, with support, teachers can adapt the methods to their context, learn to use them appropriately and successfully, and embed them into their practice.

Experimentation has been shown to significantly benefit a department's culture and ethos. As teachers experiment more, both their problem-solving skills and their morale improve. The team becomes more cohesive and responsive to challenges.

Many professional development programmes that have been linked with improved student outcomes are based in the learning teacher's own classroom.[70] Observation and feedback have been shown to be core features of effective professional development programmes.[71]

## Teacher collaboration

 Evidence

**A. Watson and E. De Geest** 2010.[72]

**What it tells us:** In their study of mathematics departments who raised achievement, Anne Watson and Els De Geest observed that:

- formal meetings were carefully planned

- departments discussed particular mathematical topics in depth at these meetings, and often this would include sharing ideas about what the important features were and how they related to other topics

- all departments did mathematics together, and this promoted pedagogic discussion best when the shared focus was on classroom tasks rather than on mathematics for personal professional development

- such discussions often revealed different perceptions of the subject matter; teachers would often review recent teaching and revise approaches for the future, and these discussions also revealed different perceptions of the subject matter

- meetings were not used as a conduit for management information. Organisational and information matters were dealt with by email or informally, not generally in meetings.

---

[70] **P. Cordingley** *et al.*, 'The Impact of Collaborative Continuing Professional Development (CPD) on Classroom Teaching and Learning. Review: How Do Collaborative and Sustained CPD and Sustained but Not Collaborative CPD Affect Teaching and Learning?', *Research Evidence in Education Library* (London: EPPI-Centre, Social Science Research Unit, Institute of Education, University of London, 2005).

[71] **P. Cordingley** *et al.*, 'The Impact of Collaborative Continuing Professional Development (CPD) on Classroom Teaching and Learning.', *Research Evidence in Education Library* (London: EPPI-Centre, Social Science Research Unit, Institute of Education, University of London, 2003).

[72] **A. Watson and E. De Geest** 2010, *op. cit.*

> The teamwork, internal networking, collaboration and use of knowledge from outside networking that took place in the departments appeared to have arisen because of the nature of the department meetings, which were collegial and professional rather than managerial and coercive.

A distinction can be made[73] between departments that are collections of people who sit in meetings together and departments that are communities. Teacher learning communities are not an end in themselves, but the means to raise student achievement, as Dylan Wiliam points out.[74] A community of practitioners is a team which has 'organized themselves for action around a shared sense of purpose'.[75]

If you have already built, or are able to build, such a community, you can make a co-ordinated effort to improve students' learning, with collaborative professional learning and collective decision making.

### Teacher development in Hong Kong

The Education Bureau (EDB), universities, and other professional organisations in the Hong Kong Special Administrative Region of China offer a variety of professional development programmes and other continuing education opportunities for in-service teachers and heads of school to address changes in the curriculum and the ongoing demands of school.

The two major types of professional development programme are courses on enhancing the overall professional knowledge of teachers and courses related to key learning areas or subject-specific areas (including mathematics and science).

Several collaborative research and development projects related to key curriculum changes also are conducted in partnership with schools and consultants or universities. Although EDB does not have official requirements for teachers to participate in professional development activities, its Advisory Committee on Teacher Education and Qualifications has set a target of

---

[73] **P. Grossman, S. Wineburg and S. Woolworth**, 'Toward a Theory of Teacher Community', *Teachers College Record* 103(6) (2001): pp. 942–1012.

[74] **D. Wiliam**, 'Formative Assessment in Teacher Learning Communities', in *Ahead of the Curve: The Power of Assessment to Transform Teaching and Learning*, edited by D. Reeves (Bloomington, IN: Solution Tree, 2007), pp. 183–206.

[75] **W. Secada and L. Adajian**, 'Mathematics Teachers' Change in the Context of their Professional Communities', in *Mathematics Teachers in Transition*, edited by B.S. Nelson and E. Fennema (Hillsdale, NJ: Lawrence Erlbaum Publishers, 1997), pp. 193–219.

150 hours of professional development over a three-year period. In addition, some schools may advise their teachers to attend a certain number of professional development courses in each academic year.

 **Consider**

What formal and informal opportunities do you have for staff to share ideas and strategies for effective mathematics teaching? How might you promote informal sharing of ideas and strategies?

## Supported: professional learning needs support

Each of the three levers for successful change – commitment to high expectations, agreed direction of travel, and high-quality professional development – can be led at a departmental level. Whatever your role within the department, whether or not you have formal responsibility or remuneration for leading the teaching and learning of mathematics, you can make a difference.

You can inspire your colleagues to raise or adhere to their high expectations. You can facilitate discussion to define great mathematics teaching. You can lead and find high-quality training. But the difference you make will be significantly increased if you have the full support of your school's senior leadership.

In working with schools to adopt the mastery approach, I find some teachers are understandably hesitant about the practicalities initially. In particular, some teachers are concerned that adopting a curriculum for mastery, where all students in a year group are learning the same concepts and skills, will result in some students getting left behind, and others being held up.

Provided the school's leadership remains committed to differentiation through depth, over time teachers discover that they can bring in additional challenges with the same concepts, so it really does have a positive impact for each and every student. It takes time and effort for teachers to effectively differentiate for depth in this way. It is important that they are supported through this time of transformation.

Schools that have seen the greatest improvement in achievement through adopting a mastery approach have been those that explicitly set out to make clear that the mastery curriculum is not 'just another scheme'. The headteacher, senior team and head of mathematics in these schools are committed to teaching for mastery, and it is this dedication that enables them to change the minds of others in the school.

This change of mindset comes about through leaders running training in staff meetings, and through leaders actually being in the classroom and teaching or team teaching. Leaders' commitment to the approach, and to embedding it across the department over time, is key to its success. What makes departmental training effective is as much to do with its coherence and the continuity of its message over time as its content or delivery.

Before you start, the school's headteacher and senior team must be fully informed about, and supportive of, a mastery approach to mathematics, including the challenges you may have to overcome.

Let's revisit the three levers for success in implementing the mastery approach, and consider the senior leadership role in each.

**1** *Buy-in:* a commitment to achievement for every single student, no matter what their background or prior attainment.

Low expectations are almost always a self-fulfilling prophecy, and it takes time to transform achievement, so there will be periods during which teachers and students aim higher and feel they are failing. By celebrating successes and reaffirming the importance of believing in every student's potential, school leadership can ensure everyone stays committed.

Potential senior team blockers: making timetabling or staffing decisions that suggest that students with low prior attainment are being 'written off' because they're unlikely to achieve 'good' grades.

**2** *Clarity:* clear, shared expectations around what they want teaching to look like, which are consistently adhered to when teaching is being observed.

One very powerful senior team contribution is where a member of the senior team teaches mathematics, and proactively ensures that they teach a group that is part of the team's collaborative experimentation. This senior leader is then in a position to talk about the challenges they faced and how they overcame them, as well as sharing anecdotal impact from their own classroom.

*Ensuring teacher quality* is second only to *leading teacher learning and development* in the effect it has on student achievement.[76] Having committed to a mastery approach, it is vital that schools establish clear, shared

---

[76] Viviane Robinson's meta-analysis of research studies is described in **V. Robinson**, *Student-Centered Leadership* (San Francisco, CA: Jossey-Bass, 2011). The methodology is explained in this paper: **V.M.J. Robinson, C. Lloyd and K.J. Rowe**, 'The Impact of Leadership on Student Outcomes: An Analysis of the Differential Effects of Leadership Type', *Educational Administration Quarterly* 44(5) (2008): pp. 635–674.

expectations around what great mathematics teaching looks like in their school context.

Studies have shown the importance of the headteacher's role as 'leading professional', encompassing involvement in and knowledge about what goes on in the classroom, including the curriculum, teaching strategies, and monitoring student progress.[77] The evidence suggests that in schools where teachers report that their leadership is heavily involved in ensuring the quality of teaching, students do better.[78]

This is not simply a matter of insisting on more classroom visits, teacher observations or more discussion of teaching and learning at staff meetings. More classroom visits and teacher feedback can make matters worse if the feedback is based on an inaccurate theory of teaching quality.

School leaders need a defensible and shared theory of effective teaching that forms the basis of a coherent teaching programme in which there is collective rather than individual teacher responsibility for student learning and well-being.

Potential senior team blockers:

- insisting on certain teaching practices being consistently applied across the school that are contrary to a mastery approach

- giving feedback on high-stakes lesson observations that fails to positively reinforce (or, worse, explicitly criticises) the practices the department is working together to implement.

**3** *Training:* high-quality, coherent opportunities for teachers to learn.

Potential senior team blockers:

- Impeding access to external networks or training courses.

- Restricting time for the mathematics team to work collaboratively, or over-burdening the team with administrative tasks that dominate this time.

It is vital that you secure senior leadership support. One of the most effective ways of doing this is to arrange for them to visit a school where teaching for mastery is already established.

---

[77] For example, school effectiveness studies such as: **P. Mortimore *et al.***, *School Matters: The Junior Years* (Salisbury: Open Books, 1988); **M. Rutter *et al.***, *Fifteen Thousand Hours: Secondary Schools and their Effects on Children* (London: Open Books, 1979).

[78] **V. Robinson**, *op. cit.*

## *Using specialist support*

A core feature that has been linked to positive student outcomes is the use of external expertise alongside school-based activity.[79] Studies indicate that professional development activity supported by specialists tends to have a positive impact for students.[80] This professional development generally builds on what teachers already know and can do, lasts at least two terms, and involves collaboration between teachers. The role of the specialist in such projects is to introduce the relevant knowledge base, and to model, observe, give feedback, coach, and discuss.

It is well worth contacting any nearby higher education institutions to find out if they are conducting any research projects you might be able to get involved in. The cost of specialist time to support teaching tends to be built into the funding for research projects.

Another option is to find other local schools that are as committed to transforming achievement as you are, and to offer to swap specialists! That way, your team will have the benefit of hearing an external advocate for a pre-agreed component of the mastery approach, and you can offer to do the same for them. There can be something very reassuring about hearing some of the same beliefs and principles from someone beyond the immediate team and school.

Membership of the Association of Teachers of Mathematics[81] and the Mathematical Association[82] will give you access to journals, conferences and other events bringing mathematics teachers together.

## Sustained: professional development takes time

By definition, mastery takes place over time. It should come as no surprise, therefore, that adopting a department-wide approach to teaching and learning mathematics for mastery is far from a quick fix.

Studies have found that the most effective professional development lasts at least two terms – more usually a year or longer. More limited change on very specific learning tasks can be achieved through shorter-term interventions, but to transform general practice, longer duration seems key.

---

[79] See above references of research carried out by the Institute of Education.

[80] **P. Cordingley et al.**, *What Do Specialists Do in CPD Programmes for Which There is Evidence of Positive Outcomes for Pupils and Teachers?* (London: EPPI-Centre, Social Science Research Unit, Institute of Education, University of London, 2007).

[81] www.atm.org.uk

[82] www.m-a.org.uk

The need to commit to staff development over a sustained period is consistently reinforced by research findings. International reviews emphasise that:

> *School leaders must ensure that staff are given time to engage with longer term programmes – to cover not only a programme's initial input but also subsequent in-class experimentation and collaboration with colleagues. Leaders must support an approach to professional development in which staff are encouraged to focus strategically and meaningfully on particular areas of learning and practice over time.*[83]

## Collaboration and continuing professional development (CPD)

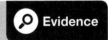 Evidence

**P. Cordingley *et al.* 2003.**[84]

**P. Cordingley *et al.* 2005.**[85]

**The study:** In a series of reviews of research literature, Philippa Cordingley and colleagues explored the impact of collaborative CPD on classroom teaching and learning.

**What it tells us:** Sustained and collaborative professional development has been shown to have a positive impact on teachers' range of teaching and learning strategies and their ability to match these to their students' needs. The research literature on professional development shows the importance of involving teachers in applying and refining new knowledge and skills and experimenting with ways of integrating them in their day-to-day practice. There is also some evidence that such professional development can result in a positive impact on student learning, motivation and outcomes. This suggests that we should embrace professional development opportunities that involve sustained collaboration, grounded in classroom observation and support.

It is vital that your team members experience a coherent programme of professional development. Colleagues might attend training courses to develop mathematics-specific skills and knowledge. They may participate in

---

[83] **P. Cordingley *et al.***, *Developing Great Teaching: Lessons from the International Reviews into Effective Professional Development* (Teacher Development Trust, 2015), p. 12.

[84] **P. Cordingley *et al.***, 'The Impact of Collaborative CPD on Classroom Teaching and Learning', *Research Evidence in Education Library* (London: EPPI-Centre, Social Science Research Unit, Institute of Education, University of London, 2003).

[85] **P. Cordingley *et al.***, 'The Impact of Collaborative CPD on Classroom Teaching and Learning', *Research Evidence in Education Library* (London: EPPI-Centre, Social Science Research Unit, Institute of Education, University of London, 2005).

conferences and events. You may subscribe to, and encourage your team to read, magazines, journals and other media, or engage in networks.

Through these activities over time, teachers in your team can become increasingly committed to achievement for every student, increasingly aligned with a shared vision for teaching and learning, and developing their classroom practice.

Such an impact is not the result of a day's training, reading an article, attending a conference, or any other one-off professional development opportunity. While these are all valuable activities, in isolation, none of them is likely to make a significant difference to the students your team teaches.

Rather, teachers work on a particular area of their practice through a longer-term programme, of which the impact in the short term should be seen as a positive indication that the longer-term experimentation and collaboration looks likely to reap rewards, rather than as an end-goal in itself.

This is not to say that one-day training courses are ineffective, as England's professional development standards explain:

> *Evidence suggests, for example, that a one-day course as a stand-alone activity without a specific focus is unlikely to have a lasting impact on pupil outcomes. That same course, however, could be used to much greater effect as part of a sustained, coherent programme which includes structured, collaborative in-school activities for teachers to refine ideas and embed approaches.*
>
> *A professional development programme is likely to involve many activities designed to sustain and embed practice, including, but not limited to: individual and collaborative teacher activity; well-designed formative assessment and evaluation; whole-school leadership; and expert input.*[86]

### Teacher development in Singapore

Singapore's Ministry of Education has placed great emphasis on teacher development over several decades. All teachers are entitled to 100 hours of professional development per year.

But arguably, it is not the quantity of the professional development teachers receive in Singapore that makes the difference. Rather, it is the coherence of their system, which means all parties are pulling in the same direction.

Singapore's National Institute of Education works closely with the ministry to provide training courses and advanced programmes, including master's

---

[86] **Department for Education**, *op. cit.*

and doctoral degrees. The ministry also provides specialised professional development courses to update teachers' content knowledge, and to update teachers on pedagogical innovations and new assessment modes in the teaching of mathematics and science.

The ministry also encourages the growth of a teacher-led culture of professional excellence and innovation among the teaching fraternity. In 2010, with this aim in mind, it established the Academy of Singapore Teachers. This teacher-led academy is tasked with fostering pedagogical leadership. It is focused on teacher collaboration in learning communities within schools and professional networks. It aims to strengthen the culture of teaching excellence and raise the standards of practice in the classroom and across Singapore's education system.

# Integrate professional learning into the working week

In a mathematics department teaching for mastery, professional development is a high priority. Teacher development is focused on deepening students' conceptual understanding over the long term.

 **Consider**

When you and your colleagues are preparing, teaching and reflecting on lessons, what professional learning is taking place?

What might you do to increase the potential professional development benefits while spending time on the following tasks:

- planning lessons

- marking exam papers

- marking exercise books?

Studies into effective professional development programmes have shown that many involve processes to encourage, extend and structure professional dialogue as well as ongoing collaborative working.[87]

When adopting a mastery approach, schools that I have worked with have committed to dedicating at least an hour a week to enable their teachers

---

[87] **P. Cordingley et al.** 2003, *op. cit.*

to engage in professional dialogue about teaching mathematics. Teachers often say this is the most significant difference their membership of the *Mathematics Mastery* partnership has made.

 **Consider**

What opportunities already exist in your department for systematic teacher learning? Could you make collaborative lesson planning work in your school? Could a weekly professional development session be timetabled for your team?

John Hattie emphasises the importance of 'teachers critiquing each other, planning together, evaluating together, and finding many other ways in which to work together'.[88]

Our solution in the *Mathematics Mastery* programme is to use teachers' usual working cycles of planning, teaching and reflecting on lessons as an opportunity for professional development. Rather than looking across a range of internet and paper-based resources each time a new topic is to be planned and taught, teachers can use this 'planning' time to learn more about the mathematical concepts involved, and the most effective ways to teach them.

 **Consider**

What is the best way for you to support teachers in your department with the mathematics and mathematics-specific pedagogy they need? Are there opportunities to re-purpose existing meeting time to use for teacher learning?

---

[88]**J. Hattie,** *Visible Learning for Teachers: Maximizing Impact on Learning* (London: Routledge, 2012), pp. 39–40.

# Summary

Successful teaching and learning can be achieved when *expert teachers* deliver lessons which have been designed together, reviewed and improved over time.

*Do the mathematics!* Teachers' own mathematics knowledge impacts on student success.

*Change is possible.* Schools can transform achievement through exhibiting strength across these three levers:

**1** *Buy-in:* share a commitment to enjoyment and achievement. To develop a coherent approach to ensure that every student enjoys and achieves in mathematics, the approach described in this book draws on effective practice in the UK and overseas, and on established research findings.

**2** *Clarity:* agree a shared understanding of effective teaching and learning. It's important to have a defensible and shared theory of effective teaching. Departmental approaches to curriculum, setting, assessment and intervention will frame the journey your department takes towards teaching for mastery.

**3** *Training:* high-quality, coherent opportunities for teachers to learn. Effective professional development is sustained, active and supported.

Integrate professional learning into the working week: schools in the *Mathematics Mastery* programme re-purpose teachers' usual working cycles of planning, teaching and reflecting on lessons as an opportunity for professional development.

# Epilogue

'Isn't this all just good teaching?'

It surprises me every time. I'll have been in conversation with a teacher about teaching for mastery, and some of the key ideas outlined in this book. Or they'll have taken part in training I'm running and seek me out at the end.

Sometimes defensive, sometimes bemused, they ask, 'Isn't this all just good teaching?'

My answer? Yes, emphatically, yes. What still puzzles me is why anyone thinks teaching for mastery would be otherwise.

Teaching for mastery involves teaching so that all students have knowledge and deep understanding of core concepts and skills. It involves teaching so that every student understands mathematics with sufficient depth to be able to solve non-routine problems.

In my experience, this is considerably easier to say than to achieve! In this book, I hope I have drawn together some of the theories, research evidence and classroom episodes that point to how it might be achieved. Yes, this is 'just' good mathematics teaching. But good mathematics teaching is far from easy.

Another question I'm sometimes asked is, 'Aren't lots of teachers doing most of this already?' Yes, thank goodness!

Teaching for mastery is about concentrating on the curriculum and the substance of education, rather than merely preparing students to jump through a series of accountability hoops.

Lots of great teachers are doing this already.

Teaching for mastery involves helping students to:

- deepen their understanding of mathematical ideas and how they fit together
- develop their powers to think mathematically
- communicate their ideas

so that they become equipped to solve new problems in unfamiliar contexts.

Lots of great teachers are doing this already.

I hope that your reflection on the ideas discussed in this book will help you to develop your own teaching and will be of some help in your work to transform the mathematics achievement of the students you teach.

Every mainstream student can acquire the depth of understanding they need for success in problem solving. Over time, everyone can acquire mastery of mathematics.

# Appendix: Lesson observation guidelines

**High expectations of engagement and achievement for every student**

| Teacher | Students |
|---|---|
| Conveys the message that progress is made through engagement and effort.<br><br>Expects every student to succeed.<br><br>Is enthusiastic about the learning expected.<br><br>Gives every student the opportunity to experience, clarify, practise and apply key ideas. | Have high aspirations, believe they can achieve and work hard in order to do so.<br><br>Want to learn and enjoy learning. |
| Follows a mastery curriculum.<br><br>Differentiates through scaffolding, questioning and use of concrete and pictorial representations – in preference to offering different tasks to different students.<br><br>Scaffolds learning by using speaking and listening activities, engaging resources and novel 'ways in' to a concept.<br><br>Extends through further developing depth of language, conceptual understanding and mathematical thinking.<br><br>Immediately acts on assessment from questioning and observation. | Explore mathematics and ask questions to deepen their appreciation of the subject.<br><br>Are challenged by solving less routine problems, demonstrating using concrete manipulatives/drawing diagrams, explaining in full sentences or asking their own questions. |

**Fewer topics, greater depth; depth of mastery for all**

| Teacher | Students |
|---|---|
| Develops conceptual understanding through multiple representations and connections.<br><br>Has a full understanding where and why this lesson falls in the sequence and in the longer-term development of students' mathematical understanding.<br><br>Anticipates and incorporates misconceptions and inaccuracies. | Have access to concrete manipulatives.<br><br>Manipulate objects or use pictorial representations to deepen their understanding.<br><br>Make links between concrete, pictorial and abstract representations.<br><br>Link new learning to previous learning in mathematics, other subjects and beyond school.<br><br>Demonstrate conceptual understanding through tackling new problems. |

| Teacher | Students |
|---|---|
| Develops communication of mathematical ideas, justifications and proofs. | Participate in pair or group discussion tasks. |
| Uses modelling to support students in developing independence in their mathematical recording, and to support writing. | Are ready to answer in-class questioning and discussion. |
|  | Speak in full sentences. |
| Considers own language and models expected language use clearly and accurately. | Use correct mathematical words and symbols. |
| Develops mathematical thinking and ability to generalise. | Do as much of the cognitive work – the writing, thinking, analysing and talking – as possible. |
| Ensures every student participates in active thinking, through a variety of appropriate questioning techniques. | Seek general patterns and create examples. |
| Encourages use of independent learning strategies. |  |
| Involves students in generalising by comparing and classifying mathematical objects or conjecturing about what might be sometimes, always or never true. |  |

**Every opportunity is used to learn mathematics**

| Teacher | Students |
|---|---|
| Ensures that lesson time is used purposefully from the very start. | Participate fully – everyone is engaged in the task, all of the time. |
| Makes clear what students should be doing at every point on the lesson, so no time is wasted. | Collaborate, discussing their thinking. |
|  | Work independently for some of the lesson. |
| Minimises teacher talk. | Demonstrate mastery and the ability to 'go it alone'. |

# Recommended reading

**Y. Ban Har**, *Teaching to Mastery Mathematics. Bar Modeling: A Problem-solving Tool* (Singapore: Marshall Cavendish, 2011).

**A. Bellos**, *Alex's Adventures in Numberland* (London: Bloomsbury, 2010).

**J. Boaler**, *The Elephant in the Classroom: Helping Children Learn and Love Maths* (London: Souvenir Press, 2010).

**P.C. Brown** *et al.*, *Make It Stick: The Science of Successful Learning* (Cambridge, MA: Harvard University Press, 2014).

**L. Gu, R. Huang and F. Marton**, 'Teaching with Variation: A Chinese Way of Promoting Effective Mathematics Learning', in *How Chinese Learn Mathematics: Perspectives from Insiders*, edited by L. Fan et al. (Singapore: World Scientific Publishing Co, 2004), pp. 309–347.

**D. Koretz**, *Measuring Up: What Educational Testing Really Tells Us* (Cambridge, MA: Harvard University Press, 2008).

**M.Y. Lai and S. Murray**, 'Teaching with Procedural Variation: A Chinese Way of Promoting Deep Understanding of Mathematics', *International Journal for Mathematics Teaching and Learning* April 2012, pp. 1–25.

**T. Nuñes, P. Bryant and A. Watson**, *Key Understandings in Mathematics Learning* (London: Nuffield Foundation, 2009).

**M. Ollerton and A. Watson**, *Inclusive Mathematics 11–18* (London: Continuum, 2011).

**X. Sun**, '"Variation problems" and Their Roles in the Topic of Fraction Division in Chinese Mathematics Textbook Examples', *Educational Studies in Mathematics* 76 (2011): pp. 65–85.

**A. Watson**, *Raising Achievement in Secondary Mathematics* (Maidenhead and New York, Open University Press, 2006).

**A. Watson and J. Mason**, *Mathematics as a Constructive Activity: Learners Generating Examples* (Mahwah, NJ: Lawrence Erlbaum Publishers, 2005).

**D. Willingham**, *Why Don't Students Like School?* (San Francisco, CA: Jossey-Bass, 2009).

# Glossary

**ACME:** The Advisory Committee on Mathematics Education is an independent committee that develops advice to influence mathematics education policy in England.

**A-level:** A subject-based qualification commonly taken at age 18 in schools in England, Wales and Northern Ireland. The 'A' stands for 'Advanced'.

**Base-10:** The numbering system we commonly use in which different symbols (the ten digits) are used for ten distinct values (0–9) and where each place to the left or right represents a power of ten.

**DfE:** Department for Education, a department of the English government.

**DfES:** Department for Education and Skills, a predecessor of the DfE.

**Dienes apparatus:** A three-dimensional manipulative, also known as base-10 blocks. These are usually made of plastic or wood, and come in four sizes, each ten times greater than the last.

**GCSE:** The qualification commonly taken at age 16 in England, Wales and Northern Ireland.

**Key stages:** The state-funded education system in England is divided into stages based on age.

> **Early Years Foundation Stage:** students aged 3–5
>
> **Key Stage 1:** students aged 5–7
>
> **Key Stage 2:** students aged 7–11
>
> **Key Stage 3:** students aged 11–14
>
> **Key Stage 4:** students aged 14–16
>
> **Key Stage 5:** students aged 16–18

**NRICH:** The NRICH website publishes free mathematics education enrichment material for ages 5–19.

**OECD:** The Organisation for Economic Co-operation and Development is a global policy forum. Its mission is to promote policies that will improve the economic and social well-being of people around the world.

**Ofsted:** The Office for Standards in Education, Children's Services and Schools, the regulator and inspectorate in England by which all state schools are subject to assessment and inspection.

**Palindromic:** When a word, line, verse, number or sentence reads the same backwards as forwards. For example, the sentence 'Madam, I'm Adam' or the number '1398931'.

**PISA:** The Programme for International Student Assessment is a triennial international survey that aims to evaluate education systems worldwide by testing the skills and knowledge of 15-year-old students.

**Primary:** relating to students aged 4–11.

**Secondary:** relating to students aged 11–16 (or 18).

**TIMSS:** The Trends in International Mathematics and Science Study is a series of international assessments of the mathematics and science knowledge of students around the world. It is conducted by the International Association for the Evaluation of Educational Achievement (IEA).

**UKMT Challenge:** Competition organised annually by the United Kingdom Mathematics Trust (an education charity).

**Year groups:**

**Year 1:** 5–6-year-olds

**Year 2:** 6–7-year-olds

**Year 3:** 7–8-year-olds

**Year 4:** 8–9-year-olds

**Year 5:** 9–10-year-olds

**Year 6:** 10–11-year-olds

**Year 7:** 11–12-year-olds

**Year 8:** 12–13-year-olds

**Year 9:** 13–14-year-olds

**Year 10:** 14–15-year-olds

**Year 11:** 15–16-year-olds.

# Index

## Acknowledgements

**American Psychological Association** for extract from *ACT: A simple theory of complex cognition*, Anderson, J. R. (1996). Reproduced with permission from American Psychological Association. **ASCD** for extracts from Kennedy, M.M. (1991) *Some surprising findings on how teachers learn to teach* in *Educational Leadership*, 49(3), 14–17. Page 17. Reproduced with permission from ASCD. **Department for Children, Schools and Families** for extract from *Report of the Expert Group on Assessment*, Department for Children, Schools and Families (2009). © Crown copyright 2009. Reproduced under the terms of the Open Government Licence v3.0. **Department for Education** for extracts from *The Framework for the National Curriculum. A Report by the Expert Panel for the National Curriculum Review* (2011). Department for Education (2011). © Crown copyright 2011. Also for extract from *Draft National Curriculum Programmes of Study* (2013), © Crown copyright 2013. Also for extract from *Final Report on the Commission on Assessment without Levels*, McIntosh, J. (2015). © Crown copyright 2015. Also for extract from *Mathematics Programmes of Study: Key Stage 3 National Curriculum in England*, Department for Education (2013). © Crown copyright 2013. Also for extracts from *Standard for Teachers' Professional Development: Implementation guidance for school leaders, teachers, and organisations that offer professional development for teachers*, Department for Education (2016). © Crown copyright 2016. All content is reproduced under the Open Government Licence v3.0. **Elsevier** for extract from Burstein, L. (ed.) (1992) *The IEA Study of Mathematics III: Student Growth and Classroom Processes*. Oxford: Pergamon Press, p.278. Reproduced with permission from Elsevier. **FLM Publishing Association** for extract from *Mathematicians as Enquirers: Learning about Learning Mathematics*, A. Watson (2008). Adapted by Anne Watson from L. Burton 2004, Springer. Reproduced with permission from FLM Publishing Association, and the author, Anne Watson. Also for extract from *Arbitrary and necessary. Part 2: assisting memory. For the Learning of Mathematicians: an international journal of mathematics*, Hewitt D. (2001). Reproduced with permission from FLM Publishing Association, and the author, D.Hewitt. **GL Assessment** for extract from *Working Inside the Black Box: Assessment for Learning in the Classroom*, © Paul Black, Christine Harrison, Clare Lee, Bethan Marshall and Dylan Wiliam, 2002. Reproduced by permission of GL Assessment. **Harvard University Press** for extract from *Measuring Up: What Educational Testing Really Tells Us*, by Daniel Koretz, Cambridge, Mass.: Harvard University Press, Copyright © 2008 by the President and Fellows of Harvard College. Also for extract from *Make It Stick: The Science of Successful Learning*, by Peter C. Brown, Henry L. Roediger, III, and Mark A. McDaniel, Cambridge, Mass.:

The Belknap Press of Harvard University Press, Copyright © 2014 by Peter C. Brown, Henry L. Roediger, III, and Mark A. McDaniel. Press of Harvard University Press, Copyright © 2014 by Peter C. Brown, Henry L. Roediger, III, and Mark A. McDaniel. **Her Majesty's Stationary Office** for extract from *Mathematics Counts*, Cockcroft, W.H. (1982). Her Majesty's Stationery Office © Crown copyright 1982. Also for extract from *Mathematics Counts: Report of the Committee of Inquiry into the Teaching of Mathematics in Schools*, Department of Education and Science (1982). Her Majesty's Stationery Office © Crown copyright 1982. Both reproduced under the terms of the Open Government Licence v3.0. **International Group for the Psychology of Mathematics Education** for extract from *Describing Elements of Mathematics Lessons that Accommodate Diversity in Student Background* (Sullivan, P., Mousley, J. and Zevenbergen, R. (2004). Reproduced with permission from Pr P. Sullivan and Pr R. Jorgensen). **John Wiley & Sons** for extracts from *Why don't students like school?* (Willingham, D. (2009). Reproduced with permission from John Wiley and Sons). Also for extract from *Mathematical Discovery: On Understanding, Learning and Teaching Problem Solving*, Polya, G. (1962). Reproduced with permission from John Wiley and Sons Inc. **Chris Kyriacou** for extract from *A Systematic Review of Strategies to Raise Pupils' Motivational Effort in Key Stage 4 Mathematics* (Kyriacou, C. and Goulding, M. (2005). Reproduced with permission from C. Kyriacou). **Ministry of Education, Sports, Science and Technology – Japan**, MEXT, Translated by A. Takahashi, T. Watanabe, M. Yoshida. Copyright © 2008 Global Education Resources LLC. Reproduced with permission from Global Education Resources LLC. Source: MEXT homepage (http://www.mext.go.jp/). Source: *"Course of Study" (MEXT). Grades 1 to 6 (Elementary school).* http://www.mext.go.jp/component/a_menu/education/micro_detail/__icsFiles/afieldfile/2010/11/29/syo.pdf and *Grades 7 to 8 (Lower Secondary School)*, http://www.mext.go.jp/a_menu/shotou/new-cs/youryou/chu/__icsFiles/afieldfile/2010/12/16/121504.pdf (accessed on 2017, October 4th). **National Academies Press** for extract from *Education and Learning to Think*, Resnick, L.B. (1987). Reproduced with permission from the National Academies Press. **National College for School Leadership** for extract from (2013) *Report on research into maths and science teaching in the Shanghai region. Research by Leaders of Education and Subject Specialists in Shanghai and Ningbo, China 11-18 January 2013*, ©2012 National College for School Leadership. Also for extract from *Report on Research into Maths and Science Teaching in the Shanghai region* (©2012 National College for School Leadership. Both reproduced under the terms of the Open Government Licence v3.0). **NCETM** for extract from *Teaching for Mastery: Questions, Tasks and Activities to Support Assessment*, Askew, A., Bishop, S., Christie, C., Eaton, S., Griffin, P.

and Morgan, D. (2015). © Crown copyright 2015. Reproduced under the terms of the Open Government Licence v3.0. **Nuffield Foundation** for extracts from *Key Understandings in Mathematics Learning. Paper 7: Modelling, Problem-solving and Integrating Concepts* (Watson, A. (2009). Reproduced with permission from the Nuffield Foundation). Also for extract from *Key Understandings in Mathematics Learning*, Nuñes, T., Bryant, P. and Watson, A. (2009). Reproduced with permission from the Nuffield Foundation. **OCR** for past paper exam questions from OCR, *GCSE (9–1) Mathematics J560/01 Paper 1 (Foundation Tier), Sample Question Paper 2014*. Reproduced with permission from OCR. **OECD** for *PISA 2015 Results (Volume I): Policies and Practices for Successful Schools* by OECD Publishing Reproduced with permission of OECD Publishing. Also for *PISA 2015 Results (Volume II) : Policies and Practices for Successful Schools* by OECD Publishing Reproduced with permission of OECD Publishing. Also for extract from *Synergies for Better Learning, OECD Reviews of Evaluation and Assessment in Education Synergies for Better Learning : An International Perspective on Evaluation and Assessment* by OECD. Reproduced with permission of OECD Publishing. **OFSTED** for extract from *Mathematics: Understanding the Score*, Ofsted (Office for Standards in Education) (2008). © Crown copyright 2009. Reproduced under the terms of the Open Government Licence v3.0. **Oxford University Press** for extract from *Mastering Mathematics: Teaching to Transform Achievement* (Drury, H. (2014). Reproduced with permission from Oxford University Press). **Solution Tree Press** for extract from Wiliam, D. (2011) Embedded Formative Assessment. Bloomington, I: Solution Tree Press, p.122. Reproduced with permission from Solution Tree Press. **Springer** for extract from Hattie, J. (2008) *Visible Learning: A Synthesis of Over 800 Meta-Analyses Relating to Achievement*. London: Routledge, p.47. Reproduced with permission of Springer. **Taylor & Francis** for extract from Day, C. (1999) *Developing Teachers: The Challenges of Lifelong Learning*. London: Falmer Press, p.4. Reproduced with permission from Taylor & Francis. **Teacher Development Trust** for extract from *Developing Great Teaching: Lessons from International Reviews into Effective Professional Development*, Cordingley, P., Higgins, S., Greany, T., Buckler, N., Coles-Jordan, D., Crisp, B., Saunders, L. and Coe, R. (2015). Reproduced with permission from the Teacher Development Trust. **The Association of Mathematics Education Teachers** for extract from *Working with students on questioning to promote mathematical thinking*, Watson, A. (2002). Reproduced with permission from the Association of Mathematics Education Teachers. **The Government of Hong Kong Special Administrative Region, Education Bureau,** for extract from Curriculum Development Council. (1999). *Syllabuses for Secondary Schools Mathematics (Secondary 1-5)*. Reproduced with permission from Mathematics

Education Section, Education Bureau, The Government of the Hong Kong Special Administrative Region. **UK Mathematics Foundation** for extracts from *Acceleration or Enrichment* (UK Mathematics Foundation (2000). Reproduced with permission from A. D. Gardiner).

Although we have made every effort to trace and contact all copyright holders before publication this has not been possible in all cases. If notified, the publisher will rectify any errors or omissions at the earliest opportunity.

# Notes

Notes